Regar
Huma
British Museum
Edited by Alexandra
Fletcher, Daniel Antoine
and JD Hill

The **British**
Museum

Published with the generous support of

THE FLOW FOUNDATION

Publishers
The British Museum
Great Russell Street
London WC1B 3DG

Series editor
Sarah Faulks

Distributors
The British Museum Press
38 Russell Square
London WC1B 3QQ

Regarding the Dead: Human Remains in the British Museum
Edited by Alexandra Fletcher, Daniel Antoine and JD Hill

ISBN 978 086159 197 8
ISSN 1747 3640

Front cover: Detail of a mummy of a Greek youth named
Artemidorus in a cartonnage body-case, 2nd century AD.
British Museum, London (EA 21810)

Printed and bound in the UK by 4edge Ltd, Hockley

Papers used in this book by The British Museum Press are
FSC® certified, elemental chlorine free (ECF) fibre sourced
from well-managed forests and other controlled sources

Further information about the Museum and its collection can
be found at britishmuseum.org

Contents

Preface

JD Hill

Human remains in museum collections can be a charged focus amidst the contested debates surrounding the legacies of colonialism and empire, the different purposes of a museum's existence and the changing understanding of the human body. The assumed primacy of western scientific research over the concerns of indigenous populations has also been a point of contention. This collection of essays offers a particular set of perspectives on these issues as seen through the lens of one major international museum. The aim of the book is to show that there are many more aspects to the collections of human remains in museums than just issues of repatriation and display. The authors are predominantly British Museum staff or those who have engaged in different ways with the human remains in the British Museum's care. None of the authors would claim that the collection seeks to offer a definitive account of the complex and broad range of questions that surround the care, display and research of human remains in museum collections, nor would they wish this volume to be read as an official statement of the British Museum's position on these subjects. While many of the authors are employed by the British Museum, this does not mean that they share the same opinions on issues such as the repatriation, display, care or research of human remains in the collection.

The motivation for publishing this book is to emphasize that for a museum of any size, it is impossible to separate out issues of repatriation or display from those of conservation, documentation and research in relation to human remains. The contributors to this volume seek to cover as far as possible the breadth of concerns related to the care of human remains. To hold a collection of any kind in trust for future generations, particularly one that includes human remains, means that those responsible for them have to consider all aspects of what that duty of care entails. Across three sections discussing the holding, conserving and researching of human remains, the chapters cover both practical and ethical issues from the relative humidity levels required for the storage of human remains to the use and publication of images. The book also reviews the claims that the British Museum's Trustees have considered in relation to the de-accession and return of some human remains in the collection. Many of the chapters highlight particular case studies that focus on one group of human remains or even the remains of one individual, such as Lindow Man. A number of authors discuss the processes and results of some areas of research on human remains in the collection, stressing the active contribution that such remains have in furthering our understanding of past societies, even if they have been in the museum's care for many years.

This book is one outcome of a continuing process of reflection and discussion concerning how the British Museum should look after the human remains in its collection. The British Museum has held human remains since its foundation in 1753 when the original museum contained biological and geological materials alongside artefacts, books, prints and drawings. In the 19th century, many of the human remains in the British Museum passed into the care of the Natural History Museum which was created out of the biological and geological collections of the original British Museum. The human remains in the Museum's care today are relatively few in comparison to the overall size of the collection. While skeletons, cremated remains and mummies from archaeological investigations form a significant proportion of the collection, there is a relatively large number of objects from the last 200 years made in part or, more rarely, in whole from human hair, teeth or bone.

The diversity of the range of human remains within the Museum's care is the key challenge in the curation, display and research of the collection. For example, different forms of human remains require different methods of storage and handling. The variety of the collection is a product of the cultures, both ancient and recent, from which they originate with different attitudes to death, human remains and mortuary practices. This divergence is also reflected in the variation of ways in which the human remains have arrived at the Museum. A significant proportion of the archaeological collections were excavated in the course of Museum projects over the last 30 years, but other remains, including many of the mummies, arrived at the Museum through gift or purchase in the 19th and 20th centuries. This also incorporates a large number of the most recent examples of human remains in the collection, and close research of the specific circumstances through which these human remains were collected often reveal complex and nuanced relationships and circumstances of their original gift or collection, before subsequently coming to the Museum at a later date.

There have been significant changes in the last 20 years as to how the British Museum cares for, displays and researches human remains, some of which have been driven by changes in legislation and governmental guidance. However, most of the developments reflect how attitudes, practices and policies have been altered by Trustees and staff following movements and debates in the fields of museum studies, archaeology and physical anthropology, in addition to the larger shifts in public attitudes to death and the display of human remains. As discussed in several chapters, the British Museum's care of human remains falls within the legislative framework of the Human Tissue Act 2004 and the British Museum Act 1963 and is led by guidance issued by the UK government's Department for Culture, Media and Sport. These policies in particular instruct how the Museum can act when human remains are subject to repatriation requests or how the Museum should care for human remains less than 100 years old. However, wider aspects of the care of human remains have developed out of in-depth discussions with staff across the Museum over the last ten years. One result of this consultation process was a review of all the human remains on display in the Museum and an evaluation of what in practice was meant by displaying human remains with care and respect. As a consequence of this review, it was agreed that some human remains should be removed from display. These discussions have also resulted in the creation of the British Museum Policy on Human Remains, which offers guidance on all aspects of the care, conservation, documentation and study of the human remains in the British Museum collection. These changes reflect how in practice each generation of British Museum Trustees and staff seek to understand what it means for a museum to care for a collection that includes human remains 'in trust': in trust not for the present, but for the future.

Part 1
Holding and Displaying Human Remains

Introduction

Simon Mays

Introduction

The last 20 years have seen advances in scientific techniques which have greatly increased the amount of information that can be obtained from the study of human remains. There has also been an explosion in the number of university higher degree courses in human osteology. Consequently, there has been a greater demand for access to collections of human remains from researchers. Furthermore, archaeology has become a favourite topic of television documentaries and news features in print and other media, with stories highlighting results of research on human remains attracting particular public interest. A corollary of this is that the public increasingly wishes, and indeed expects, to see displays featuring archaeological human remains when they visit museums. All of these developments mean that museum collections of human remains from archaeological sites are now under pressure as never before and this section deals with some of the challenges that this poses for those who curate them.

In the first chapter, Daniel Antoine discusses some of the measures taken at the British Museum to ensure the well being of its collection. Documentation of the collection is available online and is regularly updated to record destructive sampling and other aspects of the condition of the material so that changes over time can be monitored. It is intended that the amount of online information will increase, meaning that not only will researchers be able to determine more precisely in advance which burials they need to study, but in some cases they may be able to use online data directly, reducing the need to examine the material itself. This will help minimize handling damage and hence assist to safeguard the collection. The issue of whether and how human remains should be displayed in museums continues to be debated in academia, but opinion polls show that the British public is highly supportive of the display of human remains. The British Museum, in common with most other major archaeological museums in Britain, uses human remains in its public galleries to help inform visitors about the past. Human remains on display include not only bones, but mummified remains and bog bodies as well.

The topic of bog bodies is picked up in Jody Joy's contribution in Chapter Two. He discusses the display at the British Museum of Lindow Man, the Iron Age–Romano-British bog body recovered from Lindow Moss in Cheshire. Joy's main focus is on the ethical issues. The preservation of soft tissue, including facial features, means that bog bodies have the unique potential to provide visitors with an immediate connection to a particular person from long ago which helps to individualize and populate a past that may otherwise seem rather remote and impersonal. This is assisted by the presentation of the results of scientific studies which can yield detailed information about the person concerned, such as their last meal, manner of death and so forth. The importance of bog bodies for informing visitors about the past and stimulating their curiosity provides a strong ethical imperative towards their display, and they are invariably popular with the public. These considerations led the British Museum to continue displaying Lindow Man, even at a time when some other human remains were being removed from the same gallery.

Joy also provides a brief review of display issues connected with other bog bodies. When Tollund Man was recovered in Denmark in 1950, the National Museum of Denmark initially felt that the body might be too 'macabre' for public view. When the remains were finally placed on display, this assessment proved spectacularly out of tune with public attitudes with 18,000 people visiting the exhibition in ten days. This disconnect between academic discourse and attitudes of the museum-going public all too often persists today. When Lindow Man was loaned to Manchester Museum in 2008, the museum assumed that the public was becoming increasingly 'sensitive' to displays of human remains, and they attempted to use the body, and their other displays of human remains, as an opportunity to promote debate over the treatment of human remains in museums. The issue failed to gain much traction with the public, and their attempt in the exhibit to provide views of Lindow Man from different perspectives (including from an archaeologist, someone from the local community and a druid) left many visitors baffled. Public concern over the display of Lindow Man has, in reality, centred not upon whether or how his remains should be displayed, but where. Following his discovery in the 1980s, there was a local, public campaign for the 'repatriation' of the remains for display at a museum in the north-west rather than keeping them in London. Lindow Man still ended up at the British Museum, but as a compromise the remains have been loaned to Manchester Museum and other museums as part of a scheme to make exhibits more accessible around the country. Joy gives an account of the issues this raises, and emphasizes that curators should continue to consult and listen to the public regarding the display of human remains.

In the final contribution to this section, Daniel Antoine and Janet Ambers discuss some of the scientific work that has recently been carried out on the internationally important collection of human remains from the Nile valley held at the British Museum. This collection includes material from the unique late Pleistocene cemetery at Jebel Sahaba, as well as a large series of burials, some with mummified soft tissue, ranging in date from the Neolithic to the medieval period from the Fourth Nile Cataract region. The Jebel Sahaba material was excavated nearly 50 years ago and ongoing work, including application of previously unavailable methods such as radiocarbon dating of the apatite fraction of bone, illustrate the fact that old collections continue to yield new data. CT scanning is increasing the knowledge that can be gained through the non-invasive study of mummified remains. Gebelein Man, a naturally desiccated pre-Dynastic mummy, has been in the Museum collection for over 100 years, but it was only with the recent application of high-resolution CT scanning that the likely cause of death, a penetrating wound to the back, was identified. This research directly informs the visitor experience. The mummified remains, which are displayed in the public galleries, can be autopsied virtually by visitors using a touch screen, allowing the visualization of preserved internal organs.

The chapters in this section vividly illustrate why it is important to retain long-term collections of human remains in museums for both research and display purposes. Many research techniques involve the destruction of small samples of tissue, and even when remains are examined using non-destructive techniques, handling damage accumulates over time. Therefore, there is tension between the ethical requirement to preserve collections in ways which safeguard them for future generations and an imperative to allow them to be used to generate new knowledge. This tension lies at the heart of the decision-making process concerning requests for research access to human remains. A further issue, the value of human remains for enthusing and informing visitors about the past versus the need to treat remains with sensitivity and respect, lies at the heart of decisions concerning the display of human remains. This section illustrates the dilemmas that these considerations pose. It also reminds us of the importance of museums retaining expert scientific staff who are actively engaged in research. This not only helps to ensure the best curatorial decision-making concerning research access to collections, but also that displays in public galleries communicate results of research to museum visitors in an appropriate and engaging way.

Chapter 1
Curating Human Remains in Museum Collections
Broader Considerations and a British Museum Perspective

Daniel Antoine

Introduction

The British Museum holds and cares for over 6,000 human remains. The collection mostly comprises skeletal remains, but also includes bog bodies, intentionally and naturally mummified bodies, as well as objects made in part or wholly of human remains (**Pls 1–4**). The Museum has a long tradition of caring for human remains and some of the Egyptian mummies in the collection, such as that of Gebelein Man in the Early Egypt Gallery, have been on display for over 100 years. This chapter provides an introduction to the approaches taken towards the care of human remains in the British Museum collection. Broader issues and considerations relating to the care of human remains in museum collections, such as the legislation under which they fall and the display of human remains, are also discussed.

Curating human remains with care, respect and dignity

Regardless of age, origin or state of preservation, human remains in the British Museum are treated with great care and full consideration of the ethics associated with their curation. One of the most pertinent sections of the British Museum Policy on Human Remains (Trustees of the British Museum 2013) states that, during handling, storage or display, human remains should always be treated with care, respect and dignity. Ethics surrounding the display, storage and care of human remains have been the subject of much discourse, both in the media and academic literature (e.g. Lohman and Goodnow 2006; Cassman *et al.* 2007; Sayer 2010; Jenkins 2011; Giesen 2013). As noted in Sayer (2010, 130–1), both researchers and museum staff should be mindful not to objectify human remains as 'scientific objects or data'. The ever-expanding information that their analysis provides (see Part Three, this volume) and how this is conveyed through exhibitions or gallery displays, should always be balanced with a duty of care. The storage, display and handling of human remains, as well as the actions of all museum staff or researchers working with human remains, should reflect this respect. The title of this book, *Regarding the Dead*, conveys this approach as while 'regarding' can be defined as 'with respect to' or 'concerning', as a noun 'regard' has several meanings including 'look or gaze', but also 'careful thought or attention' and 'respect'. *Regarding the Dead* therefore reflects this need to balance the curation of human remains with a strong awareness of the importance of respecting and caring for such collections. Hence, human remains should never be treated or referred to as objects. Respect should always be at the forefront of anyone working with or researching human remains. The handling and display of human remains, as well as the language and terminology used to describe them, should always be appropriate and based on professional standards. The highly complex and often changing legislation that regulates the analysis, display, storage and excavation of human remains must also be taken into account.

Human remains and the law

The transfer of excavated human remains to the British Museum is conducted in accordance with legal requirements and published professional standards of archaeological

Plate 1 Egyptian cartonnage mummy-case from the 22nd Dynasty belonging to a young child whose skeletal remains show numerous healed fractures usually found in patients suffering from the rare congenital bone disorder *osteogenesis imperfecta* or brittle bone disease. British Museum, London (EA 41603)

Plate 2 The well-preserved body of Lindow Man found in a peat bog at Lindow Moss, near Manchester, c. 2 BC–AD 119. British Museum, London (1984,1002.1)

investigation. This is equally true for human remains excavated overseas. In accordance with different policies for acquisitions and human remains, the British Museum will continue to add human remains to its collection so long as it is satisfied, as far as it is possible, that the Museum can hold the remains in a lawful manner, the provenance has been clearly established, there is no suspicion of illicit trade and that the remains are of potential value to the British Museum's international audience. Such remains are most likely to be from archaeological excavations conducted in the UK and more rarely from overseas (e.g. Chapter Three, this volume).

Archaeological human remains and legislation

Human remains removed in the course of archaeological excavations in England are subject to a Ministry of Justice licence (White 2011; Parker Pearson *et al.* 2013). It is an offence under Common Law to exhume human remains without lawful authority and against Ecclesiastical Law to do so if the remains are found on consecrated ground (Garratt-Frost 1992). Several British Acts of Parliament also apply to the excavation of human remains from archaeological sites (Spoerry 1993; White 2011).[1] If there is a 'reasonable expectation' that human remains will be found during an archaeological excavation, a burial licence under Section 25 of the Burial Act 1857 should be applied for in advance (White 2011, 486). In 2005, the responsibility for buried human remains was transferred from the Home

Office to the Department of Constitutional Affairs and, subsequently, to the Ministry of Justice (White 2011; Parker Pearson *et al.* 2013). In 2008, the Ministry of Justice required that all newly excavated human remains, including archaeological remains, should be reburied after two months. This was later extended to two years to allow for scientific analysis, but did not include an option for the permanent curation of such remains in a museum (Parker Pearson *et al.* 2013, 150–3). The terms of this licence made it impossible for the British Museum to add newly excavated archaeological human remains to its collection as once registered in the collection, the Trustees are governed by various acts of parliament[2] and may only agree to the de-accession of human remains for reburial which they reasonably believe to be from a person who died after the Early Medieval period (11th century).[3]

The Ministry of Justice now acknowledges that the current burial legislation is not well suited to the needs of archaeologists and researchers, particularly as the licence requires the reburial of remains which may otherwise have international cultural, biological or archaeological significance, such as the recently re-excavated cremations from Stonehenge (Parker Pearson *et al.* 2013, 151–5). As of 2013, it is still only possible to apply for extensions to the initial two-year period, but after discussions with various interested parties such as the Advisory Panel on the Archaeology of Burials in England, the Ministry of Justice declared that it would soon be allowing for a more flexible interpretation of the 1857 Burial Act:

> However, the Ministry of Justice has looked at the provisions of the 1857 Act again and has come to the conclusion that there is room to apply the provisions with more flexibility. This will allow licences to be granted with a wider range of disposal options for exhumed remains than re-burial alone, including the retention of remains indefinitely.[4]

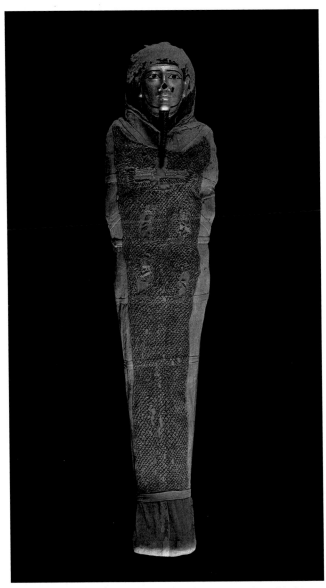

Plate 3 Mummy of Irthorru from the 26th Dynasty with a gilded mummy-mask. Irthorru was a priest of the god Min at the city of Akhmim. British Museum, London (EA 20745)

Plate 4 A bowl from Hawaii from the 18th–19th century made of wood and studded with human teeth, an example of an object made in part of human remains. British Museum, London (Oc1920,1023.1)

In the near future therefore, licences may be granted that permit the indefinite retention of human remains in appropriate repositories. This would once again allow museums to care for archaeological human remains of national and international significance. Those considering adding human remains to a museum collection should also be mindful of the implications this can have in terms of storage (e.g. space, materials and staff time), conservation, documentation and legislative considerations (see Mays 2013; McKinley 2013; Roberts 2013). As noted by Parker Pearson *et al.* (2013, 155), the numerous regulations and laws that govern the heritage sector are not static and guidance on the current legislation should be sought from the appropriate legislative authority and advisory groups, such as those discussed below.

Guidance for the care of human remains in museum collections

Following a consultation carried out in 2009 by the Ministry of Justice, English Heritage and the Church of England,[5] the Advisory Panel on the Archaeology of Burials in England

(APABE)[6] was formed to provide guidance on archaeological burials in England and to act as a unified source of advice concerning all burials in England over 100 years old and not covered by the Human Tissue Act 2004 (see below). The panel consists of professionals from a range of relevant organizations including several museums. However, it acts independently from the institutions its members are drawn from, and its principal aim is to provide information and support regarding the interpretation of two guidance documents published in 2005:

- *Guidance for the Care of Human Remains in Museums* (Department for Culture, Media and Sport (DCMS), 2005).
- *Guidance for Best Practice for Treatment of Human Remains Excavated from Christian Burial Grounds in England* (English Heritage and the Church of England 2005).

As stated on the APABE website, the panel provides advice to 'foster a consistent approach to ethical, legal, scientific, archaeological and other issues surrounding the treatment of archaeological burials', whilst taking into account relevant ethical, legal, religious, archaeological and scientific issues.[7] Other sources of advice available to institutions caring for human remains include the Human Remains Subject Specialist Network[8] and the British Association for Biological Anthropology and Osteoarchaeology (BABAO).[9] Following the Human Tissue Act 2004, collections that include human remains which are less than 100 years old also require an additional level of care to comply with the law.

Human Tissue Act 2004

Since 2004, human remains that are, or may be, less than 100 years old have been subject to the licensing requirements of the Human Tissue Act 2004. Museums are required to have a licence from the Human Tissue Authority[10] to hold and display such remains (see Woodhead 2013). The act covers all parts of a human body such as bones, teeth, organs and soft tissues, as well as any hair or nails that were removed after death. The Human Tissue Authority granted the British Museum its licence in 2008, which led to the appointment of a Designated Individual who is legally responsible for the care, movement, research and display of these particular remains. The licence applies to a comparatively small number of human remains in the British Museum collection, mostly from the Department of Africa, Oceania and the Americas, and includes artefacts that are made in part of human remains. All British Museum employees are required to contact the Designated Individual for all matters connected with human remains held under the licence, including their conservation, study, display or movement. The Designated Individual is responsible for supervising any such activity directly, or ensuring that members of staff carry out these actions in a respectful manner that complies with the requirements of the licence.

All human remains in the British Museum collection are treated with the same high standards and are kept in conditions that meet the best current practice for care and storage applicable to the nature of the remains. Practical considerations (e.g. storage space availability) and, when appropriate and possible, cultural sensitivities and objections, are also taken into account (see Part Two, this volume). Human remains covered by the Human Tissue Licence also require an additional level of documentation. An archive, maintained by the Designated Individual, contains copies of all requests, permissions and related correspondence concerning the inspection, movement, conservation, research, photography and display of such remains in the British Museum. They are also stored in clearly marked containers stating that they are, or may be, less than 100 years old and explicitly described as such on the Museum's Collection Online database.

The British Museum Policy on Human Remains

The British Museum has developed a policy with regards to the human remains in its collection which reflects recent legislative changes. The British Museum Policy on Human Remains is available online[11] and follows the recommendations of the *Guidance for the Care of Human Remains in Museums* (DCMS 2005).[12] It can be read alongside the British Museum policies on acquisition, storage, conservation and de-accessioning. The policy outlines the principles governing the respectful and lawful holding, display, study and care of human remains in the British Museum's collection (Trustees of the British Museum 2013, 3–8). Importantly, it explains the circumstances in which the British Museum Trustees may consider a request for the de-accession and transfer of human remains. A substantial body of literature exists on the issues and considerations surrounding the reburial and repatriation of human remains (e.g. Layton 1989; Fforde *et al.* 2002; Fforde 2004; Jenkins 2011). Liaising with indigenous communities and cultural descendants who have close links to the remains is an important part of the process and one that is fully recognized by the British Museum (see Chapter Four, this volume). All correspondence and documentation concerning transfer requests, as well as the outcomes, can be found on

the Museum's website.[13] Such transfers however, may not contravene any trust or condition subject to which the British Museum holds the remains and must be balanced against the Trustees' primary legal duty to safeguard the Museum's collection for the benefit of present and future generations. The public benefits of the study of human remains include furthering our understanding of funerary practices, human biology and past cultures:

> Human remains are a record of the varied ways that different societies have conceived of death and disposed of the remains of the dead. Human remains in the Collection help advance important research in fields such as archaeology, human biology, the history of disease, palaeoepidemiology, bioarchaeology, physical anthropology, forensics and genetics. Human remains, which have been physically modified by a person working within a cultural context, or which form part of an archaeological record, illuminate other objects in the collection (Trustees of the British Museum 2013, 3).

Displaying human remains

Human remains and the public

As stated in the *Guidance for the Care of Human Remains in Museums* issued by the Department for Culture, Media and Sport, visitor surveys indicate that the 'vast majority of museum visitors are comfortable with and often expect to see human remains, usually skeletons, as parts of museum displays' (DCMS 2005, 20). In 2009, as part of the Avebury Reburial Request Consultation, English Heritage and the National Trust also conducted a public opinion survey entitled 'Research into Issues Surrounding Human Bones in Museums'.[14] As stated in the document, the objectives of the research were to establish whether there was:

- Support for archaeological exhibits in museums including human bones.
- Support for the retention of archaeologically important human bones in museums used for future research (English Heritage 2009, 3).

Overall, the results indicate that the vast majority (91%) of the survey participants supported museums that wished to display and retain human bones for research purposes. In the survey, 87% of participants also agreed that displaying human burials and bones can 'help the public understand how people have lived in the past' (English Heritage 2009, 11) and 90% agreed that keeping human bones in museums for research 'helps us to find out more about how people lived in the past' (English Heritage 2009, 16). The results also showed that most of the individuals surveyed were unconcerned about the date of the skeletal remains used in displays (79%) or for research purposes (81%) as long as the bones were at least 100 years old. For skeletal remains that were over 1,000 years old, these percentages increased by a further 9% and 12% respectively (English Heritage 2009, 7–12). There was greater concern about the skeletal remains of named individuals (English Heritage 2009, 17), but no distinction was made as to whether this was assessed independently of the age of the remains. Indeed, coffins or tombstones can occasionally reveal the names of individuals that are several thousand years old, for example many of the Egyptian mummies in the British Museum collection have their names inscribed on the cartonnages. Research (e.g.

Carroll 2005; DCMS 2005) also indicates that museum visitors in Britain are comfortable with the display and study of well-preserved human remains such as mummies and bog bodies (e.g. Kilmister 2003). As noted by Parker Pearson *et al.* (2013, 155), 'archaeology as a developed profession needs to maintain a healthy debate about human remains' and therefore museums must continue to take into account and be aware of how the public views the display and storage of human remains. The British Museum regularly uses surveys to gather valuable feedback on exhibitions and gallery displays that feature human remains.

Display

The British Museum gives careful thought to the reasons for and the circumstances of the display of human remains. It has reviewed and subsequently removed some of the human remains in the galleries, several of which were part of displays that were designed many years ago (See Chapter Two, pp. 12–13). The issue of whether museums should display human remains – and if so how – has been the subject of much debate (e.g. Cadot 2009; Sayer 2010; Jenkins 2011; Woodhead 2013). The display of human remains in museums should, as far as possible, be informed and guided by current opinion as well as conceived with care, respect and dignity, and balanced against public benefit. The inclusion of human remains in a display or gallery can add to our understanding of that individual and of the population, period or culture from which they originated. Therefore:

> In the display of human remains at the Museum explanatory and contextual information will be provided. A written justification for any decision to display human remains shall be retained by the Museum and shall balance the public benefits of display against the known feelings of:
>
> a) Where these are less than 100 years old – any individual known to the Museum as having a direct and close genealogical link to the remains.
>
> b) Where they are more than 100 years old – a community which has cultural continuity with the remains in question and for whom the remains have cultural importance (Trustees of the British Museum 2013, 4).

When deciding whether to include human remains in a gallery, temporary exhibition or as part of a loan to another institution, British Museum curators ensure that care and thought have been given as to the reasons for and the circumstances of the display of the human remains in question. This process is documented during the planning stages and includes the reasoning behind the display of the human remains, how the display complies with the British Museum Policy on Human Remains and whether it satisfies the legal, ethical and practical considerations. This includes displaying the remains in conditions that are actively managed and monitored to meet standards of security and environmental control proportionate and appropriate to their age, origin and modern cultural significance (Trustees of the British Museum 2013, 4). The nature (e.g. whether a mummy, skeleton, bog body or an object made in part of human remains) and fragility of the remains, as well as that of any accompanying materials (e.g. textiles or metal objects), are taken into account when preparing a display case or gallery space so that the temperature, humidity, light and vibration conditions are appropriate to their age and state of preservation (see Chapter Six, this volume).

Images

The use of images of human remains is seldom discussed in guidance documents or most of the relevant literature and would benefit from further debate. As with the display of human remains, careful thought should be given to the use of images of human remains in publications, display panels or on web pages (DCMS 2005, 20).

When appropriate, possible cultural preferences or objections from communities which have a cultural continuity or a close genealogical link with the remains are taken into account by the British Museum when using images of human remains. This may include a process of consultation with those communities. Images of human remains on the British Museum's Collection Online database that are deemed to be culturally sensitive usually include a warning or are excluded out of consideration for the relevant cultural groups. As with all aspects of display, photographs of human remains that are used in galleries or British Museum documentation (e.g. databases, publications or educational handouts) are accompanied by explanatory and contextual information. For images of human remains that are less than 100 years, the appropriate sections of the Human Tissue Act 2004 are taken into consideration.

Photography and filming in the British Museum galleries is not prohibited and, as discussed above, the British Museum ensures that human remains are displayed with care and thought. Applications to photograph or film human remains in the British Museum collection that are not on display (e.g. for research publications or documentaries) are assessed on a case-by-case basis by the relevant curatorial staff. This involves determining how the images or film will be used and whether this will be done in a sensitive and appropriate manner that complies with the British Museum Policy on Human Remains.[15]

Loans and human remains

Before authorizing a loan to another institution that includes human remains whether for scientific research (e.g. the CT scanning of a mummy; see Chapter Three, this volume) or an exhibition, the British Museum seeks assurances from the borrower that they are able to satisfy the legal, ethical and practical obligations proportionate to the age, ethnic origin and modern cultural significance of the human remains (Trustees of the British Museum 2013, 4). This may involve adding special conditions to the loan agreement with regard to the display, storage and handling of the human remains. The loan of any human remains for detailed study or scientific analysis involves the completion of an application form (see Chapter Three, this volume), which includes a detailed method statement agreed in advance, a list of the types of examination(s) permitted and under what conditions these can be performed. Any deviation from this statement requires new written consent before being undertaken. Importantly, the form also reminds researchers of the required ethical obligations during the storage, handling and analysis of human remains (Trustees of the British Museum 2013, 4).

Documenting human remains

Information on the collections held at the British Museum, including human remains, is available on the Collection Online database[16] as well as on other pages of the Museum's website.[17] One of the key aspects of curating any collection is generating, maintaining and improving the associated records. Ancient human remains provide a unique insight into human funerary practices and cultures of the past, but they also offer a wealth of information on human biology. There is a need for more detailed, standardized and accessible information on archaeological human remains in museum collections to be made available (Giesen et al. 2013; Roberts 2013) and shared through databases such as the Museum of London's Wellcome Osteological Research Database (Giesen et al. 2013; Redfern and Bekvalac 2013). The British Museum's records of large archaeological assemblages are also being improved to meet professional standards, guidelines and methods (e.g. Buikstra and Ubelaker 1994; Brickley and McKinley 2004; Roberts 2009).[18] These additional details provide information about the nature of the archaeological assemblage and results of scientific analyses. For example, the availability, type and current location of any remaining samples used in scientific tests is documented, along with results and relevant publications. Conservation treatments and recommendations are also recorded in the Museum's conservation database.

When appropriate and possible, information about skeletal remains are also being entered into a specific database for human remains, which allows for a greater number of variables to be recorded (e.g. a wider range of measurements, biological variables and scores) than the Museum's general curatorial database. This detailed recording system will allow researchers (British Museum staff and others) to have direct access to 'raw' standardized data. This will make it possible to compare the human remains in the British Museum collection to other populations and archaeological sites and provides a guidance for what may be recorded should researchers wish to use different methods. The data on bone measurements, for example, will indicate which bones are sufficiently preserved to be measured and, if necessary, have the potential to be reanalysed using alternative measuring techniques. Many researchers request to access the human remains in the British Museum collection every year (discussed in Chapter Three, this volume) and by making standardized data available, physical access to the human remains in the collection may not always be required, minimizing risk of damage to the collection. The British Museum also intends to make more information about human remains publicly available through its web pages and encourage the publication of specialist reports (e.g. Judd 2001; 2013).

Conclusion: continuing to care for the dead

The human remains held in the British Museum collection are a unique record of how societies have conceived of death and disposed of the remains of their dead. The analysis of human remains contributes significantly to academic disciplines such as archaeology and physical anthropology and allows us to discover more about human biology and past societies. The information and insight gained through the archaeological and scientific analysis of human remains appears to be ever-increasing, particularly as scientific methods improve and develop, all of which continues to inform our understanding of past societies which can then be shared with museum visitors. Alongside these public benefits comes a responsibility to care for human remains with respect and dignity, as well as maintain a healthy dialogue regarding the dead with the visiting public and with communities that have a direct or close cultural continuity with them.

Acknowledgements

I would like to acknowledge the help and input of my colleagues from the British Museum Human Remains Working Group and the support of the Institute for Bioarchaeology.

Notes

1 Burial Act 1857; Disused Burial Grounds Act 1884; and Disused Burial Grounds (Amendment) Act 1981.

2 The British Museum Act 1963; Human Tissue Act 2004.

3 The individual must have died less than 1,000 years before the day on which section 47 of the Human Tissue Act 2004 came into force (3 October 2005).

4 Ministry of Justice 2013 (available at http://www.justice.gov.uk/downloads/burials-and-coroners/statement-exhumation-human-remains-archaeological.pdf).

5 All of whom have statutory or legal responsibilities for archaeological burials in England.

6 See http://www.archaeologyuk.org/apabe/. This replaced the Advisory Panel on the Archaeology of Christian Burials in England (APACBE).

7 See http://www.archaeologyuk.org/apabe/Science_and_the_Dead.pdf.

8 See http://www.humanremains.specialistnetwork.org.uk/home.

9 See http://www.babao.org.uk/. The BABAO website also provides information on how best to document human remains including links to the Guidelines to the Standards for Recording Human Remains by Brickley and McKinley (2004) and Human Bones from Archaeological Sites: Guidelines for Producing Assessment Documents and Analytical Reports by Mays et al. (2004).

10 See http://www.hta.gov.uk/.

11 See http://www.britishmuseum.org/about_us/management/museum_governance.aspx.

12 In accordance with this guidance, the British Museum also maintains an online inventory of all human remains within the collection, including their date, provenance, nature and acquisition history.

13 See http://www.britishmuseum.org/about_us/news_and_press/statements/human_remains.aspx.

14 http://www.english-heritage.org.uk/professional/advice/advice-by-topic/heritage-science/archaeological-science/avebury-reburial-results/ and http://www.english-heritage.org.uk/content/imported-docs/k-o/opinion-survey-results.

15 Further information on curating and displaying human remains can be found in Williams 2001, Lohman and Goodnow 2006, Cassman et al. 2007, Cadot 2009, Roberts 2009, Sayer 2010, Márquez-Grant and Fibiger 2011 and Jenkins 2011. Giesen 2013 also provides examples of different museum policies (e.g. Redfern and Bekvalac 2013; Scott 2013), including Scottish and international perspectives (e.g. Giesen and White 2013; Hall 2013; Sharp and Hall 2013).

16 See http://www.britishmuseum.org/research/collection_online/search.aspx.

17   See http://www.britishmuseum.org/about_us/news_and_press/
     statements/human_remains.aspx.
18   These guidelines will over the coming years also be used as a
     template to update previous entries.

Bibliography

Brickley, M. and McKinley, J.I. (eds), 2004. *Guidelines to the Standards for Recording Human Remains, IFA Paper No. 7,* Institute of Field Archaeologists and British Association for Biological Anthropology and Osteoarchaeology, Reading (available online at http://www.babao.org.uk/HumanremainsFINAL.pdf).

Buikstra, J.E. and Ubelaker, D.H., 1994. *Standards for Data Collection from Human Remains.* Arkansas (Arkansas Archaeological Survey Series No. 44).

Cadot, L., 2009. *En chair et en Os: le Cadavre au Musée.* Paris (École du Louvre).

Carroll, Q., 2005. 'Who wants to rebury old skeletons?', *British Archaeology* 82 (May/June), 11–15.

Cassman, V., Odegaard, N. and Powell, J. (eds), 2007. *Human Remains: Guide for Museums and Academic Institutions.* Oxford.

DCMS (Department for Culture, Media and Sport) 2005. *Guidance for the Care of Human Remains in Museums* (available online at: http://webarchive.nationalarchives.gov.uk/+/http://www.culture.gov.uk/images/publications/GuidanceHumanRemains11Oct.pdf).

English Heritage 2009. *Research into Issues Surrounding Human Bones in Museums* (available online at http://www.english-heritage.org.uk/content/imported-docs/k-o/opinion-survey-results).

English Heritage and the Church of England 2005. *Guidance for Best Practice for Treatment of Human Remains Excavated from Christian Burial Grounds in England* (available online at http://www.english-heritage.org.uk/publications/human-remains-excavated-from-christian-burial-grounds-in-england/).

Fforde, C., 2004. *Collecting the Dead: Archaeology and the Reburial Issue.* London.

—, Hubert, J. and Turnbull, P. (eds), 2002. *The Dead and their Possessions – Repatriation in Principle, Policy and Practice.* London.

Garratt-Frost, S., 1992. *The Law and Burial Archaeology.* Birmingham (Institute of Field Archaeologists Technical Paper 11).

Giesen, M. (ed.), 2013. *Curating Human Remains – Caring for the Dead in the United Kingdom.* Woodbridge.

—, McCarrison, K. and Park, V., 2013. 'Dead and forgotten? Some observations on human remains documentation in the UK', in Giesen 2013, 53–64.

— and White, L., 2013. 'International perspectives towards human remains curation', in Giesen 2013, 13–23.

Hall, M.A., 2013. 'The quick and the deid: a Scottish perspective on caring for human remains at the Perth Museum and Art Gallery', in Giesen 2013, 75–86.

Jenkins, T., 2011. *Contesting Human Remains in Museum Collections.* London.

Judd, M., 2001. 'The human remains', in *Life on the Desert Edge: Seven Thousand Years of Settlement in the Northern Dongola Reach, Sudan,* vol. 2, ed. D.A. Welsby, 458–543. London (Sudan Archaeological Research Society Publication No. 7).

—, 2013. *Gabati: A Meroitic, Post-Meroitic and Medieval Cemetery in Central Sudan, Volume 2, The Physical Anthropology.* London (Sudan Archaeological Research Society Publication No. 20).

Kilmister, H., 2003. 'Visitor perceptions of Ancient Egyptian human remains in three United Kingdom museums', *Papers from the Institute of Archaeology* 14: 57–69.

Layton, R. (ed.), 1989. *Conflict in the Archaeology of Living Traditions.* London.

Lohman, J. and Goodnow, K (eds), 2006. *Human Remains and Museum Practice.* Paris and London.

Márquez-Grant, N. and Fibiger, L. (eds), 2011. *The Routledge Handbook of Archaeological Human Remains and Legislation – An International Guide to Laws and Practice in the Excavation and Treatment of Archaeological Human Remains.* London.

Mays, S., 2013. 'Curation of human remains at St Peter's Church, Barton-upon-Humber, England', in Giesen 2013, 109–21.

—, Brickley, M. and Dodwell, N. (eds), 2004. *Human Bones from Archaeological Sites: Guidelines for Producing Assessment Documents and Analytical Reports* (available online from http://www.english-heritage.org.uk/publications/human-bones-from-archaeological-sites/humanbones2004.pdf).

McKinley, J.I., 2013. '"No room at the inn" ... contract archaeology and the storage of human remains', in Giesen 2013, 135–45.

Parker Pearson, M., Pitts, M. and Sayer, D., 2013. 'Changes in the policy for excavating human remains in England and Wales', in Giesen 2013, 147–57.

Redfern, R. and Bekvalac, J., 2013. 'The Museum of London: an overview of policy and practice', in Giesen 2013, 87–98.

Roberts, C.A., 2009. *Human Remains in Archaeology: A Handbook.* York.

Roberts, C., 2013. 'Archaeological human remains and laboratories: attaining acceptable standards for curating skeletal remains for teaching and research', in Giesen 2013, 123–34.

Sayer, D., 2010. *Ethics and Burial Archaeology.* London.

Scott, G., 2013. 'Curating human remains in a regional museum: policy and practice at the Great North Museum: Hancock', in Giesen 2013, 99–107.

Sharp, J. and Hall, M.A., 2013. 'Tethering time and tide? Human remains guidance and legislation for Scottish museums', in Giesen 2013, 65–74.

Spoerry, P., 1993. *Archaeology and Legislation in Britain.* Hertford (*RESCUE*. The British Archaeological Trust).

Trustees of the British Museum 2013. The British Museum Policy on Human Remains (available online at http://www.britishmuseum.org/about_us/management/museum_governance.aspx).

White, B., 2011. 'The United Kingdom', in Márquez-Grant and Fibiger 2011, 479–91.

Williams, E. (ed.), 2001. *Human Remains: Conservation, Retrieval and Analysis. Proceedings of a Conference held in Williamsburg.* Oxford (British Archeological Reports International Series 934).

Woodhead, C., 2013. 'Care, custody and display of human remains: legal and ethical obligations', in Giesen 2013, 31–41.

Chapter 2
Looking Death in the Face
Different Attitudes towards Bog Bodies and their Display with a Focus on Lindow Man

Jody Joy

'Death destroys individuality – but not his … When we look at Lindow Man, we are looking at the present, not the past' (Jones 2007, 23).

Since the late 1990s there has been an increasing discussion over the 'rights of the dead' and the ethics of storing and displaying human remains in British museums, and academics and museum professionals have questioned what should be done with them when they are discovered (e.g. Bahn 1984; Parker Pearson 1999, ch. 8; Swain 2002; Curtis 2003; Sanders 2009, 183–7; Alberti *et al.* 2009; Sayer 2010, ch. 3). To date, discussions have focused on issues of repatriation and reburial rather than display (Alberti *et al.* 2009, 133). In this chapter the display of human remains is considered with respect to the well-preserved ancient remains from bogs, generally known as bog bodies. Specifically, this chapter will discuss the remains of an adult male discovered in August 1984 at Lindow Moss, near Wilmslow, Cheshire, who has come to be known as 'Lindow Man' (Stead and Turner 1985; Stead 1986 *et al.*; Turner and Scaife 1995; Joy 2009) (**Pl. 1**).

Although all human remains in museums demand special treatment and should be treated with respect (see DCMS 2005), it is argued here that bog bodies are a special category as they are fleshed. Skeletons or cremated remains usually displayed in museums can be viewed at a distance, one step removed from their humanity as the features of people we recognize in everyday encounters, skin, hair, facial features and wrinkles are not preserved. Bog bodies challenge this separation as their skin and hair have been preserved by the bog and details such as facial features and even finger prints can be eerily prominent. This has the effect of bringing the past into the present as they appear to have been 'frozen in time' (Sanders 2009, 220). This is underlined through the creation of facial reconstructions (**Pl. 2**) (see Prag and Neave 1997), which often feature prominently in bog body displays. Creating facial reconstructions is not an exact science. For example, the accuracy of the facial reconstruction of Lindow Man has been questioned because it was produced solely from radiographs (Wilkinson 2007, 265). However, despite these problems, facial reconstructions can be very powerful images, acting as visual reminders that past peoples were 'just like us'.

As Melanie Giles observes (2009, 78), '… it is the appearance of these remains [bog bodies], particularly the faces of the dead, which attract our imagination'. Since they are so well preserved, it is possible to make out facial features and even to read something into the character of the individual – the furrowed brow of Lindow Man or the perceived serenity of the expression on Tollund Man's face. This creates a very different experience when bog bodies are encountered in museums and they can provoke feelings of fascination as well as distress (Jones 2007, 23). Indeed, some critics of bog body displays claim they are a kind of 'pornography of death', a source of 'grim fascination' or 'morbid voyeurism' (see Parker Pearson 1999, 183).

The unusual recovery contexts of bog bodies and their remarkable level of preservation also mean that the interpretations are richer than usual for archaeological remains. Based on the analysis of preserved skin and hair, as well as internal organs and the surrounding peat, it is

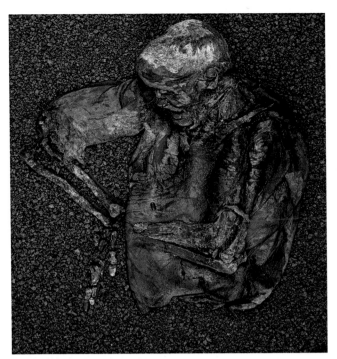

Plate 1 Lindow Man, discovered at Lindow Moss, Cheshire, August 1984, *c.* 2 BC–AD 119. British Museum, London (1984,1002.1)

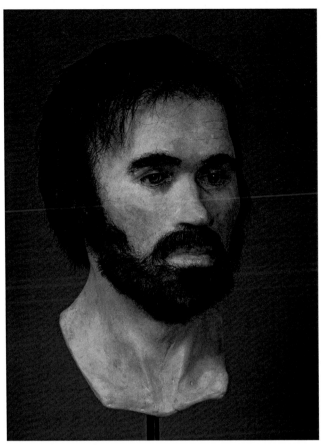

Plate 2 Facial reconstruction of Lindow Man

possible to ascertain details such as the cause of death, their last meal, general health and specifics of their environment, which results in the ability to build complex personal stories or biographies. This individualization is emphasized by giving bog bodies names such as 'Old Croghan Man' or 'Yde Girl'. Linking bog bodies to place names situates them within the present-day landscape, blurring boundaries with the distant past (Sanders 2009, 223).

As a result of these effects, bog bodies have been attributed significance beyond archaeological circles and often attract media attention. Bog bodies have been linked to regional and national identities; included in discussions of reburial and restitution, as well as religion; used as tropes for poetry; and even portrayed as characters in horror films (e.g. the 2009 film *Legend of the Bog* staring Vinnie Jones). The display of bog bodies in museums will be discussed below, as well as the reception of these displays by the general public, but first I will discuss what a bog body actually is and introduce some of the wider debates associated with the display of human remains in museums.

What is a bog body?

'Bog body' is a term that describes any human remains, many extremely well preserved, which have been recovered from a bog (an area of wet, spongy ground) (Glob 1969; van der Sanden 1996; Joy 2009, 20). Bog bodies have been found across north-western Europe, specifically Britain, Ireland, Denmark, the Netherlands and north-west Germany, and date from the Mesolithic period to the present day. Some bog bodies are deliberate burials, others are likely to be accidental drownings. It is impossible to be certain how many bog bodies have been recovered as many found in previous centuries were quickly reburied and we only have documentary evidence of their existence (referred to by Van der Sanden (1996, 20) as 'paper bodies'). The total number could, however, possibly be in the thousands.

The extraordinary preservation of bog bodies is due to a number of factors. First, bogs are cold, acidic and lacking in oxygen, which makes them relatively hostile environments for putrefaction. More important is the presence of a kind of sugar called sphagnan, which is released during the decay of the sphagnum mosses that inhabit 'raised' or 'blanket' bog environments. Sphagnan acts as a natural tanning agent, effectively turning tissues into leather. It also reacts with the digestive enzymes produced by decay-inducing bacteria, effectively immobilizing them where they come into contact with fragments of sphagnum moss (Painter 1995, 99).

The term 'bog body' usually refers to human remains dating to the Iron Age, specifically 500 BC to AD 100. This is because bog bodies dating to this time have been seen to share a number of characteristics, first identified by Glob (1969). Many show signs of a violent death, or even 'overkill', meaning that far more force or violence was used than was necessary to cause death. Several of these bodies were also deposited naked and were tied down in pools in the bog. Drawing on these characteristics, as well as descriptions of Iron Age peoples by Roman writers, Glob suggested that people deposited in bogs during the Iron Age were the victims of ritual sacrifice and were killed and placed in bogs as offerings to the gods. This interpretation has proven to be very influential and has been developed and contested by various scholars (e.g. Stead *et al.* 1986, 177–80; Ross and Robins 1989; Green 1998; Hutton 2004; Joy 2009).

The ethics of displaying human remains in museums

A discussion of the ethics of displaying human remains in Britain was driven by a call for the repatriation of

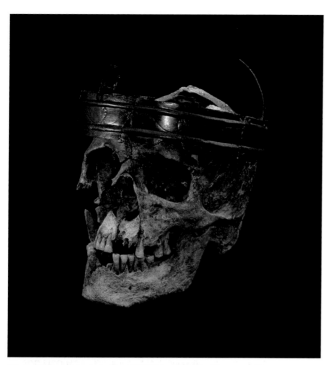

Plate 3 Crown and skull, *c.* 250 BC–150 BC, discovered in an inhumation burial, part of a large Iron Age cemetery at Mill Hill, Deal, Kent. British Museum, London (1990,0102.28)

indigenous human remains by groups in North America, Australia, New Zealand and the South Pacific (e.g. May *et al.* 2005), as well as the scandal of the unauthorized removal, retention and disposal of human tissue at Alder Hey Children's Hospital, Liverpool, during the late 1980s and early 1990s (see Jenkins 2011, ch. 1; see Chapter One, this volume).

Increasingly in the last few years, modern-day Pagan groups have vocalized their interest in ancient British human remains as they regard remains like those from the site of Avebury or Lindow Man to be their ancestors (Bienkowski 2006, 9; Restall Orr 2006, 1–4). A number of these groups have even suggested that some human remains stored in museums should be reburied (see Moshenska 2009; Thackray and Payne 2010; Blain 2011, 1025–7; HAD 2011). Although the views of Pagans requesting reburial should be respected, they represent a very vocal minority. In a recent survey commissioned by English Heritage, over 90% of museum goers who were questioned agreed that museums should be allowed to display human remains (see Chapter One, this volume; BDRC 2009, 7). There is also no single 'Pagan voice' or group which represents all Pagan views as not all Pagans support reburial (see Restall Orr 2006; Wallis and Blain 2006; Sayer 2010, 203). This makes it difficult for museums as these institutions also have to consider the views of the wider general public and other interested groups such as archaeologists and scientists.

At present there are no clear guidelines on the reburial of ancient British human remains. The Human Tissue Act 2004 only allows national museums such as the British Museum to de-accession human remains less than 1,000 years old, meaning that repatriation of accessioned ancient British remains is currently illegal. In April 2008, the British government reinterpreted the 1857 Burial Act, stating that all archaeologically excavated human remains discovered in

England and Wales should be reburied after two years (Parker Pearson *et al.* 2011). This was intended as a temporary measure until new legislation could be put in place, but it effectively meant that only two years of scientific research into newly discovered human remains, no matter how important, would be possible as no licenses were being granted for the retention of human remains in museums. After a very public campaign by archaeologists, the Ministry of Justice should soon provide a more flexible interpretation of the licence that will once again allow for newly discovered archaeological human remains to be deposited in national museum collections (see Chapter One, this volume). However, these events underline the vagaries of current legislation which are open to different interpretations.

Arguments for the continuing display of human remains in museums centre on their scientific importance, both present and future, as well as the educational advantages of displaying human remains (e.g. Payne 2010, 13). Others stress the benefit derived from seeing dead bodies in a society in which we are otherwise shielded from death (Parker Pearson 1999, 183; Curtis 2003, 30; Sayer 2011).

These debates have prompted the Department for Culture, Media and Sport (DCMS) and institutions such as the British Museum to issue guidelines for the care and display of human remains in museums (DCMS 2005; Trustees of the British Museum 2013). These guidelines suggest that displays are planned in order to encourage visitors to view human remains 'respectfully'. Respect is a variable concept and definitions diverge widely between individuals and groups with different interests (see Bienkowski 2006, 11). However, the guidelines do set out how human remains should be displayed (DCMS 2005, 20). The underlying principle of the guidelines is that the decision to show human remains should not be made lightly and careful thought must be given to the reasons for and the circumstances of the display. DCMS guidelines stipulate that 'human remains should only be displayed if the museum believes that it makes a material contribution to a particular interpretation; and that contribution could not be made equally effectively in another way'. Human remains should also be positioned so that people do not come across them 'unawares'. As one would expect, the guidelines also stipulate that 'display conditions, like storage conditions should be safe, secure and with stable, monitored environments, which are kept clean and regularly checked for pests and other potential threats'. It is also made clear that 'displays should always be accompanied by sufficient explanatory material'. This is another critical aspect of the display of human remains that is often highlighted in surveys of the general public and consultation with other interested groups (see Eklund 2007).

An example of the impact of these guidelines on museum display can be seen in the Iron Age Gallery (Room 50) at the British Museum, where Lindow Man is currently located. During a refurbishment of the gallery undertaken in 2006–7, an audit of the human remains on display was conducted. A skull (**Pl. 3**) and the bones of a child's lower arm (Morel Collection no. 1985a), which had been used to exhibit a priestly crown and a collection of bracelets, were removed as it was judged that the display of those remains did not make a 'material contribution' to the interpretation being put forward. The decoration on the crown could be viewed equally effectively on a specially constructed mount. The bracelets, and not the human remains, were of interest in a display of grave-goods from the Marne region of France. Similarly, the Manchester Museum decided to remove the head of Worsley Man from display in 2007 as he was displayed on a corridor and was not 'supported by sufficient contextual information to make sense' of his death (Giles 2009, 93). The reasons for the continuing display of Lindow Man will be set out as part of the conclusion of this chapter.

Other bog bodies

In this section the history of the discovery and display of bog bodies from elsewhere will be briefly discussed to serve as a direct comparison to the display of Lindow Man. Discussion will concentrate on Grauballe Man and Tollund Man, both discovered in Denmark in the early 1950s (Glob 1969) and well documented (Glob 1969; Asingh 2007; Asingh and Lynnerup 2007; Asingh 2009; Fischer 2012).

Discovery

Prior to the 1950s and the discoveries of Tollund Man and Grauballe Man, hundreds of bog bodies were uncovered across north-west Europe (Strehle 2007, 33). The majority were reburied. Some were taken to museums, but no attempt was made to conserve the remains permanently. Consequently, they were left to dry out causing the bodies to shrink and significantly reduce the amount and quality of information recoverable using scientific techniques (Turner 1995; Van der Sanden 1995; Asingh 2009, 49). Only with the discovery of Grauballe Man in 1952 was an effort made to preserve an entire bog body for posterity and display it to the public. This is partly due to the limitations of science at the time when Tollund Man was discovered as well as finds from the 18th and 19th centuries which were either reburied or left to dry out (see Strehle 2007, 33), but is also due to the wider attitudes of museum curators and the general public.

For example, when Tollund Man was unearthed in 1950, his remains were sent by representatives from Silkeborg Museum to the National Museum in Copenhagen. Only his head, right foot and the thumb of his right hand were conserved (Glob 1969, 35; Fischer 2012, 102), and it was normal practice at the National Museum at the time to clean any soft tissues from the bones of bog bodies (Fischer 2012, 101–2). According to Strehle (2007, 33), 'no attempt was made to conserve the whole of the body. It was seen as being too macabre to exhibit an entire corpse'. Asingh explains that it was 'on conservation-related and probably, in particular, ethical grounds that Johannes Brønsted, the National Museum's director, found the human body unsuitable for conservation and future storage as a museum artefact, and absolutely not for exhibition to the public. "It is, you know, a pretty macabre sight", was the view of a like-minded senior curator' (Asingh 2009, 12). Others may argue that it was more insensitive to only preserve selected parts of Tollund Man's body and remove soft tissues from the skeleton.

The influence of Professor Peter Glob was instrumental in transforming these attitudes as he felt that bog bodies were important for scientific research and should be displayed to the public (Glob 1969, 41; Asingh 2009, 12). Therefore when Grauballe Man was discovered by peat-cutters in 1952, Glob was soon at the site and took the remains to the new conservation workshops at the Prehistoric Museum at Århus, which had been equipped with bog bodies in mind. Grauballe Man soon came to prominence in the national and international press and Glob portrayed him as a tall, well-built man who went to his death as a willing sacrifice. According to Pauline Asingh (2009, 18, 26), this romantic interpretation appealed to a post-war Denmark, with the Danes more willing to see themselves as the descendants of a noble person who made the ultimate sacrifice, rather than the descendants of war-like and violent ancestors. Building on this publicity, and against the advice of the conservator, Glob immediately put Grauballe Man on public display. He was laid in a glass coffin and for the next ten days 18,000 people queued for long periods to view his remains (Glob 1969, 45; Asingh 2009, 24). This period of display cemented Grauballe Man in the consciousness of the public and he became something of a 'national treasure' in a way that Tollund Man had not (Asingh 2009, 24–6).

Scientific research and conservation

Soon after his discovery, Grauballe Man was the subject of an ambitious programme of scientific investigation, voraciously reported on by the press and devoured by the public. As Asingh observes, it must '… have given rise to certain ethical and humane scruples when Glob so single-mindedly handed Grauballe Man over to science. Seen with modern eyes, this was a groundbreaking, cross-disciplinary piece of work, the like of which we have first acquired a tradition for in recent decades' (2009, 37). The extent to which scientific analysis of bog bodies is now commonplace is demonstrated by the two bog bodies recovered in close succession in Ireland, Old Croghan Man and Clonycaven Man, in the early years of this century and now on display at the National Museum of Ireland. These were immediately the subject of a comprehensive scientific examination presented to the public in a popular television BBC *Timewatch* documentary, *The Bog Bodies*.

The only task that remained was the conservation of Grauballe Man's remains (see Strehle 2007). Again, this was not as simple a decision as it would seem from today's perspective, where it is standard practice to conserve bog body remains and quite common to place them on public display. As we have seen, the head and right foot of Tollund Man were conserved, but the torso was left to dry out and the soft tissues removed from the skeleton (Strehle 2007, 33; Fischer 2012, 102). Tollund Man's head was soaked in alcohol and paraffin, but it is thought to have shrunk by approximately 12% during this process (Fischer 2012, 53). Consequently the conservator at Århus, Lange-Kornbak, chose a different method, tanning Grauballe Man like leather by soaking him for 18 months in a vat of water and oak bark, followed by a further soaking in a solution of distilled water and Turkish-red oil. After a final touch up, the results of his conservation were declared satisfactory and from May 1955, Grauballe Man has been on display in the

Prehistoric Museum at Århus (Strehle 2007, 46; Asingh 2009, 67).

'Frozen in time': different approaches to the display of bog bodies

A great deal of emphasis is placed on recreating the context of discovery in the display of bog bodies, creating the impression that they have been freshly exposed and may have 'died yesterday' (Giles 2009, 90; Sanders 2009, 220). For example, a cast of the underside of Grauballe Man was created before he was conserved so that they could display him in the exact position he was found in (Glob 1969, 58). Despite the fact that the body of Tollund Man was not originally preserved, they have made a replica of his body for the current display (Fischer 2012, 105–7). An exhibit at the Landesmuseum Natur und Mensch, Oldenburg, Germany, even displayed a bog body behind a huge slice of peat (see Sanders 2009, fig. 6.3). In this instance, the bog body is almost secondary to the natural phenomenon of the peat layers.

The bodies in the National Museum of Ireland lie prone in the same way as these other bodies, but no attempt has been made to recreate the boggy environment. Rather than creating an impression of being 'freshly found', the four bodies on display are presented on their own in clear glass, creating a 'neutral' or 'forensic' appearance. The bodies are displayed alongside accompanying objects as part of a special exhibition which argues that bog bodies and artefacts were deposited close to ancient boundaries, with bog bodies acquiring a protective function (Kelly 2006). Although there are some problems with this interpretation, such as the assumption of the long continuation of ancient boundaries (see Giles 2009, 87), here the bog bodies form the pivotal part of a coherent intellectual argument. Each of the four bodies is contained within a specially designed oval-shaped 'pod' with information about the body presented alongside each display. This separates the body from the main exhibition and allows visitors to choose if they want to view the body. It also limits the number of people able to see the bodies at any one time (O'Sullivan 2007, 20). Reactions to the bog body display at the National Museum of Ireland are generally positive, although a member of the public complained to the *Irish Times* that she found the exhibition 'inappropriate' and 'upsetting' (O'Sullivan 2007, 18). Outside the display room of Windeby Girl and Rendswühren and Österby Men at the Archäologisches Landesmuseum at Schloss Gottorf, Schleswig-Holstein, Germany, is a board where visitors are invited to post comments on the display. According to Sanders (2009, 184, fig. 6.5), comments fall into two camps: those that feel bog bodies should not be displayed; and those who feel their display in museums is legitimate and worthwhile.

Summary

We can see from this brief examination of the discovery and display of bog bodies from elsewhere that until the discovery of Grauballe Man, people in Denmark had very different attitudes towards bog bodies. The influence of Glob in changing people's attitudes is clear. He established the practice of scientific examination, conservation and display of bog bodies. Glob's book, *The Bog People*, which was published in English (Glob 1969), played a key role in placing bog bodies into the international public imagination (Sanders 2009, 17). As far as the author is aware, all well-preserved bog bodies that have subsequently been discovered have been conserved and put on public display. Many old finds have also been recovered from museum stores and are on view to the public.

Lindow Man: history of recovery and display

Discovery

Receptions and reactions to bog bodies and their display will now be explored through the example of Lindow Man. On 1 August 1984, a well-preserved human leg was uncovered on the conveyor belt of a peat-cutting company located near Wilmslow in Cheshire (Turner 1986; Joy 2009). The police were informed and the leg was taken away for investigation. The county archaeologist, Rick Turner, heard about the discovery from a local reporter and went out to the site the following day to investigate. He inspected the peat-cutting and found a flap of skin, which looked to be part of a human body. He returned on 6 August and the area was excavated. A block of peat containing the body was removed and taken to the mortuary at the nearby Macclesfield General Hospital. Although archaeologists were certain that the human remains were ancient, the police were investigating a murder in the area and wanted to be certain beyond doubt that the remains were not modern. By 17 August, radiocarbon dating had shown that the body was at least 1,000 years old. In the meantime, the landowners presented the remains to the British Museum and on 21 August the body was taken to London, where on 24 September the process of removing the peat from the body began. To aid the process, X-rays were taken. Progress was slow as his body had to be kept below 4°C in order to delay the onset of decay. The remains were revealed to be the upper torso of an adult male. It took five days to excavate the body from the peat and progress was filmed for a BBC *QED* documentary. A correspondent from *The Sunday Times* was also present (Stead 1986). The discovery was announced to the press in the second week of the excavation (see **Pl. 4**) and it received worldwide coverage. The press named the body Pete Marsh, but he was called Lindow Man by the scientists investigating his remains (Stead 1986, 16). Reports on the initial discovery and scientific investigation concentrated on his antiquity, scientific discoveries and the context of his death, specifically its violent nature and how he ended up in the bog. Depending on the expert consulted, Lindow Man was variously portrayed as a murder victim (Nurse 1984) or as a ritual sacrifice (Gillie 1984). When the *QED* film was screened in April 1985, it was watched by more than 10 million people. Early in 1986 the programme also won the British Association for the Advancement of Science award.

The remains of Lindow Man were then the subject of a comprehensive scientific investigation. This continued until December 1986 (see Stead *et al.* 1986). However, throughout the process, the primary concern appears to have been to conserve the body. As Stead states, '… to excavate, record, investigate and display, but essentially to preserve it' (1986,

14). In the middle of December 1984, Lindow Man was handed over to the conservators who had to devise a suitable method of conserving his body (see Omar and McCord 1986; Omar *et al.* 1989; Daniels 1991; Daniels 1996). A number of methods were considered, but the conservators eventually settled on freeze-drying. This had been routinely used on waterlogged wood since the 1970s, but this was the first time that the method had been used to preserve a human body. Freeze-drying removes moisture by sublimation. Unlike air drying, this preserves cell structure and reduces shrinkage. The possibility of shrinkage was further reduced by first of all soaking Lindow Man's remains in a solution of polyethylene glycol (Omar and McCord 1986). Initial assessments of the freeze-drying process were positive. The shrinkage of the body was less than 5%. Although the body was now less flexible, it could be handled more easily. There was also a noticeable lightening of skin colour and no discernible odour coming from the body (Omar and McCord 1986, 20).

Exhibition

Lindow Man was first put on public display at the British Museum in July 1986 as part of the *Archaeology in Britain* exhibition, situated in Rooms 49–50. The exhibition closed in February 1987 and at the request of the Director of the Manchester Museum, Lindow Man was loaned to the Manchester Museum for six months until October 1987. The loan proved extremely popular with up to 2,000 visitors per day and it was extended into 1988. It was during this time that a campaign to return Lindow Man to the north-west began, headed by local woman Barbara O'Brien. Headlines such as 'Pete should stay in the North', 'He is ours', 'The body snatchers' and 'Tug-o-war over body from the bog' appeared in local and national newspapers throughout the summer and autumn of 1987. Local MPs even became involved. Debate also turned to the 'north–south divide' with local opinions such as 'London has everything. He should be kept here…' being forcefully expressed (Anon. 1987). Perhaps the most memorable feature of the campaign was the song *Lindow Man we Want you Back Again*, performed by pupils from Lindow Primary School in November 1987.

Despite the campaign in the north-west, as outlined above, the legal title to Lindow Man had been handed over to the British Museum by the landowners shortly after his discovery and Lindow Man was returned to the British Museum in 1988. On his return he was redisplayed in the Central Saloon Galleries 36 and 37. The showcase was positioned alongside and facing the Hinton St Mary mosaic. In this location the body was subject to high levels of natural light (see Bradley *et al.* 2008). Concerned about the effect of the light on his body, the display was altered. Fluorescent lights were switched off and a solid back and canopy were added to the display case in an attempt to shield the body from light. The showcase was also reoriented so that the canopy sheltered Lindow Man from light spilling through the skylights. Other than a second loan to Manchester Museum from March–September 1991, Lindow Man remained in the Central Saloon until 1997 when he was moved to his current position in the Iron Age Gallery (Room 50).

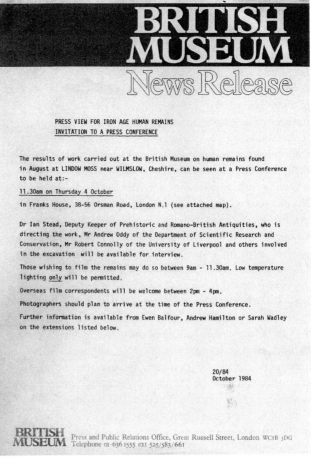

BRITISH MUSEUM
News Release

PRESS VIEW FOR IRON AGE HUMAN REMAINS
INVITATION TO A PRESS CONFERENCE

The results of work carried out at the British Museum on human remains found in August at LINDOW MOSS near WILMSLOW, Cheshire, can be seen at a Press Conference to be held at:-

11.30am on Thursday 4 October

in Franks House, 38-56 Orsman Road, London N.1 (see attached map).

Dr Ian Stead, Deputy Keeper of Prehistoric and Romano-British Antiquities, who is directing the work, Mr Andrew Oddy of the Department of Scientific Research and Conservation, Mr Robert Connolly of the University of Liverpool and others involved in the excavation will be available for interview.

Those wishing to film the remains may do so between 9am - 11.30am. Low temperature lighting only will be permitted.

Overseas film correspondents will be welcome between 2pm - 4pm.

Photographers should plan to arrive at the time of the Press Conference.

Further information is available from Ewen Balfour, Andrew Hamilton or Sarah Wadley on the extensions listed below.

20/84
October 1984

BRITISH MUSEUM Press and Public Relations Office, Great Russell Street, London WC1B 3DG Telephone 01-636 1555 ext 525/583/661

Plate 4 Press release announcing the discovery of a bog body at Lindow Moss

Interpretation of death

The interpretation of Lindow Man's death has been the source of much debate (see Joy 2009, ch. 4). In two articles published in the *Times Literary Supplement,* the historian Ronald Hutton (2004) and the former British Museum curator and current head of research JD Hill (Hutton 2004; Hill 2004), discussed the dominant interpretation by leading authorities on Iron Age religion that Lindow Man was the victim of a ritual sacrifice, in particular that he suffered a 'threefold death' and died in the Iron Age (e.g. Ross and Robins 1989; Green 1998, 177). This was the account presented on the original display panel positioned alongside Lindow Man and the weight of these interpretations have caused the death of Lindow Man to be widely interpreted as the ultimate proof of the occurrence of human sacrifice in prehistoric Britain.

However, as Hutton (2004) argues, the proof is far from definitive. Current dating evidence, which dates Lindow Man's death to 2 BC–AD 119 (Gowlett *et al.* 1989), means he is equally likely to have died in the Roman period as in the Iron Age. This is important as it removes the death of Lindow Man in time significantly away from the deaths of many of the continental bog bodies discussed as sacrificial victims by Glob (1969). There are also discrepancies in the account of the extent of Lindow Man's injuries. In the original report of his discovery and subsequent scientific investigation, Iain West, a pathologist at Guy's Hospital, suggests Lindow Man was struck on the head twice (West 1986) and suffered a heavy blow to the back which resulted in a broken rib. The animal sinew found around his neck was used as a garrotte and caused his neck fracture, and at the same time it quickened the flow of blood from a deep cut to his neck. This violent death is interpreted by West as being suggestive of a ritual sacrifice and this reading was taken up by Stead in the conclusion of the report (West 1986, 80; Stead 1986, 180). These different injuries were later interpreted as a 'three-stage' or 'triple death' (Ross and Robins 1989, 45–9). However, in the same report (Connolly 1986), and an earlier article (Connolly 1985), Robert Connolly of Liverpool University provided a very different account and interpretation of Lindow Man's injuries. According to Connolly, the wound to the neck and the broken rib occurred after his recovery from the bog. Connolly agrees with West that the two blows to the top of the head were not immediately fatal, but rendered Lindow Man unconscious. His broken neck was caused not by the use of the animal sinew as a garrotte, but rather by a heavy blow to the back of the head and the animal sinew is interpreted as a necklace. The 'ligature marks' around his neck could have been caused by the sinew as the body bloated when it was submerged in the pool. Following this account of Lindow Man's injuries, Connolly (1985, 17) concludes that Lindow Man is more likely to have been the victim of a violent robbery than a ritual sacrifice.

Lindow Man could therefore have been the subject of a ritual sacrifice or an unfortunate robbery victim. Other interpretations are also possible. For example, the animal sinew could have been used as a tether and Lindow Man could therefore be an executed prisoner. In 2010, following these debates, the exhibition panel detailing the account of Lindow Man's death was updated for his display at the British Museum (see below).

Recent exhibitions

Recent refurbishment of the prehistoric galleries prompted the British Museum to offer Lindow Man on loan to the Manchester Museum for a period of one year from 19 April 2008–19 April 2009. This loan was organized as part of the British Museum's Partnership UK scheme, which makes British Museum exhibits more accessible to people throughout the country. The two earlier exhibitions at Manchester had presented the 'life and times' of Lindow Man, as well as the latest scientific discoveries (see Sitch 2009, 51). The 2008 exhibition was very different, as Bryan Sitch asserts: 'the Manchester Museum wanted to engage a new generation of people from Manchester and the North-West with one of Britain's most famous archaeological discoveries, to stimulate public debate about how human remains are treated in museums and other public institutions, to display the body in a respectful manner and to explore different interpretations of the body' (Sitch 2010a). Consultation was at the heart of the Manchester Museum's preparations for the 2008–9 exhibition as, in a series of meetings, they sought the views of a variety of interested groups, including archaeologists, Pagans and members of the local community (see Sitch 2007).

The result, *Lindow Man: A Bog Body Mystery*, was an innovative and thought-provoking exhibition, which sought to illustrate how Lindow Man means different things to different people by presenting his story through the eyes of seven individuals, including the peat-digger who found him, an archaeologist, a forensic scientist, two museum curators, someone from the local community and a Druid (Sitch 2010b). In addition to interview extracts and Iron Age artefacts loaned by the British Museum, the exhibition was supported by personal objects including peat spades, laboratory equipment, a Pagan wand and items contemporary to the time of his discovery, such as a Care Bear (Sitch 2009, 52). Reaction to the exhibition was mixed. Some critics liked the multivocal approach and the fact that no 'right way' of interpreting Lindow Man was presented (Burch 2008). Others criticized the apparent lack of information on the Iron Age, stating that the exhibition was more about the 1980s than the life and times of Lindow Man (Schofield 2008). Comments left by visitors to the exhibition were similarly contrasting (see Sitch 2009, 52–3). While many liked the inclusion of modern-day perspectives and objects, more traditional museum goers clearly expected a straightforward presentation of Iron Age life and some struggled with the polyvocal approach. This problem was recognized by the Manchester Museum and more Visitor Service Assistants were put in place to provide assistance throughout the course of the exhibition.

After the exhibition at the Manchester Museum, Lindow Man then went on display at the Great North Museum, Newcastle, in the exhibition *Lindow Man: Body of Evidence* (August–November 2009). In stark contrast to the Manchester exhibition, this was a more traditional exhibition, complete with models of roundhouses, the prominent display of Iron Age objects and an interactive video exploring how Lindow Man had died. It is interesting that this exhibition has generated far less debate than *Lindow Man: A Bog Body Mystery* amongst academics and the public.

Summary

We have seen how Lindow Man has been the subject of major public and media attention. At the time of his discovery, people were fascinated to learn about the discoveries being made about his life on a daily basis. This is reflected in the huge audience figures for the BBC documentary charting the scientific investigation of his body. Interestingly, there was no debate at the time concerning whether Lindow Man should be conserved and put on public display, and discussions focused rather on how to preserve his remains. Later on, a strongly held sentiment that his remains should stay in the north-west meant that public and press attention focused on this debate. The decision by the Manchester Museum in a recent exhibition to present his remains in a different way was arguably sparked by wider debates in the discipline concerning how museums should care for human remains. As public reactions to this exhibition demonstrate, debates driven within the museum profession do not necessarily marry with the concerns and reactions of the public (see Jenkins 2011). This is demonstrated by the lack of attention and debate surrounding the more traditional exhibition of Lindow Man at the Great North Museum and underlined by public enquiries to the British Museum relating to Lindow Man. A very high proportion of public enquiries regarding

Lindow Man, roughly 75%, are from university students investigating the ethics of displaying human remains in museums. Questions from members of the public tend to concern details about Lindow Man's life and death, rather than whether or not he should be on display which is not questioned.

We can also see how Lindow Man has been appropriated into wider debates with diverse motivations (see Sayer 2010, 70). Many academics have based their careers on particular interpretations of bog bodies and professional reputations have been built and put on the line. Furthermore, although there was clear local affection for Lindow Man, as museum documentation and the opinions of people interviewed at the time in the local press make clear, the campaign to return him to the North-West was also driven by underlying tensions between a regional and a national museum and their right to major archaeological discoveries, as well as the north–south divide in Britain, in particular the view that 'all the good things go to London'. Finally, Restall Orr (2006) and others used the display of Lindow Man at Manchester Museum as a platform to put forward particular views on religion and the reburial of archaeological remains.

Displaying Lindow Man

In this final section, the present display of Lindow Man is described and assessed. As a conclusion, in the light of recent debates concerning display and reburial, the argument for his continuing display will be put forward.

The present display of Lindow Man

Lindow Man has been on permanent display at the British Museum for over 20 years and has been in his current location in the Iron Age Gallery, with his display largely unaltered, since 1997. He is displayed in a square case which is at hip-level. Two sides of the square are accessible to the public, while the other two sides support a canopy over the display case (**Pl. 5**). On one of these two sides is a photograph of the find spot, Lindow Moss. Surrounding the case is a metal handrail, which now supports two small information panels. To one side of the display on a nearby wall is a third, much larger display panel with a further image of Lindow Moss on it. Lindow Man sits on a bed of specially treated bark chippings, which are inert for conservation reasons but are designed to replicate the dark peat of a bog. Although he was originally deposited face-down in the bog, he has been inverted for display to lie face-up.

Although the display case is over 15 years old, it is very reliable and it maintains temperature to within 1° of 20°C and relative humidity to within 2% of 55%. These conditions are constantly monitored by museum staff. The intensity of light in his display case is now carefully controlled to between 30–50 lux, as it was discovered that previous exposure to strong light had caused his skin to lighten (Bradley *et al.* 2008).

Assessing Lindow Man's display

The current display was put in place before the DCMS guidelines for the display of human remains were drawn up. Nevertheless, it fortunately follows the recommendations found in the DCMS guidelines. In addition to careful environmental monitoring, Lindow Man is positioned in one corner of the gallery, away from the main thoroughfare and therefore fulfilling one of the guidelines stipulated by the DCMS and already outlined in this chapter that where possible human remains should be displayed in an area of the gallery which is specially partitioned or in an alcove (DCMS 2005, 20). However, the current space is not ideal and with unlimited resources it would be completely revised. For example, although the lack of space restricts the number of people able to view the body at any one time, it often becomes overcrowded. This is not helped by the fact that his remains are only visible from two sides. The height of the case also makes it difficult for wheelchair users and children to view Lindow Man's remains. Finally, the position of the main information panel, on the opposite wall, often causes confusion as people search for information about Lindow Man. Following some of the methods employed to display the bog bodies at the National Museum of Ireland, Lindow Man could be displayed in his own pod, allowing people to make a choice of whether or not to view his remains. His case would ideally be accessible all the way round with the height lowered slightly to improve visibility. Lindow Man is already positioned alongside a cabinet displaying artefacts associated with 'making a living', many dating to the 1st century AD. This case is full of objects, such as spindle whorls and weaving combs, which were used by people in their day-to-day lives. On the back of his exhibition case there is also a display panel detailing the types of houses most people lived in. Although no explicit connection is made, it is hoped that visitors make this association between Lindow Man and everyday life in the past. To clarify this link, a small exhibition space on the subject of life in the 1st century AD could be established, separate from the current gallery and with Lindow Man at its centre. This would reinforce the connection between people and the artefacts on display.

To achieve these aims, Room 50 needs to be completely rearranged and any major revisions to Lindow Man's display will have to wait for the next gallery refurbishment. In the meantime, small improvements have been made. Questionnaires show that visitors expect to see sufficient explanatory material when human remains are put on display. They want to know when the person died; how old they were; how they died; what sort of life they led; and what they looked like. Some people have also indicated that stories about the lives of past peoples are important to them. DCMS guidelines also stipulate that displays of human remains should have 'sufficient explanatory material' (DCMS 2005, 20). With this in mind, as well as the issue of people searching for the wall panel, information accompanying Lindow Man has been updated. In addition to the large panel explaining the context of his discovery and the circumstances of his death, two smaller panels were added explaining the scientific investigation and preservation of his body, as well as outlining the questions surrounding the extent of his injuries (**Pl. 5**).

Conclusions: why should Lindow Man remain on display?

In a recent discussion questioning if museums should display the dead, Alberti *et al.* ask 'what is it that you can say about

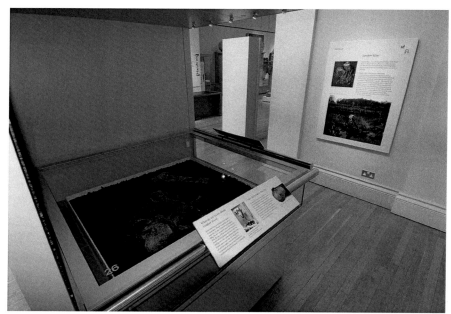

Plate 5 Display of Lindow Man (August 2013) showing the arrangement of case and text panels in the Iron Age Gallery at the British Museum

the past or another culture which you can only say by having human remains on display' (Hill, quoted in Alberti *et al.* 2009, 139). The answers provided by Alberti *et al.* (2009, 139) range from 'nothing', 'sometimes quite a bit', to 'lots'. The position adopted here is that expressed in the DCMS guidelines and the middle-ground conveyed by Alberti *et al.* (2009), namely that it is right to display the dead but only in those circumstances where the argument being put forward cannot be made by other means. Bog bodies are argued to be one of these special cases because they are recognizable as real people, providing an actual and tangible link to the past. These qualities mean that links to past practices and material culture can be made which would otherwise not be possible, with Lindow Man for example described as 'the everyman of British prehistory' (Joy 2009, 5). As they look like they may have died yesterday, their display also provides a context in which mortality and humanity can be explored. It is these qualities which also mean that great care and attention must be made to reduce the possibility of bog bodies being the subject of a kind of voyeurism. To some extent it is unavoidable, but risks can be mitigated by adopting approaches set out by the DCMS guidelines and examples such as the display at the National Museum of Ireland.

Questionnaires show that visitors to the British Museum expect to see human remains on public display (e.g. Eklund 2007, 41), and evidence from broader studies demonstrates that museum-goers are largely supportive of the display of the dead (BDRC 2009; Sayer 2010, 96–7). However, as has been demonstrated by recent debates and by the example of Grauballe Man, public reactions can change quickly. Scientists, professional archaeologists and museum curators cannot make an exclusive claim to human remains. Equally, we cannot ignore wider debates and concerns by hiding behind the importance of science. Consultation with the public and other interested parties is very important if the archaeology and presentation of human remains is to continue to be relevant in the future (see Moshenska 2009, 815; see Chapter One, this volume). It is the responsibility of museum curators to listen to and consult the public through questionnaires and debate, to continue to promote research of human remains and to disseminate new research and ideas through popular publications and museum displays.

Returning to Lindow Man, the details we have been able to reconstruct about his life and death are compelling and trigger genuine fascination amongst visitors. Like other bog bodies, Lindow Man is especially thought provoking because he is fleshed. It is possible to imagine how he may have looked as a living human being. His face is full of character with a deeply furrowed brow and small ears. Many visitors comment on the fact that he looks no different from people today. It is this link to past people that Lindow Man communicates best and would be impossible to replicate if he was not on display.

Acknowledgements

I would like to thank Julia Farley and Bryan Sitch for providing information and commenting on previous drafts of this chapter. Thank you also to the editors for their useful feedback. All errors remain my own.

Bibliography

Alberti, S.J.M.M., Bienkowski, P., Chapman, M. and Drew, R., 2009. 'Should we display the dead?', *Museum and Society* 2009 7(3), 133–49.

Anon. 1987. 'Pete should stay in the north', *Wilmslow Express Advertiser*, 13 August 1987.

Asingh, P., 2007. 'The man in the bog', in Asingh and Lynnerup 2007, 15–31.

—, 2009. *Grauballe Man: Portrait of a Bog Body*. Århus.

— and Lynnerup, N. (eds), 2007. *Grauballe Man: An Iron Age Bog Body Revisited*. Højbjerg.

Bahn, P.G., 1984. 'Do not disturb? Archaeology and the rights of the dead', *Oxford Journal of Archaeology* 3(1), 127–39.

BDRC 2009. *Research into Issues Surrounding Human Bones in Museums* (http://www.babao.org.uk/index/cms-filesystem-action/eh%20opinion_survey_report.pdf, accessed July 2012).

Bienkowski, P., 2006. 'Persons, things and archaeology: contrasting world-views of minds, bodies and death', paper delivered at the conference 'Respect for Ancient British Human Remains: Philosophy and Practice', Manchester Museum, 17 November 2006 (http://www.museum.manchester.ac.uk/medialibrary/documents/respect/persons_things_and_archaeology.pdf, accessed July 2012).

Blain, J., 2011. 'Neo-shamanism: pagan and "neo-shamanic"

interactions with archaeology', in *The Oxford Handbook of the Archaeology of Ritual and Religion*, ed. T. Insoll, 1017–31. Oxford.

Bradley, S., Fletcher, P., Korenberg, C., Parker, J. and Ward, C., 2008. 'A review of the colour and condition of Lindow Man 20 years after conservation', *Studies in Conservation* 53, 273–84.

Brothwell, D., 1986. *The Bog Man and the Archaeology of People*. London.

Burch, S., 2008. 'Lindow Man: a bog body mystery, Manchester Museum [exhibition review]', *Museums Journal* 108(7), 46–9.

Connolly, R.C., 1985. 'Lindow Man – a prehistoric corpse', *Anthropology Today* 1(5), 15–17.

—, 1986. 'The anatomical description of Lindow Man', in Stead *et al.* 1986, 54–62.

Curtis, N.G.W., 2003. 'Human remains: the sacred, museums and archaeology', *Public Archaeology* 3, 21–32.

Daniels, V. D., 1991. 'From peat to public: two bog bodies "live" again', *Museum International* 43 (2), 118–20.

Daniels, V., 1996. 'Selection of a conservation process for Lindow Man', in *Human Mummies: A Global Survey of their Status and the Techniques of Conservation*, ed. K. Spindler, H. Wilfing, E. Rast-Zissernig, D. zur Nedden and H. Nothdurfter, 173–81. New York.

DCMS (Department for Culture, Media and Sport) 2005. *Guidance for the Care of Human Remains in Museums* (http://webarchive. nationalarchives.gov.uk/+/http://www.culture.gov.uk/reference_library/publications/3720.aspx, accessed July 2012).

Eklund, K., 2007. 'Displaying the dead: visitor attitudes towards the display of human skeletal remains at the British Museum', unpublished MA dissertation, University of London.

Fischer, C., 2012. *Tollund Man: Gift to the Gods*. Stroud.

Giles, M. 2009. 'Iron Age bog bodies of north-western Europe. Representing the dead', *Archaeological Dialogues* 16(1), 75–101.

Gillie, O., 1984. 'Scientists unwrap Iron Age Briton', *The Sunday Times*, 16 September 1984.

Glob, P. V., 1969. *The Bog People: Iron Age Man Preserved*. London.

Gowlett, J.A.J., Hedges, R.E.M. and Law, I.A., 1989. 'Radiocarbon accelerator (AMS) dating of Lindow Man', *Antiquity* 63, 71–9.

Green, M., 1998. 'Humans as ritual victims in the later prehistory of Western Europe', *Oxford Journal of Archaeology* 17(2), 169–89.

HAD 2011. *Reburial Handbook*, March 2011, Version 5 (http://www. honour.org.uk/system/files/HAD+Reburial+Handbook+v1_0. pdf, accessed July 2012).

Hill, J.D., 2004. 'Lindow Man's moustache – another version of death in the peat bog', *Times Literary Supplement*, 5 March 2004, 15.

Hutton, R., 2004. 'What did happen to Lindow Man?', *Times Literary Supplement*, 30 January 2004, 12.

Jenkins, T., 2011. *Contesting Human Remains in Museum Collections: The Crisis of Cultural Authority*. London.

Jones, J., 2007. 'Riddle of the bog', *Guardian*, 21 June 2007, G2, 23–5.

Joy, J., 2009. *Lindow Man*. London.

Kelly, E.P., 2006. *Kingship and Sacrifice: Iron Age Bog Bodies and Boundaries*. Dublin (Archaeology Ireland Heritage Guide no. 35).

May, S.K., Gumurdul, D., Manakgu, J., Maralngurra, G. and Nawirridj, W., 2005. '"You write it down and bring it back…that's what we want" – revisiting the 1948 removal of human remains from Kunbarlanja (Oenpelli), Australia', in *Indigenous Archaeologies: Decolonising Theory and Practice*, ed. H.M. Wobst and C. Smith, 110–30. London.

Moshenska, G., 2009. 'The reburial issue in Britain', *Antiquity* 83, 815–20.

Nurse, K., 1984. 'Man victim of muggers', *Daily Telegraph*, 5 October 1984.

Omar, S. and McCord, M., 1986. 'The handling and conservation of Lindow Man', in Stead *et al.* 1986, 17–20.

—, McCord, M. and Daniels, V., 1989. 'The conservation of bog bodies by freeze-drying', *Studies in Conservation* 34, 101–9.

O'Sullivan, J., 2007. 'Bog bodies', *Heritage Outlook* (Winter 2006–Spring 2007), 18–20.

Painter, T.J., 1995. 'Chemical and microbiological aspects of the preservation process in sphagnum peat', in Turner and Scaife 1995, 89–103.

Parker Pearson, M., 1999. *The Archaeology of Death and Burial*. Stroud.

—, Schadla-Hall, T. and Moshenska, G. 2011. 'Resolving the human remains crisis in British archaeology', *Papers from the Institute of Archaeology* 21, 5–9.

Payne, S., 2010. 'A child's gift to science', *British Archaeology* 112, 12–13.

Prag, J. and Neave, R., 1997. *Making Faces: Using Forensic and Archaeological Evidence*. London.

Restall Orr, E. 2006. 'Human remains: the acknowledgement of sanctity', paper delivered at the conference 'Respect for Ancient British Human Remains: Philosophy and Practice', Manchester Museum, 17 November 2006 (http://www.museum.manchester. ac.uk/medialibrary/documents/respect/human_remains_the_acknowledgement_of_sanctity.pdf, accessed July 2012).

Ross, A. and Robins, D., 1989. *The Life and Death of a Druid Prince: The Story of an Archaeological Sensation*. London.

Sanders, K. 2009. *Bodies in the Bog and the Archaeological Imagination*. Chicago.

Sayer, D., 2010. *Ethics and Burial Archaeology*. London.

—, 2011. 'Who's afraid of the dead? Archaeology, modernity and the death taboo', *World Archaeology* 42(3), 481–91.

Schofield, J., 2008. 'Lindow Man: Manchester Museum gets bogged down' (http://www.manchesterconfidential.co.uk/Culture/Architecture/Lindow-Man-Manchester-Museum-gets-bogged-down, accessed July 2012).

Sitch, B., 2007. 'Lindow Man consultation, Saturday 10th February 2007' (http://www.museum.manchester.ac.uk/aboutus/ourpractice/lindowman/fileuploadmax10mb,120485,en.pdf, accessed in January 2009).

—, 2009. 'Courting controversy – the Lindow Man exhibition at the Manchester Museum', *University Museums and Collections Journal* 2, 51–4.

—, 2010a. *Case Study: Lindow Man Temporary Exhibition* (http://www.umg.org.uk/2010/08/27/case-study-lindow-man-temporary-exhibition/, accessed July 2012).

—, 2010b. 'Consultation or confrontation: Lindow Man a bog body mystery', in *The Museum Community: Audiences, Challenges, Benefits*, ed. N. Aberby, A. Adler and A. Bhatia, 392–419. Edinburgh.

Stead, I.M., 1986. 'Excavation and examination', in Stead *et al.* 1986, 14–16.

— and Turner, R.C., 1985. 'Lindow Man', *Antiquity* 59, 25–9.

—, Bourke, J.B. and Brothwell, D. (eds), 1986. *Lindow Man: The Body in the Bog*. London.

Strehle, H., 2007. 'The conservation of Grauballe Man', in Asingh and Lynnerup 2007, 32–50.

Swain, H., 2002. 'The ethics of displaying human remains from British archaeological sites', *Public Archaeology* 2, 95–100.

Thackray, D. and Payne, S., 2010. *Avebury Reburial Request Summary Report, April 2011* (http://www.english-heritage.org.uk/content/imported-docs/a-e/avebury-reburial-request-summary.pdf, accessed July 2012).

Trustees of the British Museum 2013. The British Museum Policy on Human Remains (available at http://www.britishmuseum.org/about_us/management/museum_governance.aspx).

Turner, R.C., 1986. 'Discovery and excavation of the Lindow bodies', in Stead *et al.* 1986, 10–13.

—, 1995. 'Recent research into British bog bodies', in Turner and Scaife 1995, 108–22.

— and Scaife, R.G., 1995. *Bog Bodies: New Discoveries and New Perspectives*. London.

Van der Sanden, W.A.B., 1995. 'Bog bodies on the continent: the developments since 1965, with special reference to the Netherlands', in Turner and Scaife 1995, 146–67.

—, 1996. *Through Nature to Eternity: The Bog Bodies of Northwest Europe*. Amsterdam.

Wallis, R.J. and Blain, J., 2006. 'The Sanctity of Burial: Pagan Views, Ancient and Modern, paper delivered at the conference 'Respect for Ancient British Human Remains: Philosophy and Practice', Manchester Museum, 17 November 2006 (http://www.museum.manchester.ac.uk/aboutus/ourpractice/respect/fileuploadmax10mb,136200,en.pdf, accessed July 2012).

West, I., 1986. 'Forensic aspects of Lindow Man', in Stead *et al.* 1986, 77–80.

Wilkinson, C. 2007. 'Facial reconstruction of Grauballe Man', in Asingh and Lynnerup 2007, 260–71.

Chapter 3
The Scientific Analysis of Human Remains from the British Museum Collection
Research Potential and Examples from the Nile Valley

Daniel Antoine and Janet Ambers

The British Museum has nine curatorial departments[1] which manage the Museum's collection, as well as a Department of Conservation and Scientific Research that houses research and conservation laboratory facilities. British Museum scientists, along with the curatorial staff, further the understanding of the collection, together with the cultures and periods from which they originate, through an extensive programme of research and analysis. This chapter will discuss how the scientific investigation of human remains held in museum collections can – with the development of fresh approaches and scientific methods – benefit from new research and continue to further our understanding of the past. It also describes how the British Museum collection is made available to other researchers. The chapter concludes with examples of current research in the Department of Ancient Egypt and Sudan, including new work on long-held collections and the innovative technology used to display the results.

Holding for the future: new advances in scientific analysis

The human remains held in the British Museum collection have been and continue to be part of numerous research projects, initiated by both the Museum and external researchers, and the scientific analysis of these remains is furthering our understanding of past cultures, human biology and ancient diseases (see Part Three, this volume). The importance of the scientific investigation of archaeological human remains has been the subject of much literature (e.g. English Heritage and the Church of England 2005; Bekvalac *et al.* 2006; Mays 2013). A considerable amount of biological information can be discovered through the analysis of skeletal remains (e.g. Buikstra and Ubelaker 1994; Brickley and McKinley 2004; Roberts 2009), mummified remains (see below and Chapter Nine, this volume), or even a single tooth (e.g. Hillson 1996; Antoine *et al.* 2009). This goes beyond simply determining the age-at-death or biological sex of an individual. Human remains can inform us of various aspects of past biology, such as child growth and development, biological affinities between individuals or populations, past diets and the occurrence of ancient diseases or trauma (e.g. Larsen 1997; Roberts 2009; Roberts and Manchester 2005; Waldron 2008). As stated in the *Guidance for the Care of Human Remains in Museums* published by the Department for Culture, Media and Sport (see Chapter One, this volume), 'Many human remains have undoubted potential to further the knowledge and understanding of humanity through research, study and display' (DCMS 2005, 20). New research can help refine or advance previous interpretations, furthering our understanding of the past and allowing new questions to be addressed.

An example is given by the examination of the skeletal remains from the site of Jebel Sahaba, which is central to several projects investigating the early inhabitants of the middle Nile valley, including their biological affinity (e.g. Irish 2005; Crevecoeur 2012). Located near the Second Nile Cataract, this Palaeolithic cemetery was excavated by Fred Wendorf in 1965–6 as part of the UNESCO Aswan High Dam Salvage Project (Wendorf 1968). Along with the associated archives, this assemblage was generously donated to the British Museum in 2001 and now forms part of the Wendorf Collection. The skeletal remains from this site are well known for showing signs of violent death, including several individuals bearing cut marks or found with embedded lithics. Jebel Sahaba is generally regarded as representing the earliest evidence of collective violence or warfare, and is one of the earliest known burial sites in the Nile valley (Anderson 1968; Wendorf 1968; Judd 2007; Antoine *et al.* 2013). The date of the skeletons from Jebel Sahaba was originally determined by radiocarbon dating of the collagen fraction of the bone, a technique conventionally used to avoid cross-contamination with carbonates in groundwaters. However, the collagen was poorly preserved, a common problem in arid environments (Saliège *et al.* 1995; Sereno *et al.* 2008; Zazzo and Saliège 2011) and questions remained as to the reliability of the original date (Antoine *et al.* 2013). The site was recently redated using the apatite fraction – one of the minerals found in bone – instead of the poorly preserved collagen (a protein). The new radiocarbon dates confirmed that the burial site belongs to the Epipaleolithic (i.e. Upper Palaeolithic) period and that the skeletal remains held in the Museum are one of the rare examples of a sizeable population from the Late Pleistocene (Antoine *et al.* 2013).

Other analytical methods now in use were not available 20 years ago – for example, the possibility of studying the genome of ancient pathogens was in its infancy. The study of ancient biomolecules and the extraction of ancient DNA are now allowing us to further investigate the epidemiology of ancient diseases (e.g. Brown and Brown 2011). Schuenemann *et al.* (2013), for example, recently sequenced the genome of *Mycobacterium leprae* in British, Swedish and Danish medieval skeletons with leprosy. While standard archaeological methods provide an insight into the lives of individuals suffering from leprosy, such as whether they were stigmatized and buried in separate burial sites, we can now also directly compare the genetic composition of past and present *Mycobacterium leprae* genomes and study the evolution of such pathogenic organisms (Schuenemann *et al.* 2013). Another technique, stable isotope analysis, has transformed research on ancient diet through the chemical analysis of isotopes found in human tissues such as bones and teeth. Carbon and nitrogen isotopes can reflect the diet during life and are particularly informative when considering the relative intake of marine, plant and terrestrial animal proteins consumed (see Roberts 2009; Brown and Brown 2011), whilst other isotopes such as those of oxygen and strontium, can indicate geographic origin. Older methods are also being superseded or revised, with new radiocarbon calibrations and techniques, like that of apatite dating described above, providing new age estimates (e.g. Roberts 2009, 214–16). High resolution 3D imaging techniques such as CT scanning have revolutionized the use of X-rays to analyse mummified remains. However, while new research is transforming our understanding of ancient human remains, access has to be carefully managed in order to protect collections for present and future generations. Academic publications indicate that human remains held in British institutions play a vital role in research (Mays 2010), but that some museum collections are under an increasing

amount of pressure with the majority of work based on only a few skeletal assemblages (Roberts and Mays 2011; Roberts 2013). The scholarly justifications for any destructive sampling must therefore be carefully considered and the British Museum must attempt to balance the competing needs of present day scholars requesting access to the collection, the necessity to preserve material for future generations and the overriding imperative to ensure that human remains are always treated in an ethical and respectful way.

Access to human remains for scientific analysis

The British Museum receives a large number of requests to examine, and often to sample, all types of collection material, including human remains, for scientific purposes. The Museum recognizes the importance of making the collection available to external researchers, so that its artefacts can be included in broader research projects and compared to other collections. While such research is one of the prime justifications for the existence of museums, a fine line has to be maintained between this need and the duty of care implicit in the British Museum Act 1963[2] to protect the collection for present and future generations. As discussed in Chapter One, human remains also require special ethical considerations, as well as great care and respect (e.g. Sayer 2010). When permitting research on this part of the collection, the British Museum reminds researchers of their ethical obligations with regard to human remains and expects them to follow the relevant principles of the British Museum Policy on Human Remains (Trustees of the British Museum 2013, 4).

In order to safeguard the collection, and to ensure that any human material is treated in a suitably respectful manner, all such requests are subject to a rigorous review process following a formal application procedure. Researchers or others visitors wishing to view, study or otherwise have access to human remains in the Museum's collection that are older than 100 years and not on public display are required to apply in writing to the appropriate curatorial department. Before arranging access, the curator responsible for the collection will take into account the merit, feasibility and appropriateness of the proposal, as well as the state of preservation and fragility of the remains. All applications must also comply with the British Museum Policy on Human Remains. For any request involving access to human remains that are, or may be, less than 100 years old, care is also taken to ensure compliance with the Human Tissue Act 2004 and written permission from the Designated Individual named on the Museum's licence is required (see Chapter One, this volume). No requests for access to any human remains in the collection that are the subject of a claim for transfer are considered while the outcome of the claim is pending.

All handling and investigative methods are undertaken in such a way that the risk of contamination which might affect analysis in the future is avoided and copies of all data collected are retained within the Museum records so that unnecessary repeated handling can be avoided. The scientific analysis of human remains forms an integral part of modern archaeological research that sometimes necessitates destructive sampling. The extraction of ancient DNA or stable isotopes, for example, requires the destruction of small amounts of bone or dental tissue. Authorizing destructive sampling should be considered carefully and useful advice can be found in the *Guidance for Best Practice for Treatment of Human Remains Excavated from Christian Burial Grounds in England*, published by English Heritage and the Church of England. Annexe E6 on the 'Ethics of destructive sampling of human remains' (English Heritage and the Church of England 2005, 34) includes several pertinent points that are applicable to all human remains:

- Can non-destructive techniques be used to address the research question(s)?
- Is there a realistic prospect of producing results?
- The area to be sampled should be carefully considered and samples should not be taken from areas that may affect future research. Sampling areas with signs of pathological change should be avoided unless it is the focus of the study.[3]
- Prior to sampling, the bones or teeth to be analysed should be fully recorded, measured and the resultant data inputted into an appropriate database. When possible, and particularly if the skeleton is intended for museum display, researchers should produce a high-resolution impression or cast of the part(s) that will be damaged or destroyed.[4]

As discussed in Chapter One, the Museum keeps a record of all destructive sampling (and the location of any remaining samples) and research on human material that includes any form of destructive sampling[5] requires the completion of a specific application form.[6] In addition to a detailed list of the collection(s) to be accessed or sampled, the form includes sections on the technical reasons for the request and a description of the intended methods of analysis. This must be completed by all external researchers or students, irrespective of whether the examinations/ analyses are taking place at the British Museum or off-site, and whether or not they are collaborating with Museum staff. The application form, the application process, the rationale behind it and the conditions that may apply, as well as the assessment criteria, are all available online,[7] together with some examples of the loan conditions which may be applied should the analysis require the human remains to go off site (e.g. for techniques that are not available at the British Museum, such as CT scanning). Decisions as to whether to permit access are based on expert opinions gathered during the review process, which is conducted jointly by the appropriate curator(s), members of the British Museum's scientific team with expertise in the area and, if there are any concerns about the vulnerability of the material to physical damage, by conservation specialists. Colleagues from other institutions may also be called on for advice if necessary, particularly if the application is part of a larger research project with samples requested from other museums.

The British Museum's assessment criteria for analysis

When making an application, researchers are encouraged to make an honest assessment of the likelihood of the success or failure of the project. The information collected is then considered against a number of criteria to assess the suitability of the application. These criteria are listed on the 'Scientific Study of the British Museum Collection' web page and include:

- The scholarly merit of the proposal.
- The feasibility of the project.
- The appropriateness of the proposed scientific techniques/methods to answer the questions posed.
- Experience and expertise of the research team in applying these techniques/methods.
- Previous work undertaken on similar material.
- The fragility of the material in question.
- Sample sizes required in relation to the size and rarity/ uniqueness of the object.
- Other immediate or long-term impact on the object(s), including risks associated with exposure of object(s) to ionizing or non-ionizing radiation.
- Experience of the research team in working with museum material.
- Anticipated outputs of the research (publications, etc).
- Health and safety implications.

The samples requested should not duplicate previous research unless there have been significant developments in that particular field or the methods have considerably changed (e.g. new radiocarbon dates may be required if the previous ones are no longer deemed to be reliable and improved techniques have become available). Reviewers must also determine if the proposed project has a defined aim of substantial scholarly merit; if that aim can yield new or more advanced knowledge than currently exists; and if it can feasibly be achieved by the applicants using proven methods. All of this may sound straightforward, but it is not unknown for the destructive sampling of human remains to be requested with few or poorly defined aims that repeat work which has already been reliably carried out, or even for samples to be requested speculatively without guaranteed access to appropriate equipment. Unless the investigation method is totally non-invasive and can be proven to hold no risks for the materials concerned (something which is extremely difficult, given that even unpacking skeletal material can put it at risk, hence jeopardizing potential future research; see below), it is also seldom appropriate for any collection material, and almost never appropriate for human remains, to be used in tests of novel or only partially developed techniques. If an application is made to apply an unusual or novel method to British Museum material, the technique would first need to have been demonstrably proved using suitable test materials and even then small-scale pilot studies on collection material may be suggested as a first step prior to a full-scale study. Factors such as preservation and taphonomic conditions should be taken into account, including whether or not previous research on similar material (e.g. preservation, location or period) has been successful. If an application for access meets these primary requirements, consideration then moves to the suggested methodology and the experience and expertise of the applicants in using these methods.

The Museum has a duty of care to ensure that only the most productive and least destructive techniques are applied to material in the collection, and that any investigation is carried out in a way that does not jeopardize the potential for future research. This can seem severe to individual applicants, who may only have access to a limited range of equipment, but it is nonetheless an ethical necessity. For similar reasons it is expected that research teams demonstrate a track record of success in the use of the techniques to be applied, that adequate provision is in place to ensure that all relevant equipment is available and that they have a good publication record and clear plans are in place for suitable and rapid publication of the results. At this stage, attention is also paid to ensuring that adequate health and safety measures can be put in place to protect both external researchers and British Museum staff. For many applications this is largely a box-ticking exercise, but with increasing reliance on technology and the development of portable equipment using ionizing and non-ionizing radiation (as exemplified by X-ray fluorescence [XRF] and laser scanning respectively) the safety risks can be very real.

Non-destructive methods of examination are always preferred if possible, but it must be remembered that even techniques which appear to be non-destructive may in fact have a considerable negative impact. Something as apparently mundane as opening a box and removing items from a secure storage environment (for details of the types of storage considered appropriate for human remains see Chapters Five and Six, this volume) places that material at increased risk. For this reason handling is kept to a minimum, the condition of the material assessed throughout the process and the use of examination methods which create reliable real or virtual copies of items is encouraged as these may prevent the need for further direct examination. Even those scientific techniques generally termed non-destructive are not always truly non-invasive. The clearest example of this is probably X-radiography, long considered an ideal technique for the study of human remains. Questions are now being asked about the effects of radiation exposure on already fragmented strands of ancient DNA. Research by Grieshaber et al. (2008), while not finding any statistical evidence to show that exposure to radiation decreases the amount of amplifiable DNA, did suggest that the doses to which such materials are exposed need to be carefully considered.[8] Similarly, 3D scanning methods can seem an ideal panacea for the study and comparison of form or surface morphology without the need for physical contact, particularly as the data would also then be available for future scholars. However, all scanning methods require some means to measure distances, usually in the form of laser or visible light, and all such interventions have the potential to cause damage, particularly to surface layers. This can be ameliorated by careful control of the intensities used and only levels which fall within the standard British Museum guidelines for light exposures are permitted.

Should sampling be truly unavoidable, a balance needs to be struck between the risks involved, ethical considerations, the importance of the possible results and the size of sample required in relation to the size, rarity or uniqueness of the remains. In some cases it may be concluded that it is better to forgo knowledge for the moment and to wait for the development of new and less destructive techniques rather than to go ahead with the level of sampling currently needed. In all cases only the minimum quantities of material necessary to address the research questions can be justified. Within the British Museum, sampling is always supervised or undertaken by museum staff and is preceded by the recording of the original state of the specimen and accompanied by full documentation (including images) of the sampled areas. When sampling is permitted, the investigators are usually asked to return any material which is not destroyed by analysis to the museum (normally within a year of sampling, although this is negotiable if necessary). Such materials, including chemical extracts and mounted samples, are then available for study by other groups and can alleviate the need for further sampling in the future. Where two or more requests for much of the same work are received, applicants may be asked to collaborate. Collaboration with British Museum scientists may also be suggested, particularly in cases where the Museum has a research interest in the area, the material is very fragile or the suggested analytical equipment/techniques (or more suitable non-destructive techniques) are available in the British Museum's laboratories. The British Museum also requires copies of all results for inclusion in its collection database and retains the right to make all findings available to other researchers five years after they are received, regardless of whether they have been published elsewhere, thus ensuring that data becomes available to other scholars. This right does not exist to deny researchers the fruits of their work, and is not always exercised, particularly if publication is imminent or has been delayed, but is a response to the large amounts of work undertaken on museum objects in the past which has never been disseminated. Ultimately, the British Museum has a duty of care towards its collection rather than to individual researchers and so must seek to make such information publicly available. In an effort to further our understanding of the collection, the British Museum staff are also involved in many research projects, examples of which can be found below and in Part Three of this volume.

Scientific analysis of human remains from the Nile valley

With over 2,000 human remains, the Department of Ancient Egypt and Sudan curates one of the largest collections of ancient human remains in the British Museum (Antoine 2010a). The collection reflects the varied funerary practices and burial traditions of the Nile valley and includes naturally mummified remains preserved by the very dry environment (**Pl. 1**) and intentionally mummified remains from the pharaonic and Roman periods (**Pl. 2**), as well as skeletal remains (**Pl. 3**) from both Egypt and Sudan (e.g. Judd 2001; 2013). A large part of the collection was recovered during the Merowe Dam Archaeological Salvage Project. The construction of a new dam at the Fourth Nile Cataract (in modern Sudan) resulted in a major international rescue campaign during which the Sudan Archaeological Research Society (SARS),[9] in conjunction with the British Museum, excavated several burial sites from the Neolithic to medieval period. As part of a division of finds, a collection of over 1,000 skeletal remains and

Plate 1 Naturally mummified remains of an adult male from the late Predynastic Period c. 3500 BC. British Museum, London (EA 32751)

Plate 2 Mummy of an adult woman from the 3rd Intermediate Period wrapped in linen bandages with a glazed composition bead-net, winged scarab amulet and gilded mummy-cover around lower legs. British Museum, London (EA 6697)

naturally mummified bodies was generously donated to SARS by the National Corporation for Antiquities and Museums of Sudan.[10] In turn, SARS donated the collection to the British Museum, where it is now curated. This collection is currently the focus of an extensive research programme that will allow us to gain a unique insight into the inhabitants of the Fourth Nile Cataract region, from the Neolithic to the medieval period. Over the coming years, this should reveal how changes in environment, culture, diet and living conditions may have had an impact on the biology and state of health of the inhabitants of the Fourth Cataract region. This remarkable collection includes over 50 mummies from the medieval period that were naturally mummified by the hot and arid conditions. They have, over

Plate 3 Early Dynastic burial of an adult male from Tarkhan, Egypt, 1st Dynasty, c. 3000 BC. British Museum, London (EA 52887)

the past two years, been the focus of an extensive conservation programme using passive methods (i.e. that avoid chemicals and consolidants) so as not to affect their future research potential (see Chapter Six, this volume). These mummies are also part of larger, mostly skeletonized, assemblages and their analysis is adding to the physical anthropology data derived from the skeletons and revealing aspects of the medieval period that do not usually survive in the archaeological record. This includes unique examples of medieval Christian tattoos (**Pl. 4**) and wonderful textiles. Unlike most Egyptian pharaonic and Roman mummies, the Fourth Nile Cataract mummies were preserved by chance and were not eviscerated. CT scans have shown that their internal organs, as well as the contents of their digestive tracts, are still present (Taylor and Antoine 2014). By analysing their skin, hair and internal organs, we are now building a picture of the medieval period that goes beyond the data derived from skeletal remains and should provide unique insights into body adornment, soft tissues pathology, diet and parasitology.

The analysis of the skeletons from these sites is also revealing valuable biological information, including evidence of pathological abnormalities rarely described in the archaeological literature. Several skeletons from site 4-L-2 (*Kerma ancien* Period, 2500–2050 BC) have smooth-walled lesions on the bodies of the vertebrae that make up the neck, the cervical vertebrae. Tortuosities and aneurysms, two abnormalities of the vertebral artery, are the most likely cause of such lesions. Indeed, the vertebral artery, which passes along both sides of the cervical vertebrae, can occasionally become dilated, coiled or looped. The tortuous segment – or tortuosity – can cause a pressure defect in adjacent vertebrae, as can the localized enlargement triggered by the weakening of the arterial wall in an aneurysm (Waldron and Antoine 2002). In both conditions, the adjacent bone reacts to the pressure exerted by the abnormally shaped artery by moving away, thus creating a smooth-walled lesion. This is often accompanied by an enlargement of the holes that guide the artery along the side of the cervical vertebrae, the transverse foramen (see Waldron and Antoine 2002; Antoine 2010a; 2010b). Without the preservation of soft tissues, differentiating between

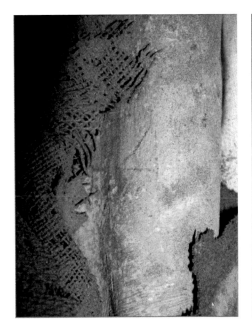

Plate 4 Example of a Christian tattoo from medieval Sudan (left) found on the upper leg of a naturally preserved adult female mummy (site 3-J-23; SK140) and enhanced using infrared reflectography (right), *c.* AD 700. It represents a monogram (motif made by combining and overlapping letters) of the Archangel Michael and is one of the first known surviving examples of tattoos from medieval Sudan. British Museum, London (EA 83133)

tortuosities and aneurysms can be difficult as they can both affect the cervical vertebrae in the same way. These abnormalities are linked to pathological changes in the arterial wall (such as the build-up of cell debris or fatty materials like cholesterol), trauma to the neck or may be congenital in origin (Waldron and Antoine 2002).

Other examples from the Nile valley have been found at Hierakonpolis[11] (C-Group, 2055–1700 BC; Antoine 2010b) and Kawa[12] (Meroitic, 400 BC–AD 400; Antoine 2010a), and apart from a few additional sites (e.g. Waldron and Antoine, 2002), these lesions are seldom reported on in the archaeological and anthropological literature. This is probably due to the relatively subtle changes associated with such abnormalities and, without the careful analysis of the cervical vertebrae, evidence for them is likely to be missed. In order to gain a clearer idea of the prevalence of such lesions, many sites and collections would need to carefully reanalysed, once again highlighting the importance of maintaining research collections. The data collected to date, particularly on the skeletons recovered from the ongoing British Museum excavations at Kawa, suggest that a higher than expected percentage of young individuals (20–35 years old at death) were affected by abnormalities of the vertebral artery. This differs from the patterns observed in modern populations, where these abnormalities (particularly tortuosities) are found in fewer, and usually older, individuals (Waldron and Antoine 2002). Further work is required to

investigate why this might be and the possible reasons behind differing epidemiological patterns.

Modern analytical techniques such as CT scanning are only now advancing our understanding of long-held parts of the British Museum collection, some of which were added many decades ago and have been on display for over a century. The body of a man who was buried during the late Predynastic period in about 3500 BC at the site of Gebelein in Upper Egypt, for example, is on display in the Early Egypt Gallery (Room 64). Known as Gebelein Man,[13] he was placed in a crouched position in a shallow grave (**Pl. 1**) and the arid environment, as well as direct contact with the hot sand, naturally dried and mummified his remains. This remarkably well-preserved mummy offers a unique insight into the funerary practices of the late Predynastic era, a period that precedes the unification of Egypt in around 3100 BC.[14] Chance discoveries of such well-preserved bodies in ancient times may also have encouraged the belief that physical preservation was a necessary part of the afterlife and may have encouraged ancient Egyptians to develop the practice of artificial mummification. Gebelein Man has been in the British Museum collection for over 100 years and on display for much of that time, but very little was known about him. In 2012 he was CT scanned for the first time and high resolution X-rays were used to create 3D visualizations so that his muscles, bones, teeth and internal organs could be carefully examined. A virtual autopsy table,[15] an

Plate 5 The Virtual Autopsy display next to Gebelein Man (left) in the Early Egypt Gallery with a close up (right) of the interactive touchscreen and the secondary display screen above it

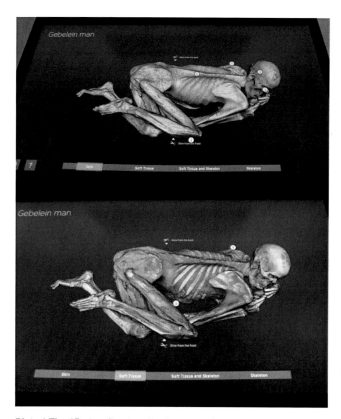

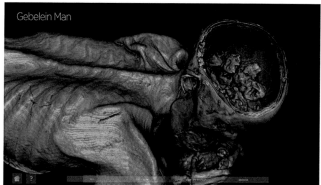

Plate 7 A virtual cutting plane revealing Gebelein Man's remarkably preserved 5,500 year old brain

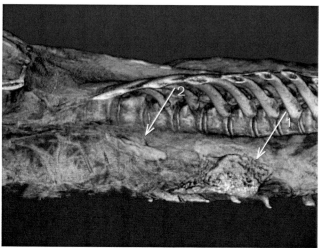

Plate 8 Cutting plane revealing the excellent preservation of Gebelein Man's internal organs, including what appears to be his lungs (1) and one of his kidneys (2)

Plate 6 The 3D visualization display of the CT scan of Gebelein Man (top) allowed visitors to virtually remove layers and observe the excellent preservation of the underlying muscles and skeleton (bottom)

interactive tool based on medical visualization, was used to convey the results of the research to the public in a new Room 64 display next to Gebelein Man (**Pl. 5**). This temporary exhibition[16] allowed visitors to explore for themselves true 3D visualizations (as opposed to animations) of the original CT scan data by using an interactive touchscreen. The software made it possible to separate the different tissues of the body, allowing users to virtually remove the skin, revealing the remarkably well-preserved underlying muscles (**Pl. 6**) and analyse the skeleton. The cutting function let visitors discover that his extraordinarily well-preserved brain (**Pl. 7**) was still present in the skull and internal organs (**Pl. 8**), often removed when the ancient Egyptians began to artificially mummify bodies, were clearly visible. Information points at relevant locations in the

Plate 9 One of 14 information points built into the interactive display to help visitors discover some of the significant findings

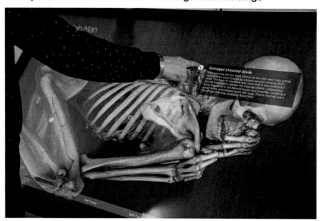

3D models were used to guide the visitors, allowing them to discover the more significant findings (**Pl. 9**). The morphology of his pelvis (**Pl. 10**) confirmed he was a male and fusion lines on the head, the humerus and the femur indicate that he was a young man of probably 18–21 years old when he died (**Pl. 11**). Consistent with his age, his teeth, fully visible for the first time, showed light wear and he had no apparent dental problems. These new scans also allowed us to visualize something more unexpected. A cut in the skin over his left shoulder blade and the apparent damage to the underlying bone (**Pl. 12**) had never been explained and may have occurred post-mortem. Indeed, many of the bones appear to have been broken after burial and the skin is cracked in a number of places, probably as a consequence of the rapid desiccation that preserved his body. Nonetheless, the 3D visualization of the CT scan shows that the cut on the shoulder blade was different and goes beyond the skin and into the muscle tissue (**Pl. 13**). It was probably caused by a sharp pointed object 1.5–2cm wide and the force of the blow was such that it also damaged the underlying scapula (**Pl. 14**) and shattered one of the ribs immediately below it, embedding bone fragments into his muscle tissue (**Pl. 15**). The fragmentation pattern, particularly that of the rib, indicates that the damage occurred when the bone was fresh, as dry bone usually breaks in a different way. A lot of force would also have been required to shatter the rib into such small fragments. The analysis of ancient human

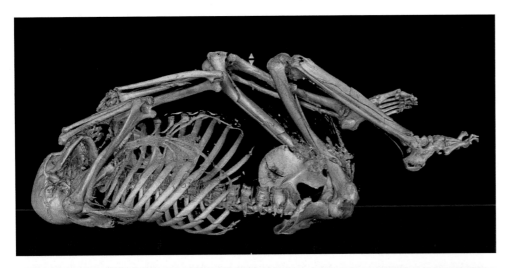

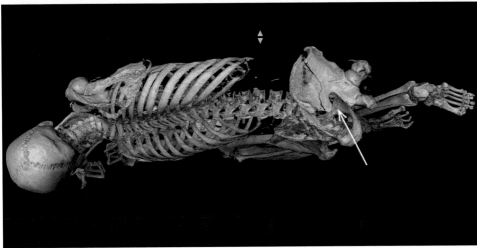

Plate 10 Imaging Gebelein Man's skeleton (top) revealed that numerous bones had been broken post-mortem. The pelvis (bottom) has a male morphology, including a narrow sciatic notch (arrow)

remains rarely reveals the cause of death, but the cut on his back, as well as the damage to the shoulder blade and rib, are characteristic of a single penetrating wound.[17] The weapon is likely to have penetrated into his left lung and may have damaged the surrounding blood vessels. There is no other evidence of trauma or defensive wounds, and the absence of any signs of healing, as well as the severity of the injuries, suggest that this can be considered to be the cause of death. Based on the forensic analysis, the weapon would have been approximately 1.8cm wide at the rib (**Pl. 16**). As the cut was clean and the skin is not lacerated, the weapon was probably not a projectile point, such as an arrow or spear-head, which would have damaged the skin further when removed. Flint knives are also too wide to fit the forensic evidence and a metal blade is the most likely weapon. Metal knives from that period were mainly made of copper and silver, and are rarely found because the precious metals would have been recycled rather than discarded (Friedman and Antoine 2012). Weapons were symbols of power and status and were often depicted in the art of this period as well as being commonly found in graves, but evidence of actual violence is rare (Friedman and Antoine 2012). The lack of defensive wounds suggests the injury was not the result of warfare and may have been caused by interpersonal violence. Gebelein Man has been on display for many decades, but it is only now through the use of science and modern technology that we are beginning to understand more about him. Not only have we been able to

Plate 11 The fusion line on the head of the femur (arrow) indicates that this bone was in the process of completing its growth. Based on modern fusion times, he was most probably between 18 to 21 years old when he died

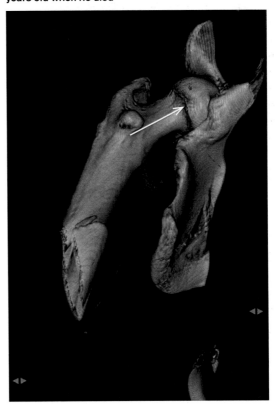

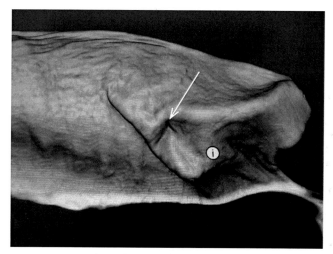

Plate 12 Cut mark (arrow) on the damaged left shoulder blade

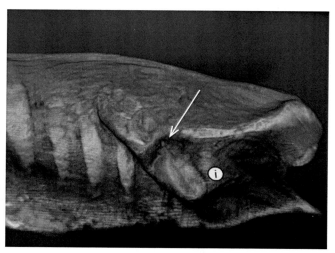

Plate 13 Internal view revealing how the cut (arrow) penetrates into the muscle tissue of the left shoulder blade

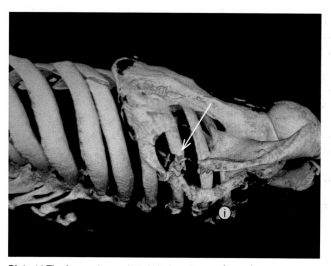

Plate 14 The bones immediately below the cut (arrow) are damaged, with the scapula (shoulder blade) broken in several places

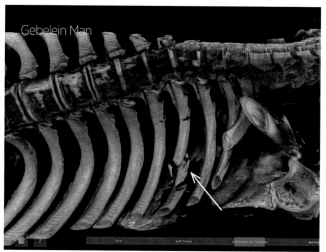

Plate 15 View from inside the chest cavity directly under the cut (arrow) and damaged shoulder blade. The area of the 4th rib immediately below the entry site is shattered into small angular fragments, suggesting a high velocity impact normally associated with a direct hit on fresh bone

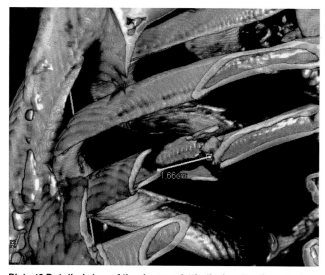

Plate 16 Detailed view of the damaged 4th rib showing the approximate width (yellow) of the damaged area. Measurements suggest the weapon used was 1.5–2cm wide at the rib level (image courtesy of Professor Anders Persson)

discover that he was young when he died but, unexpectedly, he appears to have been stabbed in the back. He is also remarkably preserved, offering the possibility of studying organs that were usually removed in later intentionally mummified remains. Importantly, the virtual autopsy table has also allowed visitors to explore the CT scan data interactively and discover for themselves how we have been able to gain this information and improve our understanding of life in Predynastic Egypt.

Conclusions

The methods and analytical tools available to researchers and curators are always evolving, allowing long-held collections to be reanalysed and thus refine our understanding of the past. With the emergence of more advanced dual energy CT scanners, for example, we should be able to generate even higher resolution images and perhaps one day virtually read text on objects (e.g. amulets) found within mummy wrappings. Some of the British Museum mummified remains are currently being analysed using this new generation of CT scanners, which will increase our understanding of ancient Egyptian funerary practices and generate more detailed information on the biology of the inhabitants of the Nile valley (Taylor and Antoine 2014). The analysis of human remains must be managed in a way that protects collections for future generations and, mindful of their ethical obligations, museums must make sure that the human remains held in their care are always treated with respect and dignity (see Chapter One, this volume).[18] New research also offers an opportunity to share discoveries with British Museum visitors and describe the methods used to analyse ancient human remains, as well as the information such methods allow us to access. Highlighting the importance of research and the role that human remains can play in our understanding of the past is an essential part of the dialogue museums should be having with the public if they are to continue to receive support for the display and scientific analysis of human remains in their collections.

Acknowledgements

We would like to acknowledge the help and input of our colleagues from the British Museum Human Remains Working Group and the Department of Conservation and Scientific Research, as well as the support of the Institute for Bioarchaeology. The help and support of the National Corporation for Antiquities and Museums of Sudan is also gratefully acknowledged. For their help and work in developing the Virtual Autopsy, we would also like to thank our colleagues from the British Museum and from the Department of Ancient Egypt and Sudan, particularly Dr Renée Friedman and Dr John Taylor, as well as David Hughes and Thomas Rydell (Interactive Institute and Visualization Center C), Professor Anders Ynnerman (Linköping University) and Professor Anders Persson (Center for Medical Image Science and Visualization).

Notes

1 http://www.britishmuseum.org/about_us/departments.aspx.
2 http://www.legislation.gov.uk/ukpga/1963/24/contents.
3 The following areas should be avoided: all standard osteological landmarks, the mid-point of long-bone shafts or joint surfaces. Complete cross-sections, rendering maximum length/width/breadth measurements obsolete, should not be allowed (i.e. bones should not be cut in half).
4 For robust bones and teeth, impressions may be taken following the method described in Hillson (1992).
5 This also includes any non-destructive analysis that uses radiation sources outside the 400–700nm (visible light) range and exposure to light levels above 500 lux (other than the use of simple photographic flash lights).
6 EE2 Application to Conduct Scientific Analysis of British Museum Collection Material.
7 http://www.britishmuseum.org/the_museum/departments/conservation_and_scientific/facilities_and_services/collection_scientific_study.aspx. Applications should be made on form EE2 (downloadable from the right hand side of the page).
8 In the case of the Jericho skull (Chapter Eight, this volume), this was considered before the CT scanning. The date of the cranium and the nature of the modifications made destructive sampling for DNA analysis not advisable and scanning was recommended.
9 http://www.sudarchrs.org.uk/index_links.htm.
10 http://gmsudan.com/20110408/the-national-corporation-for-antiquities-museums-ncam/.
11 http://www.hierakonpolis-online.org/.
12 The site of Kawa is located between the Third and Fourth Nile Cataracts in modern Sudan and is currently being excavated by Derek Welsby from the British Museum, in conjunction with the Sudan Archaeological Research Society. The site was occupied from the reign of Akhenaton (mid-14th century BC) until the 4th century AD and the excavation of the Kushite phase (800 BC–AD 400) is ongoing.
13 http://www.britishmuseum.org/explore/highlights/highlight_objects/aes/p/gebelein_man.aspx.
14 http://www.britishmuseum.org/explore/highlights/article_index/a/ancient_egypt_the_predynastic.aspx.
15 http://www.britishmuseum.org/whats_on/past_exhibitions/2012/virtual_autopsy.aspx and http://www.britishmuseum.org/channel/exhibitions/2012/virtual_autopsy_gebelein_man.aspx.
16 The Virtual Autopsy was on display in Room 64 from 16 November–3 March 2013 as part of a very successful trial and will return on permanent display in 2014.
17 The findings were confirmed by forensic expert Professor Anders Persson of the Center for Medical Image Science and Visualization: http://www.cmiv.liu.se/.
18 Additional advice on the scientific analysis of human remains and guidance on best practice regarding destructive sampling can also be found in several online documents including the *Guidance for the Care of Human Remains in Museums* (DCMS 2005), *Guidance for Best Practice for Treatment of Human Remains Excavated from Christian Burial Grounds in England* (English Heritage and the Church of England 2005) and, in particular, *Science and the Dead: A Guideline for the Destructive Sampling of Archaeological Human Remains* (Advisory Panel on the Archaeology of Burials in England 2013, http://www.archaeologyuk.org/apabe/Science_and_the_Dead.pdf).

Bibliography

Anderson, J., 1968. 'Late Paleolithic skeletal remains from Nubia', in *The Prehistory of Nubia*, ed. F. Wendorf, vol. 2, 996–1040. Dallas.

Antoine, D., 2010a. 'Life and death in the Nile valley: bioarchaeological research at the British Museum', *Ancient Egypt* 10(5), 46–51.

—, 2010b. 'Pain in the neck? An abnormality from HK27C', *Nekhen* 22, 23.

—, Hillson, S. and Dean, M.C., 2009. 'The developmental clock of dental enamel: a test for the periodicity of prism cross-striations in modern humans and an evaluation of the most likely sources of error in histological studies of this kind', *Journal of Anatomy* 214, 45–55.

—, Zazzo, A. and Friedman, R., 2013. 'Revisiting Jebel Sahaba: new apatite radiocarbon dates for one of the Nile valley's earliest cemeteries', *American Journal of Physical Anthropology* Supplement 56, 68.

Bekvalac, J., Cowal, L. and Mikulski, R., 2006. 'Scientific research on archaeological human remains in the United Kingdom: current trends and future possibilities', in *Human Remains and Museum Practice*, ed. J. Lohman and K. Goodnow, 111–16. Paris and London.

Brickley, M. and McKinley, J.I. (eds), 2004. 'Guidelines to the standards for recording human remains', IFA Paper No. 7, Institute of Field Archaeologists and British Association for Biological Anthropology and Osteoarchaeology, Reading [online], available online at http://www.babao.org.uk/HumanremainsFINAL.pdf.

Brown, T. and Brown, K., 2011. *Biomolecular Archaeology: An Introduction*. Chichester.

Buikstra, J.E. and Ubelaker, D.H., 1994. *Standards for Data Collection from Human Remains*. Arkansas (Arkansas Archaeological Survey Series No. 44).

Crevecoeur, I., 2012. 'The Upper Paleolithic human remains of Nazlet Khater 2 (Egypt) and past modern human diversity', in *Modern Origins: A North African Perspective*, ed. J-J. Hublin and S.P. McPherron, 205–19. New York.

DCMS (Department for Culture, Media and Sport) 2005. *Guidance for the Care of Human Remains in Museums* (available online at: http://webarchive.nationalarchives.gov.uk/+/http://www.culture.gov.uk/images/publications/GuidanceHumanRemains11Oct.pdf).

English Heritage and the Church of England 2005. *Guidance for Best Practice for Treatment of Human Remains Excavated from Christian Burial Grounds in England* (available online at: http://www.english-heritage.org.uk/publications/human-remains-excavated-from-christian-burial-grounds-in-england/).

Friedman, R. and Antoine, D., 2012. *Murder and Mayhem in Predynastic Egypt*. British Museum blog (available online at http://blog.britishmuseum.org/2012/12/06/murder-and-mayhem-in-predynastic-egypt/).

Giesen, M. (ed), 2013. *Curating Human Remains – Caring for the Dead in the United Kingdom*. Woodbridge.

Grieshaber, B., Osborne, D., Doubleday, A. and Kaestle, F., 2008. 'A pilot study into the effects of x-ray and computed tomography exposure on the amplification of DNA from bone', *Journal of Archaeological Science* 35(3), 681–97.

Hillson, S., 1992. 'Impression and replica methods for studying hypoplasia and perikymata on human tooth crown surfaces from archaeological sites', *International Journal of Osteoarchaeology* 2, 65–78.

—, 1996. *Dental Anthropology*. Cambridge.

Irish, J.D., 2005. 'Population continuity vs. discontinuity revisited: dental affinities among Late Paleolithic through Christian era Nubians', *American Journal of Physical Anthropology* 128, 520–35.

Judd, M., 2001. 'The human remains', in *Life on the Desert Edge: Seven Thousand Years of Settlement in the Northern Dongola Reach, Sudan*, ed. D.A. Welsby, vol. 2, 458–543. London (Sudan Archaeological Research Society Publication No. 7).

—, 2007. 'Jebel Sahaba revisited', in *Archaeology of Early Northeastern Africa*, ed. K. Kroeper, M. Chlodnicki and M. Kobusiewicz, 153–66. Poznan.

—, 2013. *Gabati: A Meroitic, Post-Meroitic and Medieval Cemetery in Central Sudan, Volume 2, The Physical Anthropology*. London (Sudan Archaeological Research Society Publication No. 20).

Larsen, C.S., 1997. *Bioarchaeology: Interpreting Behaviour from the Human Skeleton*. Cambridge.

Mays, S., 2010. 'Human osteoarchaeology in the UK 2001–2007: a bibliometric perspective', *International Journal of Osteoarchaeology* 20, 192–204.

—, 2013. 'Curation of human remains at St Peter's Church, Barton-upon-Humber, England', in Giesen 2013, 109–21.

Roberts, C.A., 2009. *Human Remains in Archaeology: A Handbook*. York.

Roberts, C., 2013. 'Archaeological human remains and laboratories: attaining acceptable standards for curating skeletal remains for teaching and research', in Giesen 2013, 123–34.

— and Manchester, K., 2005. *The Archaeology of Disease* (3rd edn). New York.

— and Mays, S., 2011. 'Study and restudy of curated skeletal collections in bioarchaeology: a perspective on the UK and its implications for future curation of human remains', *International Journal of Osteoarchaeology* 21, 626–30.

Saliège, J.F., Person, A. and Paris, F., 1995. 'Preservation of 12C/13C original ratio and ^{14}C dating of the mineral fraction of human bones from Saharan tombs, Niger', *Journal of Archaeological Science* 22, 301–12.

Sayer, D., 2010. *Ethics and Burial Archaeology*. London.

Schuenemann, V.J., Singh, P., Mendum, T.A., Krause-Kyora, B., Jäger, G. *et al.*, 2013. 'Genome-wide comparison of medieval and modern *Mycobacterium leprae*', *Science* 341, no. 6142, 179–83.

Sereno, P.C., Garcea, E.A.A., Jousse, H., Stojanowski, C.M., Saliège J-F. *et al.*, 2008. 'Lakeside cemeteries in the Sahara, 5000 years of Holocene population and environmental change', *PLoS ONE*, 3, e2995.

Taylor, J.H. and Antoine, D., 2014. *Ancient Lives, New Discoveries: Eight Mummies, Eight Stories*. London.

Trustees of the British Museum 2013. The British Museum Policy on Human Remains (http://www.britishmuseum.org/about_us/management/museum_governance.aspx).

Waldron, T., 2008. *Palaeopathology*. Cambridge.

— and Antoine, D., 2002. 'Tortuosity or aneurysm? The palaeopathology of some abnormalities of the vertebral artery', *International Journal of Osteoarchaeology* 12, 79–88.

Wendorf, F., 1968. 'Site 117: a Nubian final Paleolithic graveyard near Jebel Sahaba, Sudan', in *The Prehistory of Ancient Nubia*, ed. F. Wendorf, vol. 2, 954–95. Dallas.

Zazzo, A. and Saliège, J.F., 2011. 'Radiocarbon dating of biological apatites: a review', *Palaeogeography, Palaeoclimatology, Palaeoecology* 310 (1–2), 52–61.

Part 2
Caring For, Conserving and Storing Human Remains

Introduction

Gaye Sculthorpe

My perspective on the care of human remains in the British Museum is influenced by two interrelated factors. The first derives from my unique position as a curator at the British Museum who is also a descendant of peoples (Tasmanian Aborigines) whose ancestral remains were once held in the Museum until they were recently repatriated (see Chapter Four, this volume). Secondly, having only recently arrived in the museum world of the United Kingdom from Australia, I am aware of some of the different issues at play in both countries when caring for human remains in museum collections.

The curation and conservation of human remains in the British Museum occurs within the legislative frameworks of the Human Tissue Act 2004, the British Museum Act 1963, guidelines from the UK's Department for Culture, Media and Sport as well as internal Museum policy and practices (see Chapter One, this volume) which has been discussed in the preceding section. This part of the book explores in more detail some specific aspects of the curation, care and conservation of remains. Curation involves decisions about what to collect or remove from the collection, as well as undertaking documentation, research and exhibitions. Caring for remains involves decisions from the moment of excavation or acquisition about packing, transport, storage, conservation and display and includes overall attitudes to care. These papers deal with issues relating to caring for human remains which have been in the museum for many years as well as newly excavated materials, and in all cases contemporary standards of care must be maintained.

Unlike in Australia and New Zealand where museums collected human remains of indigenous minorities from largely within their own country, a distinctive feature of the British Museum collection is the range of countries, cultures and time periods from which human remains derive. However, remains come not only from a number of foreign countries, but many remains – indeed the majority – come from within the United Kingdom and most are from archaeological contexts. Although the legislation governing their management is the same, and museum policies cover all remains held, the practice of curation and care differs in some aspects across museum departments due to the context of collection, whether the remains were used in cultural contexts not intended for mortuary disposal and whether or not there are contemporary groups with particular cultural interests in the remains.

For some indigenous peoples, the most contentious issue relating to the care of human remains is whether or not a museum should continue to hold such material. For the British Museum, this is particularly the case with human remains from Australia, New Zealand and the Hawaiian Islands. Representatives of Aboriginal Australian communities first made requests for the repatriation of human remains from the British Museum in the 1980s as part of a broader ongoing campaign to return ancestral remains from museums and other institutions around the world.

As the United Kingdom was the colonizing force in Australia, in the 19th century human remains and sometimes heads of known individuals were taken back to the United Kingdom as 'trophies', curiosities or in the purported interest of science or medicine. Over many decades, Indigenous Australians have been making concerted efforts to document, track down and repatriate such remains with some success. Human remains have been located in various museums and institutions as well as in unmarked graves in public cemeteries.[1] Repatriation of these remains is of high importance to the originating communities and is evidence of strong ongoing cultural beliefs in having the remains of the dead treated in a culturally appropriate manner, including mortuary disposal of remains in the area of origin.

In Chapter Four, Natasha McKinney discusses both the nature of human remains from Oceania in the Museum's collection and the varying levels of documentation detailing their original cultural context and collection. While most remains in the Oceanic collections are in the form of skeletal remains, some of the remains have been modified for cultural purposes including for certain kinds of display and exchange in their originating communities. These include decorated skulls from Papua New Guinea, preserved heads from Papua New Guinea and West Papua, *rambaramp* figures from Vanuatu and various objects made from modified or unmodified human remains such as bone flutes from New Zealand or feather sceptres from Hawaii.

Human remains from Oceania in the British Museum collection are not numerous, but are generally of high cultural importance to representatives of those living cultures from which they derive. Most of these remains were collected in various colonial contexts rather than excavated from archaeological deposits as is the case in other museum departments. McKinney notes how some exchanges of material may have been influenced by new colonial interactions which may complicate considerations of their cultural significance. Furthermore, unlike in some other departments of the Museum, human remains are no longer actively collected in the Department of Africa, Oceania and the Americas. In regard to human remains from Oceania, there is scope for improving documentation of these collections, but there is no active internal research programme at present.

Since the introduction of the Human Tissue Act 2004 (see Chapter One, this volume), repatriation of human remains from the British Museum can now be considered in very specific circumstances, which are outlined elsewhere in this volume. The second part of McKinney's paper considers in detail recent repatriation requests for human remains from Oceania. McKinney outlines the particular circumstances in each case and discusses the particular reasons whereby some requests have been successful (human burial bundles from Tasmania and skeletal remains from New Zealand) and others unsuccessful (tattooed heads from New Zealand and preserved heads from the Torres Strait). Her chapter highlights some of the difficulties Trustees have in dealing with repatriation requests when there is a paucity of original documentation about the circumstances of collection or the customary mortuary processes involved.

As McKinney notes, the Museum Trustees have the responsibility for making any decisions about repatriation in accordance with current legislation and the policies they develop. The decision-making process involves close consideration of information from various sources including

advice from staff, external experts commissioned to write reports and at times, face-to-face discussions with representatives of those communities requesting the return of ancestral remains. Unlike many other museums, correspondence, reports and extracts of minutes of Trustee meetings considering these requests are made available publicly on the Museum's website offering a degree of transparency to the decision making process. Issues of repatriation will no doubt continue to arise from time to time and will often be contentious or difficult due to the issues outlined above.

With all human remains in the Museum, it is the aim of conservation work to extend the 'life' of remains so that the physical attributes and associated information retain their integrity. However, conserving human remains for the future requires not only attention to the intrinsic physical attributes of the remains, but also to particular storage and collection management techniques. In Chapter Five, Daniel Antoine and Emily Taylor discuss the practical aspects of handling, storing and transporting human remains. Importantly, they note the risks associated in working with human remains, such as the possible existence of pathogenic bacteria and the presence of heavy metals such as lead which necessitates careful preparation and thought before moving or transport. Remains may need to be removed from their original site to another country for study, therefore an awareness of relevant legislative and customs requirements is essential and they highlight the important role of the museum courier, the carrier as well as liaison and agreement with any lenders.

Significantly, Antoine and Taylor also note that the greatest potential hazard to the physical state of remains is internal to the museum: that of prior pesticide treatments which may not be recorded in museum documentation. Therefore, an integrated approach to care is required that involves not only curators, but conservators, physical anthropologists and scientists to understand the residues involved and to protect staff from possible contamination. The chapter also outlines how storage and collection management techniques affect the recording of museum registration numbers, the labelling of remains and boxes, the physical layout of bones within storage and the types of storage materials that can usefully and appropriately be employed.

In Chapter Six, Barbara Wills and her co-authors illustrate the range of factors that are considered in assessing the appropriate approaches to the conservation of remains which are applicable to remains in any museum. These include an understanding of the rituals of deposition, the burial environment, health and safety concerns such as those surrounding lead coffins, past reconstructions and whether the remains will be stored, displayed or made available for loan, for example in exhibitions that include Egyptian mummies.

In a number of case studies, the Museum conservators detail the specific treatment methods chosen and the rationale behind those decisions. They highlight the differences involved when dealing with the preparation of objects for display (using an example of remains from the Paleolithic era), naturally preserved remains (such as a bog body), purposefully preserved remains (Egyptian mummies), spontaneously preserved remains (such as examples from the Nile valley) and when improving storage of remains (in this case a mummified hand from western China) which have associated fibres, textile fragments, other tissues and loose soil. While each case has unique circumstances that need to be considered, Wills *et al.* also note the need to follow international and national protocols, discuss approaches with curators and physical anthropologists and to always take a minimalist approach to any physical intervention.

A key overarching requirement for care in a museum environment is the need to maintain stable environmental conditions and having appropriate storage materials and systems. Wills *et al.* usefully include a table outlining both desirable and acceptable environmental conditions for the storage and display of ancient Egyptian mummies, bog bodies and skeletal material. They also provide useful technical information relating to cleaning, dealing with past reconstructions, removing old museum registration numbers and details of materials that can be usefully employed in the treatment, packing, transport and storage of human remains.

Chapters Five and Six highlight two common elements: the need for vigilance through regular survey of the remains in the collection and the need to give attention to the psychological issues involved. Working with human remains is both a privilege and a responsibility, and those engaging in this work need to be psychologically prepared and supported in carrying out their duties. Training needs to take into account both professional and emotional aspects of caring for such materials.

Across the world, each cultural group has its own attitude to the treatment of the dead and human remains which differs widely across space and through time. There may be cultural beliefs and practices that could at times sit uncomfortably within museum policy in continuing to hold some remains. Museum staff have expert knowledge in the conservation and practical aspects of care, handling, transport and storage which they apply to human remains. Yet, by the nature of the diverse communities and associated beliefs from which remains originate, they cannot be fully cognisant of all contemporary cultural sensitivities and beliefs associated with those remains. An open dialogue with relevant communities is an important opportunity for the Museum to engage with and learn from other cultures rather than be regarded as a source of knowledge about those cultures. Such dialogue may lead to increased documentation and understanding of the remains concerned and how they should be cared for in the broadest cultural sense. The British Museum seeks where possible and appropriate to accommodate these concerns while the remains are in its care.

Within the legal requirements of the United Kingdom and policy decisions made by the Trustees, the British Museum continues to acquire and hold certain human remains as part of research directed towards an increased understanding of the ancient and modern world. It aims for the highest standards of physical care and also transparency in information when dealings with all remains. For a small number of human remains, dialogues about whether the Museum should continue to hold certain remains are likely to be ongoing.

Notes

1 See, for example, C. Forde 'How a tribal chief got buried in Liverpool', *The Times Higher Education*, 10 June 1997.

Chapter 4
Ancestral Remains from Oceania
Histories and Relationships in the Collection of the British Museum

Natasha McKinney

Introduction

The region known as Oceania is a diverse part of the world. Dominated by the Pacific Ocean, it encompasses thousands of islands and atolls, from the Caroline Islands in the west, to Rapa Nui in the east, and the large land masses of Australia, New Guinea and New Zealand. The sequence of human settlement varies greatly for these different areas. Current evidence appears to indicate that the Australian continent was first settled over 60,000 years ago, whereas the outer limits of Polynesia were reached much more recently, with New Zealand being settled last, around 900 years ago.

The people of Oceania, their physical characteristics, societies and practices have engaged the attention of westerners from the earliest moments of contact. From the 16th century onwards, European explorers began recording the similarities and differences between the people they encountered, speculating about their relationships to each other and to the wider world. Oceanic peoples also sought to define the explorers in their own cultural terms and memorialized their visits in oral histories. Over time, missionaries, colonial officials, settlers and later anthropologists were amongst those who continued to observe, question and record, each with their own agenda. Their success depended on the relationships they created and often the prevailing political conditions of the time.

Museum collections originate from these varied encounter situations. Collected human remains often appear to represent the most invasive of cross-cultural investigations, and in recent decades have rightly stimulated discussion amongst museum professionals concerned about their correct curatorship and care, in addition to requests for repatriation. A major preoccupation has been engagement with cultural descendants. In Pacific institutions, indigenous people may be involved with the museum on a variety of levels – as staff, researchers, consultants, visitors and collectively as local communities – enabling curatorship to be more closely aligned with indigenous priorities and observances. In Britain, museums with Oceanic collections must frequently overcome the barrier of distance in order to establish relationships which might similarly add cultural integrity to curatorial practice, and maintain a sense of the contemporary relevance of collections to those with whom they are most closely connected.

While it is a misconception that all indigenous groups in the Pacific are interested in the repatriation of human remains from overseas and local institutions, this has been a priority in Australia, New Zealand and the Hawaiian Islands in particular. In these countries, the issue of repatriation of artefacts and human remains forms part of wider efforts to regain control of cultural heritage. National governments have recognized that dispossession – of lands, property and rights – during the colonial area was a historical wrong which can to an extent be rectified in the present through formalized restitution processes (Jenkins 2011). Repatriation programmes have been incorporated into the activities of those departments responsible for cultural heritage, and by extension in national and state museums as potential repositories for returned remains.

The first part of this chapter gives a brief overview of the breadth and diversity of the British Museum collection, describing the remains within the context of mortuary practices across the Pacific. The second part covers the three repatriation claims for human remains processed by the British Museum since the Human Tissue Act 2004 came into force, all of which have related to the Oceanic collections. This gives some insight into the varied collection histories of the remains, and the relationships of the respective communities to them.

An overview of human remains in the Oceanic collections at the British Museum

The earliest collected human remains in the British Museum's Oceanic collection are from the Pacific voyages of James Cook, undertaken between 1768 and 1779. While human remains continued to enter the collection until the 1960s, in most cases the material had not been collected from its original source later than the early decades of the 20th century. A significant proportion of the remains derive from actual exchanges, rather than through archaeological excavations or other means. Human remains from Oceania are not actively being added to the Museum's collection today.

The collection consists of over 200 remains, almost half of which are from Papua New Guinea, including the Trobriand Islands, the Admiralty Islands, New Britain and New Ireland. Other items are from Australia and the Torres Strait Islands, West Papua, the Solomon Islands and the Santa Cruz group, Vanuatu, Kiribati, Fiji, Samoa, Tonga, the Society Islands, the Marquesas Islands, Rapa Nui, Hawaii and New Zealand. There are over 80 skulls or crania, most of which are decorated or modified, in addition to charms, ornaments and implements such as spatulas and fish-hooks. Details of the collection can be accessed via the Museum's Collection Online database (http://www.britishmuseum.org/research/collection_online/search.aspx); images of some remains are not shown due to relevant cultural sensitivities.

This section describes some of the human remains in the collection, in order to give an insight into the cultural diversity of the Pacific and the ethnographic and cultural value of these collections. Discussion of particular remains enables the appreciation of the social priorities of a particular group in relation to the dead, while the collection history reveals the complexities of interactions between Pacific peoples and outsiders. Pacific scholars have been consulted to ensure that there are in general no cultural objections to the publication of images of the remains shown in this chapter.

Decorated skulls from Papua New Guinea

A significant proportion of the Oceanic human remains are from Papua New Guinea. The European colonization of New Guinea began relatively late in comparison to other parts of the Pacific, becoming formalized in the late 19th century, with Dutch, German and British involvement. While the colonial authorities placed restrictions on practices such as exposing corpses on open platforms and the use of traditional repositories such as caves and trees, traditional mortuary practices continued in New Guinea well into the 20th century, in contrast to other parts of the Pacific where suppression occurred much earlier.

Plate 1 Human skull over-modelled with clay, Sepik River, Papua New Guinea, *c.* 1850–1919. British Museum, London (Oc1919,0718.20)

One such practice was the decoration of skulls for display in or near the communal house for men, sometimes on specially constructed boards and racks. In some places, such as the Sepik region of northern Papua New Guinea, this involved the 'over-modelling' of the skull with clay, the recreation of features such as the eyes with cowrie shell, seeds or imported beads and the painting of the face. The skulls of kin or enemies were treated in this way, and the modelled clay features were intended to create an actual resemblance to the deceased (Greub *et al.* 1985). When displayed on racks as part of large assemblages, they testified to the strength of a particular clan and frequently attracted the interest of outsiders.

In 1919, the Museum acquired a collection of over 200 objects from Mr Frank Streeten. Almost all of the objects are from mainland Papua New Guinea and appear to have been collected by Streeten himself, although there are no specific details about this. Amongst the masks, axes and arrows, there are 11 over-modelled human skulls (**Pl. 1**) and an armlet made of human vertebrae. The remains are noted as being from the Sepik River. The style of the skulls' decoration suggests that they may be linked to the Iatmul people of the Middle Sepik. The Iatmul use similar designs on the faces of carved wooden spirit figures, initiates and masks, *mai*, worn during ceremonies as they do on decorated skulls. The designs are thought to have a protective function (d'Alleva 1998). Amongst the Iatmul and other groups in New Guinea, head-hunting was formerly of central importance to the well being of a community, and its suppression led to anxiety and fundamental change. It was considered a necessary redress where relatives had been killed and was regarded as a means of maintaining balance, fertility and prosperity. The display of the heads represented the success and strength of both individual warriors and the clan.

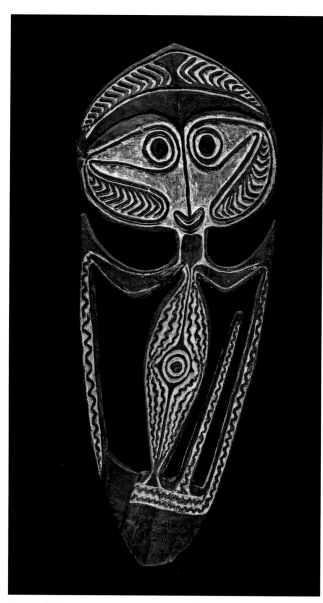

Plate 2 *Agiba*, wooden skull rack, Aird River Delta, Papuan Gulf, Papua New Guinea, late 19th century. British Museum, London (Oc1906,1013.5)

In the Papuan Gulf region of southern New Guinea, the taking of a head was also used to mark certain junctures such as the completion of a new communal men's house or war canoe. The Kerewa people of the western Papuan Gulf displayed the skulls of head-hunting victims by hanging them from carved, anthropomorphic boards known as *agiba*. These could only be carved by men who had committed a homicide (Haddon 1918). An *agiba* was collected from the Aird River Delta in the Papuan Gulf in 1904 during the Cooke-Daniels Ethnographic Expedition to New Guinea (**Pl. 2**), in addition to several skulls with long cane loops which had been used to secure them for display (British Museum, Oc1906,1013.93, Oc1906,1013.955.b and Oc1906,1013.1607). Over 1,800 objects from this expedition along the south coast were donated to the Museum in 1906 by the anthropologist and medical doctor Charles Gabriel Seligman and the expedition sponsor Major Cooke-Daniels. The collection also includes another type of decorated skull, which has a wooden projection from the nose in the form of an open

oval and cylindrical sections of wood covered with coix seeds extending from the eye sockets (Oc1906,1013.578).

Preserved heads from Papua New Guinea and West Papua

Missionaries and colonial officials confiscated 'trophy heads' as part of efforts to control and pacify particular areas, and were also the means by which this type of human remains ultimately became part of the collections of overseas museums. In some cases these individuals also engaged in scientific endeavour, writing extensive articles about the communities that they were living amongst and supplying information to others. In the Western Province of Papua New Guinea, certain groups employed a method of preserving heads which attracted particular interest. Reverend E. Baxter Riley, in charge of the Fly River Mission at Daru from 1902, carried out an interview with two men taken into custody at the same time as several 'stuffed heads' had been seized by a Government Patrol Officer. At Baxter Riley's request, they described the techniques of preparation in detail. The interview formed the basis of an article by Baxter Riley, published in the 1923 volume of the anthropological journal *Man*, with accompanying articles on the same topic by anthropologist A.C. Haddon and Resident Magistrate Leo Austen. Baxter Riley was given permission by the Resident Magistrates to send two of the heads to museums in Cambridge and Manchester (see Baxter Riley 1923).

There are two heads of this type in the British Museum from the Fly River area. The heads were prepared using the techniques recorded by Baxter Riley, which according to Austen were techniques reserved for enemies. First they were 'cooked' in order to loosen fat and flesh, then the skull was removed and cleaned before being repositioned and the skin stuffed with bark, vegetable fibre and clay (Vandyke-Lee 1974; Haddon 1923; Baxter Riley 1923). The first (Oc1927,0407.1) is recorded as being from the Lake Murray District. In 1927 this head was donated by Miss Beatrice Ethel Grimshaw, an Irish journalist who had been working in Papua New Guinea since 1907. The head was most likely collected in the 1920s, when she joined an exploring party to the Fly River, which Lake Murray lies beyond (Laracy 1983). In this case, the nose has been replaced with a bound rattan loop, the lower mandible hangs around the neck and there are ear ornaments made of long leaf strips, possibly from the sago palm. The head is painted with a red vertical band down the centre of the face, which broadens to encircle the mouth.

The second (Oc1934,1203.1) is noted to have been 'taken by head-hunters of Suki Creek, lower middle Fly River, from a village lower down the river in 1931' (British Museum Register 1934). The head was donated by Captain F.C. Bradley of the Royal Navy. This head exhibits certain typical features described in the 1923 articles. For example, it seems to have a stone, nut or seed inside the skull, which rattles when moved. The ears, with attachments similar to those described above, are intact in accordance with the description of the removal of the skull from the scalp from Baxter Riley's informants. This is achieved without removing the ears and thus the ear ornaments of the victim remain in place. A wooden peg protrudes from the back of the skull. This later enabled the head to be suspended using the peg and the nose formed with a rattan loop, for drying over a fire and for display in the ceremonial house (Baxter Riley 1923). A third head, which appears to have been preserved using the same techniques was acquired as part of the 1944 bequest of collector H.G. Beasley. This head (Oc1944,02.2072) is recorded as being from the Marind Anim people, of the south-eastern part of former Dutch New Guinea – now the Indonesian province of West Papua. In 1913 and the years that followed, hundreds of old skulls and 'fresh heads' were destroyed in the territory of the Marind Anim by the Dutch authorities, as they responded to complaints from the British government that the Marind Anim were carrying out intensive head-hunting in the areas to the east which were part of British New Guinea (Corbey 2010). Punishments also included imprisonment and death.

A rambaramp from Vanuatu

The human remains from Island Melanesia in the British Museum also include decorated and over-modelled skulls, and a single more elaborate memorial in the form of a *rambaramp* from Vanuatu (Oc1895,0396.1, **Pl. 3**), which was received as a donation in 1895. These human figures are funerary effigies from the island of Malekula in northern Vanuatu. Only the skulls of high-ranking individuals were kept and presented as *rambaramp*, which consist of an over-modelled skull and a body made of plant materials with elements made from clay (Layard 1928). In Malekula, men belong to grade societies, within which they can achieve a higher rank by participating in elaborate ceremonial rites. A person's grade status was indicated by insignia such as ornaments made from a boar's tusk, shell armlets and plaited armbands, the use of a particular coloured paint or a painted design for a particular part of the body as well as other body decorations. These were faithfully represented after death in the creation of the *rambaramp*.

In this case, the face and body are painted with orange, blue and black vertical bands. The upper arm on each side has painted-on armbands representing armbands made of black coconut shell and white shell beads, the beads arranged to form geometric patterns. On the left arm there is a boar's tusk armlet. On each shoulder, two small heads moulded from clay face outwards, each having a thick bunch of vegetable fibre projecting upwards from the top of their heads out of cane tubes. These are replicas of heads seen on the dancing sticks associated with one of the three main grade societies (Deacon 1970). *Rambaramp* were displayed in the communal men's house until they rotted away, at which time the skull was transferred to the clan ossuary.

Bone flutes from New Zealand

With the exception of the preserved human heads from New Zealand discussed below, the remains from Polynesia in the British Museum collection are in the form of objects. Māori cultural treasures are considered to have a sacred, or *tapu* quality, which derives from the material used as well as the process of making itself, and the individuals with whom the object has been associated during its existence. Objects made from human bone are particularly *tapu*. The bones of

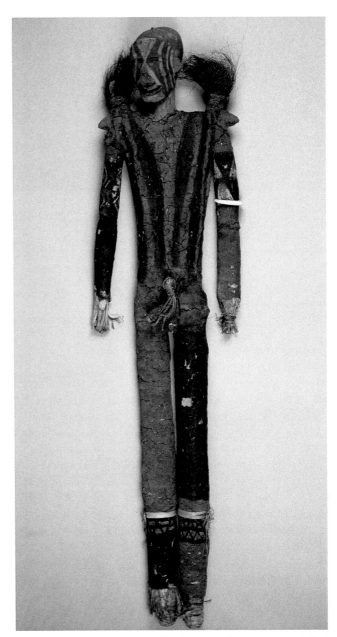

Plate 3 *Rambaramp*, funerary effigy incorporating an over-modelled skull, Vanuatu, c. 1850–93. British Museum, London (Oc1895,0316.1)

enemies could be used to make a range of objects, serving both a practical and derisory function. These included fish hooks, personal ornaments and musical instruments, which are represented in the collection, as well as needles and cloak pins (Te Awekotuku 1996). There are four human bone flutes in the collection, all of the type known as *koauau*, which are straight flutes typically carved from one piece of wood or bone, made in the early to mid-19th century (Oc1850,0206.1, Oc1896,-.930, Oc.1716, Oc,LMS.145). One of the flutes is known to have originally belonged to a chief, Titore Tākiri of the Ngāpuhi tribe in the far north of the North Island (**Pl. 4**). Titore[1] developed a friendship with Captain F.W. Sadler, who regularly sailed between the Bay of Islands and Sydney during the 1830s, and gifted several prestigious objects to him. These included a rare type of nephrite neck ornament, a nephrite club, a bone cloak pin and a flute. The objects were sold to the Museum in 1896 by Captain Sadler's granddaughter. The flute is elaborately carved with human figures. Another flute (Oc,LMS.145),

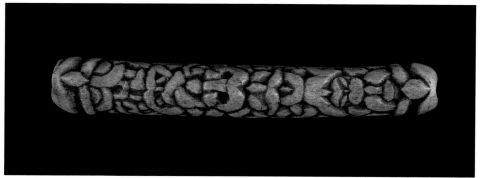

formerly in the collection of the London Missionary Society, is relief-carved with a lizard. This may be a reference to human mortality, as lizards were regarded as being symbolic of death and misfortune (Te Awekotuku 1996, 48). It is thought to have been made in the early 19th century in the Taranaki region of the North Island (Starzecka, Neich and Pendergrast 2010).

Feather sceptres from the Hawaiian Islands

The Hawaiian collection in the British Museum also includes human bone fish hooks, personal ornaments incorporating bone, wooden bowls inlaid with human teeth and carved human figures made of wood, with real human teeth set in the mouth. Another striking object type is the *kāhili*, which are often described as sceptres or standards because of their form and their association with those of high rank. They consist of a straight staff, topped with neatly arranged feathers. They were owned by chiefs, *ali'i*, but were carried by their attendants, and were also used in funeral processions (Buck 1957). In the past, the staff was formed of a wooden or whalebone core, mounted with rings of turtle shell, bone or ivory. The feathers of tropic birds, frigate birds and the Hawaiian honeycreepers and honeyeaters were amongst the types which were tied in bunches to form the cylindrical plume. In contrast to the derisory use of teeth or bone to inlay bowls or as fish hooks, the use of leg bones to make *kāhili* was an honour to the deceased (Buck 1957). One of the two sceptres which definitely include human bone is thought to have been collected on James Cook's third Pacific voyage (1776–9), when he visited the Hawaiian Islands and where he met his death (Oc,HAW.167, **Pl. 5**). A robust bone, probably the right humerus,[2] forms the core of the staff and the rounded joint is visible at the base. The upper section is covered with rings of turtle shell, neatly sectioned and flush with the surface of the bone; black feathers form the plume. A *kāhili* of this kind carried the name of the ancestor whose bones they were, and was used at the funerals of his descendants as a continuing commemoration (Buck 1957).

Claims for human remains from Oceania

When considering repatriation claims, an institution must operate within the legal boundaries pertaining to the de-accession of collection material. The British Museum Act 1963 clearly states that objects may only be disposed of in a very limited range of circumstances.[3] However, from October 2005, Section 47 of the Human Tissue Act 2004 gave the Board of Trustees of the British Museum and eight other national museums the power to authorize the de-

accession of human remains less than 1,000 years old. The return of human remains, whether subject to a claim or not, was not made mandatory, however. A decision to authorize de-accession could be made by Trustees 'if it appears to them to be appropriate to do so for any reason' (Section 47, Subsection 2). In order to ensure that decisions would be made in a diligent and transparent manner, the British Museum developed a policy on human remains, approved by the Trustees in October 2006 and updated in 2013. The policy relates closely to the recommendations in the *Guidance for the Care of Human Remains in Museums,* a Code of Practice which was released by the Department for Culture, Media and Sport and which aims to support all UK museums in managing collections of human remains and in exercising the power to de-accession (DCMS 2005; see Chapter One, this volume).

The policy describes the criteria under which the Trustees will consider a request for the transfer of human remains, with the aim to ensure that the Museum is liaising with the most appropriate community (see paragraphs 5.14–5.16, Trustees of the British Museum 2013). It requires claimants to demonstrate that there is a continuity of cultural beliefs and practices between themselves and the community from which the remains originate (termed 'Cultural Continuity'), and that the remains are culturally important to the claimant community in the present. It is suggested that the significance or 'Cultural Importance' of the remains may relate to the fact that the remains were removed in a manner which was inconsistent with the customs and practices of the people concerned, or that customary mortuary processes or ceremonies were interrupted by the collection of the remains (see section 5.15.4[4]). Consideration of these important points has been central to all three of the claims to date, with the Trustees making specific reference to the circumstances of collection and how these related to the documented practices of the respective groups in the minutes of their decisions (see http://www.britishmuseum.org/about_us/news_and_press/statements/human_remains.aspx for further details of each of the claims described here).

The Tasmanian cremation ash bundles

In July 2005, the Tasmanian Aboriginal Centre (TAC) restated a claim first made in 1985 for the return of two cremation ash bundles, which had entered the Museum's collection in 1882. Wrapped in animal skin, the remains were in the form of amulets, which could be worn to ward off illness and as mementoes of the relative whose ashes they held. The ash bundles were very likely collected by George Augustus Robinson during the period which he spent as 'conciliator' in Tasmania between 1829 and 1839.[5] Robinson's remit was to reduce the violence between settlers and the Aborigines so that land could be acquired by the settlers through the use of more peaceful methods. Robinson's activities included moving as many groups as possible away from mainland Tasmania to a new settlement, Wybalenna, on Flinders Island to the north-east, a place which Robinson later managed. Separated from their lands and customary practices, many Tasmanians died of disease in poor living conditions (Robinson, *Australian Dictionary of Biography* 1967).

The ash bundles were the only two known to exist, but they appear from Robinson's own accounts to have once been in fairly common usage (TAC 2005). In Robinson's journal entry for 9 July 1829, he describes observing a woman preparing a bundle. From her basket she took two circular pieces of kangaroo skin, into which she gathered the ashes from a recent cremation of a man. She drew together the skins by threading the sinews of a kangaroo tail through perforations around the circular edge, pulling them tight to create the charm – one for her sick husband and one for herself (Plomley 2008). On several occasions during his travels around Tasmania, Robinson described seeing the amulets being made or used. A possible link has been identified between Robinson's journal entries in late May and early June 1838 and the collection of one of the amulets (Plomley 1962). On 25 May 1838 Robinson writes about a woman referred to as Ellen,[6] who was dying of consumption. She wore an amulet around her neck and a human bone charm to alleviate back pain. Robinson tried to acquire the bone charm without success (Ellen replied that he had one already). Robinson reports Ellen's death on 13 June. On the original label and the British Museum registration slip for the amulet formerly registered with the number Oc1882,1214, the date 'June 26th 1838' is noted. Because this date is close to that of Ellen's death, it has been suggested that the bundle was a possession of hers and may have been taken without consent (perhaps explicitly so) (Plomley 1962, 10).

Following their probable collection by Robinson, the ash bundles were donated to the Museum in 1882 by the Royal College of Surgeons (Lincoln's Inn Fields, London), having been purchased as part of the extensive collection of the Staffordshire surgeon, Dr Joseph Barnard Davis, before his death in 1881. Davis, a renowned craniologist, had purchased the bundles from Rose Robinson, the widow of George Augustus Robinson (1791–1866), in 1867 as part of the Australian collections of her late husband.

On 23 March 2006, the Museum's Trustees decided to accept the claim for the return of the ash bundles. Several key points were pertinent to the decision (British Museum 2006). In collecting the remains, Robinson had caused the mortuary process, as practised by Tasmanians, to be interrupted, which prevented the remains from eventual natural disposal within the ancestral landscape. Importantly, the nature of the interruption (which in this case, is likely to have meant acquisition by coercion or without consent) was inconsistent with Tasmanian practices

Plate 5 *Kāhili*, feather sceptre with human bone handle, Hawaiian Islands, 18th century. British Museum, London (Oc,HAW.167)

– that is, it does not appear that Tasmanian Aborigines ever willingly traded or exchanged these sacred items with outsiders. Robinson's own accounts detail people's reluctance to part with them. In accordance with the British Museum Policy on Human Remains, independent advice was provided to the Trustees in the form of reports on the wider scientific value of the remains and the cultural value of the remains to the claimant group (British Museum 2006). Dr Robert Foley, Professor of Human Evolution at the University of Cambridge, noted that the research potential of cremation ash is currently limited, in contrast to intact skeletal material (Foley 2005). The cultural and spiritual significance of the remains to the Tasmanian Aboriginal people was ultimately judged to outweigh the public benefit of retaining them (Besterman 2005; Akerman 2006). The ash bundles were repatriated to Tasmania in September 2006 by two representatives from the TAC.

The kōiwi tangata (human remains) from New Zealand

In June 2006 a repatriation request was made for seven preserved human heads and nine skeletal remains from New Zealand. The claim was received from the Museum of New Zealand Te Papa Tongarewa, which in 2003 was mandated by the New Zealand government to establish a repatriation programme seeking the return of human remains from international and domestic institutions to Māori tribes.

The Māori practice of preserving the heads of ancestors has parallels elsewhere in Polynesia and the wider Pacific. The head was considered the most sacred part of the body, and the heads of chiefs, warriors or particularly revered kin were treated in this way. Warriors' heads might be preserved at a battle site, so that they could be mourned over once returned home as well as to prevent them from being taken by their enemies (Starzecka 1992). Enemy heads were preserved and displayed for the purposes of derision and bore witness to the prowess of a particular group (Orchiston 1967). Facial tattooing, *moko*, communicated individual identity and enhanced the impressive appearance of Māori men. This aesthetic appeal was retained in death by careful preparation of the heads through a process of steaming in an earth oven and drying with the aid of sun and sometimes smoke, and the reinforcement of nose and cheeks with small wood strips and flax (Orchiston 1967). For some early European visitors to New Zealand, the heads, now referred to as *toi moko*, were immediately recognized as potential curios and attempts were made to trade them away from their owners.[7] The desire to obtain European muskets later increased the willingness of Māori to engage in this trade, to the degree that some heads are thought to have been prepared deliberately for sale.

The seven heads now in the British Museum collection were all likely traded out of New Zealand in the early decades of the 19th century. While a certain amount is known about the history of four of the heads within Britain, it has not been possible to trace any of the heads to a specific exchange or location in New Zealand and links to a particular tribe have not been made.[8] The Trustees of the British Museum concluded their decision on this claim in April 2008. In deciding against the repatriation of the *toi moko*, they stated that it was not clear to them that the process of mortuary disposal had been interrupted or disturbed by their original collection (British Museum 2008). In addition, it was unclear whether the importance of the remains to an originating community outweighed the importance of the remains as information sources about human history. In this particular matter the Trustees were informed by a report by Dr Lissant Bolton, head of the Oceania section (and now Keeper of the Department of Africa, Oceania and the Americas), resulting from consultation work carried out in New Zealand. The report concluded that Māori may favour the identification of the specific tribe to which the heads are related *prior* to any repatriation to New Zealand, and the need to definitively provenance remains before any burial of remains in a particular tribal area was of great concern (Bolton 2007). The independent reports argued equally strongly for the scientific value of the remains and conversely their cultural importance to Māori (Endicott 2007; Besterman 2007). In contrast to the preserved heads, the nine human bone sections and fragments which were part of the claim were judged by the Trustees to be more clearly intended for mortuary disposal and so the claim for these was accepted. In November 2008 the repatriation was carried out from the British Museum by staff from Te Papa Tongarewa, according to Māori protocols. There is ongoing contact between research staff at both institutions in relation to human remains and other aspects of the Māori collection.

The Torres Strait Islands claim

A third claim was received in June 2011 for two human skulls from the Torres Strait Islands, which are politically part of Australia. The claim was submitted by the Torres Strait Islands Repatriation Working Group, as representatives of the Torres Strait Islander Traditional Owners, specifically of the islands of Nagir and Mer. The two skulls were collected by marine biologist Alfred Cort Haddon, on his first field research visit to the Torres Strait Islands in 1888–9. At this time Haddon was Professor of Zoology at the Royal College of Science, Dublin, but his experiences in the Torres Strait Islands increased his interest in ethnography, and he later led the Cambridge Anthropological Expedition to the Islands (1898). The first skull was identified by Haddon as a young man named Magau, who had died at the end of 1887. Haddon purchased this skull in August 1888 while on the island of Nagir. The type of skull is known as a *pada kuik* and was used for divination. Haddon published accounts of the preparation of Magau's skull, his funeral ceremony and the collection of his skull (Haddon 1904, 258–9; Haddon 1893, 154–6). The second skull is one of five purchased by Haddon on Mer in 1889. Haddon describes 'one or two' of these skulls being decorated for him. This type of skull was known as a *lamar marik*, and the skull, which is now in the Museum, was used by Haddon to demonstrate the exact method of divination as carried out on Mer (Haddon 1908, 266–8; Haddon 1932, 92–3). The preparation and decoration of skulls after death in this manner was the task of close relatives of the deceased. The skulls were then presented back to the immediate kin at a funeral ceremony which took place a few months following death. Skulls were presented in specially made baskets, and were then kept in the family home or a clan repository (McKinney 2011).

The Trustees decided in December 2012 that this claim would not be accepted. In this case they felt the evidence was insufficient for them to agree to repatriation and that it was unclear that the process of mortuary disposal had been interrupted (British Museum 2012). The independent report by bioarchaeologist Professor Simon Hillson of University College London stated that the remains were relatively rare in collections, and were an important resource which may contribute to studies of the early human settlement of Australia through morphological and possibly genetic analysis (Hillson 2012). Anthropologist Dr Richard Davis of the University of Western Australia wrote an extensive report on the cultural significance of the remains, contextualizing the skulls within Torres Strait Islander mortuary practice of the late 19th century (Davis 2011). Importantly, Davis notes that the preparation of skulls following death was not only a process intended to ensure the proper passage of the person's spirit, but that the stages in the mortuary ceremonies served to re-establish the deceased's new spiritual identity in relation to their kin and community. This process contributed to the skull's efficacy. Laws relating to the disposal of dead bodies and Christian burial practices led to the cessation of mortuary rituals including the preparation of skulls, as they had been carried out prior to 1900. However, Davis points out that the secondary stage of mortuary ceremonies today takes the form of a tombstone unveiling, which as in the past is prepared for long in advance and is accompanied by feasting and dance. These points reinforce the claimants' case for both Cultural Continuity and Cultural Importance as described in the Museum's policy (as discussed above). However, in stating that it was unclear whether the process of mortuary disposal had been interrupted by collection, the Trustees implied that the active participation of Islanders in exchanges with the collector, Haddon, may have influenced their decision against repatriation.

In the Torres Strait Islands case, as in the Tasmanian example, the accounts of the collectors themselves played a pivotal role in discussions and ultimately the decision of the claim. A major challenge in assessing claims is the interpretation of the available documentation, which is often fragmented or extremely limited, as in the New Zealand case. Collectors' own assessments of particular exchanges must be balanced with knowledge relating to customary practices in relation to the dead and traditional exchange systems. Consideration should also be made of the fact that contact and colonization led to major disruptions in Oceanic societies, whereby exchanges sometimes took place while established spheres of authority and exchange systems were in a state of flux.

Conclusion

This brief discussion of the Oceanic human remains in the British Museum highlights the significant diversity in the treatment of the body after death in different parts of the Pacific as well as for different members of society. In many places, the process of colonization and conversion to Christianity has meant that today burial and cremation are the most common practices regardless of a person's social status. However, as seen in the Torres Strait, the nature of ceremonies associated with death and commemoration may have strong resonance with the past and represent new formulations of cultural identity.

The British Museum's Oceania collection in its present state will continue to grow in importance rather than size or scope, as the gap of time increases since remains were prepared in these ways and some of the associated beliefs and practices were current. In the future it is hoped that opportunities for collaborative research with indigenous scholars and communities will bring new perspectives and insights into parts of the collection, and that relationships with cultural descendants will continue to be positive and multifaceted.

Notes

1 In historic records, including those of the Museum, this chief is referred to as Titore or variations of this name, such as 'Tetoro'.

2 Information from British Museum Curator of Physical Anthropologist, Daniel Antoine, 2010.

3 See Section 5 of the British Museum Act 1963, and the British Museum Policy on De-accession of Registered Objects from the Collection (Trustees of the British Museum 2010).

4 Or section 5.14.4 in the 2006 policy under which the three claims were considered.

5 Robinson is often referred to by his later title, 'Protector of the Aborigines', a role which he took up in 1839 at Port Phillip, Victoria.

6 Ellen's Aboriginal names were Pealurerer and Nertateerner (TAC 2005; see Plomley 1987, 885, and also 859 and 880).

7 On James Cook's first Pacific voyage, the naturalist Joseph Banks forcibly acquired a head at Queen Charlotte Sound in the South Island in January 1770 (Banks 1962, 457). The whereabouts of this head is unknown.

8 The analysis of tattooing styles in relation to region is a continuing area of research at Te Papa Tongarewa.

Bibliography

Akerman, K., 2006. *A Brief Assessment of the Cultural Significance of Cremation Ash Bundles* (unpublished report). Retrieved from http://www.britishmuseum.org/pdf/Final_Dossier.pdf

Austen, L., 1923. 'Karigara customs', *Man* 23, 35–6.

Banks, J., 1962. *The Endeavour Journal of Joseph Banks, 1768–1771, Vol.1.* Sydney and London.

Baxter Riley, E., 1923. 'Dorro head-hunters', *Man* 23, 33–5.

Besterman, T., 2005. *Report for the Trustees of the British Museum: Request from the Australian Government for the Return of Two Cremation ash bundles from Tasmania* (unpublished report). Retrieved from http://www.britishmuseum.org/pdf/Final_Dossier.pdf

—, 2007. *Report to the Board of Trustees of the British Museum: Request from Te Papa Tongarewa for the Return of Sixteen Māori kōiwi tangata to New Zealand* (unpublished report). Retrieved from http://www.britishmuseum.org/about_us/news_and_press/statements/human_remains/repatriation_to_new_zealand.aspx

Bolton, L., 2007. *Repatriation Request from Karanga Aotearoa (Repatriation Unit), Te Papa Tongarewa (Museum of New Zealand): Report on Discussions held in New Zealand* (unpublished report). Retrieved from http://www.britishmuseum.org/about_us/news_and_press/statements/human_remains/repatriation_to_new_zealand.aspx

British Museum 2006. *Request for Repatriation of Human Remains to Tasmania: Minutes of Meeting of the Trustees – March 2006.* Retrieved from http://www.britishmuseum.org/about_us/news_and_press/statements/human_remains/repatriation_to_tasmania.aspx

— 2008. *Request for Repatriation of Human Remains to New Zealand: Minutes of Meeting of the Trustees – April 2008.* Retrieved from http://www.britishmuseum.org/about_us/news_and_press/statements/human_remains/repatriation_to_new_zealand.aspx

— 2012. *Request for Repatriation of Human Remains to the Torres Strait Islands, Australia.* Retrieved from http://www.britishmuseum.org/about_us/news_and_press/statements/human_remains/repatriation_to_torres_strait.aspx

British Museum Act 1963. Retrieved from http://www.legislation.gov.uk/ukpga/1963/24/contents

British Museum Register 1934 (Archives of the Department of Africa, Oceania and the Americas).

Buck, P.H., 1957. *Arts and Crafts of Hawaii.* Honolulu.

Corbey, R., 2010. *Headhunters from the Swamps: The Marind Anim of New Guinea as seen by the Missionaries of the Sacred Heart, 1905–1925.* Leiden.

D'Alleva, A., 1998. *Art of the Pacific.* London.

Davis, R., 2011. *Report on the Cultural Significance of Torres Strait Islander Ancestral Remains held by the British Museum* (unpublished report). Retrieved from http://www.britishmuseum.org/about_us/news_and_press/statements/human_remains/repatriation_to_torres_strait.aspx

DCMS (Department for Culture, Media and Sport) 2005. *Guidance for the Care of Human Remains in Museums.* London.

Deacon, A.B., 1970. *Malekula: A Vanishing People in the New Hebrides.* Oosterhout N.B.

Endicott, P., 2007. *Report on the Prospects and Potential Value of Scientific Research on Human Remains from New Zealand held in the British Museum* (unpublished report). Retrieved from http://www.britishmuseum.org/about_us/news_and_press/statements/human_remains/repatriation_to_new_zealand.aspx

Foley, R., 2005. *Report on the Scientific Significance of Two Cremation Ash Bundles from Tasmania held in the British Museum* (unpublished report). Retrieved from http://www.britishmuseum.org/pdf/Final_Dossier.pdf

Greub, S., Kaufmann, C., Schuster, M., Hauser-Schäublin, B. and Schmid-Kocher, C., 1985. *Authority and Ornament: Art of the Sepik River, Papua New Guinea.* Basel.

Grimshaw, B.E., 1910. *The New New Guinea.* London.

Haddon, A.C., 1893. *The Secular and Ceremonial Dances of Torres Straits.* Leiden.

—, 1904. *Reports of the Cambridge Anthropological Expedition to Torres Straits, Vol. 5, Sociology, Magic and Religion of the Western Islanders.* Cambridge.

—, 1908. *Reports of the Cambridge Anthropological Expedition to Torres Straits, Vol. 6, Sociology, Magic and Religion of the Eastern Islanders.* Cambridge.

—, 1918. 'The Agiba cult of the Kerewa Culture', *Man* 18, 177–83.

—, 1923. 'Stuffed human heads from New Guinea', *Man* 23, 36–9.

—, 1932. *Head-hunters: Black, White, and Brown.* London.

Hillson, S., 2012. *Decorated Human Skulls Oc,89+.96 and Oc,89+.97* (unpublished report). Retrieved from http://www.britishmuseum.org/about_us/news_and_press/statements/human_remains/repatriation_to_torres_strait.aspx

Human Tissue Act 2004. Retrieved from http://www.legislation.gov.uk/ukpga/2004/30/contents

Jenkins, T., 2011. *Contesting Human Remains in Museum Collections: The Crisis of Cultural Authority.* New York.

Laracy, H., 1983. 'Grimshaw, Beatrice Ethel (1870–1953)', *Australian Dictionary of Biography*, National Centre of Biography, Australian National University (http://adb.anu.edu.au/biography/grimshaw-beatrice-ethel-6494/text11135, accessed 17 March 2014).

Layard, J.W., 1928. 'Degree-taking rites in South West Bay, Malekula', *The Journal of the Royal Anthropological Institute of Great Britain and Ireland, Vol.58*, 139–223.

McKinney, N., 2011. *Request for the De-accession of Human Remains from the Torres Strait Islands, Australia: Briefing Note for Trustees* (unpublished report). Retrieved from http://www.britishmuseum.org/about_us/news_and_press/statements/human_remains/repatriation_to_torres_strait.aspx

Orchiston, D.W., 1967. 'Preserved heads of the New Zealand Maoris', *The Journal of the Polynesian Society 76*, no. 3, 297–329.

Plomley, N.J.B., 1962. *A List of Tasmanian Aboriginal Material in Collections in Europe. Record of the Queen Victoria Museum, Launceston.* Launceston, Tasmania.

— (ed.), 1987. *Weep in Silence: A History of the Flinders Island Aboriginal Settlement, with Flinders Island Journal of George Augustus Robinson, 1835–1839.* Hobart.

—, 2008. *Friendly Mission: The Tasmanian Journals and Papers of George Augustus Robinson, 1829–1834.* Launceston, Tasmania.

Robinson, George Augustus (1791–1866) (1967). *Australian Dictionary of Biography.* Retrieved from http://adb.anu.edu.au/biography/robinson-george-augustus-2596/text3565

Ryan, P., 1972. *Encyclopaedia of Papua and New Guinea.* Melbourne.

Starzecka, D.C., 1992. 'Mokomokai: Preserved human heads of the Maori'. Unpublished seminar paper, British Museum (Museum of Mankind).

—, Neich, R. and Pendergrast, M., 2010. *The Maori Collections of the British Museum.* London.

Tasmanian Aboriginal Centre 2005. *Tasmanian Aboriginal Cremation Ash Bundles and the Circumstances in which they were Collected by George Augustus Robinson.* Unpublished report: TAC.

Te Awekotuku, N., 1996. 'Maori: people and culture', in *Maori Art and Culture*, ed. D. Starzecka, 26–49.

Trustees of the British Museum 2006. The British Museum Policy on Human Remains (retrieved from http://www.britishmuseum.org/pdf/Human%20Remains%206%20Oct%202006.pdf).

— 2010. British Museum Policy on De-accession of Registered Objects from the Collection (retrieved from http://www.britishmuseum.org/pdf/Deaccession_2010-03-04.pdf).

— 2013. The British Museum Policy on Human Remains (available online at http://www.britishmuseum.org/about_us/management/museum_governance.aspx).

Vandyke-Lee, D.J., 1974. 'The conservation of a preserved human head', *Studies in Conservation* 19, no.4, 222–6.

Chapter 5
Collection Care
Handling, Storing and Transporting Human Remains

Daniel Antoine and Emily Taylor

The handling and storage of the human remains held in the British Museum collection follows the recommendations set out in the *Guidance for the Care of Human Remains in Museums* published by the Department for Culture, Media and Sport (DCMS 2005, 18–19). All human remains are treated with respect, care and dignity and are stored in conditions that are actively managed and monitored to meet the required standards of security, access management and environmental control which are proportionate and appropriate to their age, origin and modern cultural significance (Trustees of British Museum 2013, 3–4). The working practices presented here are drawn from the *British Museum Guidance for the Care, Study and Display of Human Remains*, an internal guidance document prepared by the British Museum Human Remains Working Group,[1] and takes into account a range of considerations from possible cultural preferences in the way human remains are stored to health and safety implications. This chapter will discuss the issues faced by staff curating human remains, with a strong emphasis on skeletal remains as these represent the majority of the collection held at the British Museum.

Risks associated with human remains

> Pathogenic bacteria and viruses that were once the cause of death of individuals excavated in archaeological or osteoforensic contexts do not represent a health risk to archaeologists and museum personnel. In contrast, organic pesticides and heavy metals represent a real threat (Arriaza and Pfister 2007, 214).

The possible risks to British Museum staff involved in the excavation, storage, handling or analysis of human remains are carefully evaluated in advance by the completion of a risk assessment (see English Heritage and the Church of England 2005, 45; Arriaza and Pfister 2007, 205–21; Cassman *et al.* 2007; see also Chapter Six, Appendix 1). For human remains from English burial grounds, which represent the largest proportion of remains in the British Museum collection, the most likely sources of risk to health appear to be the presence of pathogens, psychological stress and contamination by heavy metals such as lead (English Heritage and the Church of England 2005, 45). With human remains that are less than 100 years old, the risk of any of these factors affecting staff or researchers working with human remains may be relatively high and such work is carefully assessed on a case-by-case basis (English Heritage and the Church of England 2005, 45; see also Galloway and Snodgrass 1998; Cox 2000; Crist 2001; Konefes and McGee 2001). For human remains that are over 100 years old, the risks are regarded as significantly lower and possible dangers associated with pathogens such as anthrax and smallpox appear to have been overestimated (English Heritage and the Church of England 2005, 45). The risk of staff being exposed to tetanus and leptospirosis during an excavation is greater, but it is on par with the risk associated with gardening (English Heritage and the Church of England 2005, 45). Heavy metals, such as lead, are used in some coffins and may result in a risk of poisoning (Cox 2000; English Heritage and the Church of England 2005, 45).[2] Normal hygiene procedures, such as hand washing, must be observed at all times and gloves ought to be worn when preserved soft tissues are present. Additional protection, such as suitable filter masks, may be necessary in dusty environments or during laboratory sampling of bone for analysis. Bone dust is an irritant and can lead to sensitization with regular exposure (English Heritage and the Church of England 2005, 45). Suitable masks should be used when working with powdery bone or when drilling bone/teeth for scientific sampling (Díaz-Jara *et al.* 2001). Other environments where the wearing of masks may be advisable include areas such as crypts where dust, lead and high concentrations of fungal spores may be present (see Cox 2000).

The British Museum also holds human remains from around the world, which were buried and have survived in very different environments. The risks associated with their handling appear to be similar to those concerning human remains from English burial grounds. For most human remains, pathogens are extremely unlikely to survive for over 100 years or remain infective for long enough to present a genuine threat to curators, researchers or conservators working on burials from archaeological contexts (see Arriaza and Pfister 2007, 205–6). The majority of living organisms found in ancient human remains are probably the result of recent contaminations or represent soil microorganisms. Viruses found in relatively recent mummies from the 16th century have good structural preservation, but their viability was shown to have been lost and they are unable to cause disease or reproduce (Arriaza and Pfisterl 2007, 205–6). Even under 'ideal' cold and stable conditions, the remains of 19th-century smallpox victims preserved in the permafrost of the Arctic, as well as those from the 1918 Spanish influenza outbreak buried in the permafrost in Alaska, did not contain any viable viruses (Arriaza and Pfister 2007, 205–6). An amoeba-infecting *Pithovirus sibericum* virus was recently revived after lying dormant and remaining infectious for 30,000 years in the Siberian permafrost (see Legendre *et al.* 2014), but the conditions found in most archaeological sites are unlikely to suit the long-term survival of pathogens. In contrast, very little is known about the preservation of prions (proteinaceous infectious particles with no nucleic acids) that cause BSE and Creutzfeldt-Jacob disease. Prions may have the potential to survive long term, but they have not, as of yet, been recovered from archaeological specimens (Arriaza and Pfister 2007, 206–7). Staff and researchers working on very recent material (less than 100 years old) or at historical cemeteries (particularly from New Guinea where the prion disease *kuru* is endemic), should be aware of this risk and are advised to wear protective equipment (Arriaza and Pfister 2007, 206–7; see also Galloway and Snodgrass 1998; Konefes and McGee 2001). Crist (2001), however, also discusses the risks associated with working on recently buried human remains from historical graves and concludes that:

> The absence of living cells after death, fragility of most microorganisms, and unfavourable post-mortem conditions are all important factors that significantly reduce, and may exclude, the likelihood of infection from skeletonised human remains (Crist 2001, 98).

Any outbreak of moulds, fungi or the presence of anthrax endospores may also be a risk, but healthy adults have a low probability of being adversely affected by these, and the likelihood of contracting anthrax appears to be small (Sledzik 2001, 71–7). Nonetheless, outbreaks of mould should be avoided as susceptible individuals can be at risk of developing mould-induced hypersensitivity pneumonitis, an inflammation of the lungs caused by repeatedly breathing in a foreign substance (Arriaza and Pfister 2007, 207). The prevalence of this condition is low, but cases of sensitization among museum staff working on materials other than human remains have been published. Indeed, the risk is not specific to human remains and mould growth on human remains poses the same risks as any other mould growth (see Kolmodin-Hedman *et al.* 1986; Wiszniewska *et al.* 2009).

The greatest potential hazard with human remains appears to involve the use of pesticides on museum collections. Pesticides have been used to preserve mummies in some museum collections and the conservation records or treatment history of any human remains should be checked for such risks. These details may not always be available as the treatment may have occurred prior to acquisition or may not have been noted. Where the use of pesticides is suspected, human remains should be handled with gloves. If the remains are fragmented and dusty, dust-filtering masks should also be worn to avoid ingesting any toxins present within the dust (see Arriaza and Pfister 2007, 216–17). This also applies to human remains in which prions may be present (see above). Funerary practices may also add unexpected biological hazards. Examples include highly toxic chemicals such as arsenic (e.g. bright yellow pigments used to decorate some Andean mummies), lead (e.g. human remains recovered from lead-lined coffins) or mercury (e.g. present in some Peruvian funerary textiles) (Arriaza and Pfister 2007; Konefes and McGee 2001).

Handling human remains: considerations and care

Psychological stress and high staff turnover can be associated with work on well-preserved and/or relatively recent human remains (English Heritage and the Church of England 2005, 45), and some individuals may not wish to work with, or feel comfortable handling human remains for cultural, religious or personal reasons. For some, this may include all forms of human remains (e.g. skeletal, cremated, mummified or bog remains and objects made wholly or in part of human remains), or may only apply to well-preserved remains such as mummies. British Museum staff who are likely to be involved in the handling of human remains are offered the opportunity to discuss any concerns they may have with an appropriate member of staff as this may have implications for working with specific collections and in specific storage areas. Prior to coming into contact with such collections, it is useful to determine what category of human remains they feel comfortable handling, whilst taking into account the origin, age and degree of preservation of the remains. This can be ascertained by discussing images in publications or on the British Museum's Collection Online database, rather than the human remains themselves. It is also important to determine to what extent a person is prepared to handle human remains. Unless they are involved in specific tasks such as conservation and display mounting work, or the analysis of human remains for research purposes, handling does not usually involve any direct contact.

When human remains require handling, this must be done with great care and respect, in a dedicated or appropriate environment and preferably over a clean cushioned surface to prevent damage (see Roberts 2013; Cassman and Odegaard 2007a; 2007b). Anyone handling human remains should have received appropriate training (e.g. in physical anthropology, bioarchaeology, conservation or museum handling) and should be made aware of their ethical obligations with regard to human remains. The condition and fragility of the human remains is assessed and taken into account before they are transported, unpacked and handled. The use of analytical or measuring equipment by researchers can result in wear and tear in heavily studied collections (see Chapter Three, this volume) and should be supervised and carefully monitored. For example, in order to avoid marking bone, metal recording instruments such as measuring callipers are, as far as possible, avoided and the use of plastic (coated) equivalents is encouraged. It is also no longer advisable to write information on human remains (such as site codes or registration numbers) as this may be regarded as inappropriate by some cultures. Advice on how to clean/process human remains is sought from a trained conservator on a case-by-case basis and passive conservation is encouraged so as not to affect the research potential of the human remains (see Chapters Three and Six, this volume). The use of resins as consolidant and/or adhesives should also be avoided and only applied by a trained conservator under the guidance of a person with the appropriate anatomical knowledge, such as a physical anthropologist. In particular, teeth should never be glued into their sockets as roots are a source of valuable biological information and should remain observable. Overall, there are no substitutes for training and detailed guidance from an experienced physical anthropologist or conservator (see Chapter Six, this volume; Cassman et al. 2007; Cassman and Odegaard 2007a; 2007b).

The storage of human remains

Providing appropriate storage is also an essential part of caring for museum collections. Museums and research collections may, depending on space and resource availability, develop different storage solutions for the human remains in their collection (e.g. Cassman and Odegaard 2007c; Mays 2013; McKinley 2013; Redfern and Bekvalac 2013; Roberts 2013; Scott 2013). As the human remains themselves vary in their specific nature, coming from many different cultural contexts and burial environments, so do the storage solutions. In the British Museum, different types of human remains are stored in environmental conditions appropriate to their specific nature (see Chapter Six, this volume). Although the storage conditions may vary, the basic duty of care remains the same and the Museum aspires to follow strict storage guidelines. All materials used in storage (including boxes, bags, labels and pens) are, as far as possible, inert and of conservation grade with long-term stability. Ideally, inert metal shelving is used. These should be raised at least 100mm above the floor to protect from accidental flooding and pests, and to allow for cleaning. Boxes or other appropriate containers used to store human remains should always be clearly labelled with

a registration number and other pieces of relevant information. Labels should also state that these boxes or containers enclose human remains. If the human remains are less than 100 years old and covered by the Human Tissue Act 2004, this must be clearly stated on the outside of the box (see Chapter One, this volume).

The human remains in the British Museum collection are stored in a respectful way that ensure their long-term preservation. Whenever appropriate and possible, the British Museum may also be guided by the cultural preferences and sensitivities of communities that have cultural continuity with the remains, or for whom the remains have cultural importance (see Giesen and White 2013). This may cover the selection of materials used to pack the human remains, the location of the remains within the storeroom and the position, orientation or articulation of the remains. Decisions to keep objects associated with human remains together are determined by cultural context and made on a case-by-case basis. Wherever possible, associations between human remains and funerary objects are maintained (e.g. a dedicated space for the human remains within a general storage area). For composite objects made in part of human remains, specific advice is usually sought from a trained conservator. Human remains in the British Museum's care are also regularly inspected to ensure they are stored appropriately and do not show signs of deterioration. Condition assessments are undertaken by trained and authorized staff as appropriate for the collection stored (see Cassman and Odegaard 2007b). The Museum may also have in its care recently excavated human remains that are not yet registered parts of the collection, in addition to human remains that the Museum is studying or storing temporarily. These are stored and handled using the same principles.

In most circumstances, human remains are kept in discrete areas away from the main activity of the store. All storerooms holding human remains should be:

- Secure with access restricted/monitored.
- Watertight and sealed from potential pests and dust.
- Kept clean and monitored for pests, damage and other potential threats.
- Maintained as areas where no food or drinks are permitted.
- Regularly monitored regarding the relative humidity and temperature.
- In conditions where light (both daylight and artificial light) is kept to a minimum as this may damage the human remains, boxes and labels.

The majority of the human remains held in the British Museum collection are skeletal remains and, when appropriate and possible, they are stored in wire-stitched carton rigid boxes (e.g. 505mm x 250mm x 243mm) and elements are bagged separately using clear polythene bags (500 gauge), with Tyvek® labels in each bag (see examples in Chapter Six, this volume). Frequently accessed collections may be stored differently to ease access and minimize handling (e.g. trays or inert boxes with supportive inert packing). When appropriate and possible, teeth should not be stored in occlusion (i.e. upper and lower teeth positioned against each other) and no pressure should be applied to the teeth as this may cause the enamel to peel away. Unless there

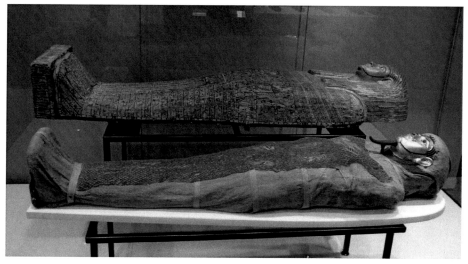

Plate 1 The mummy of Irthorru (26th Dynasty, British Museum, EA 20745) displayed on a handling board for the exhibition *Journey through the Afterlife: Ancient Egyptian Book of the Dead* at the Western Australian Museum, May 2013

are any cultural objections, a robust and complete skull should be stored resting on its top (upside-down with the teeth/maxilla pointing upwards), using appropriate support if necessary (e.g. acid-free tissue 'doughnuts'; see Chapter Six, this volume). If suitable, the mandible should be stored separately with the teeth facing up and nothing should rest on top of the dentition. The heavier long bones of the arms and legs should be placed at the bottom of a box so that they are flat and do not cross (i.e. parallel to each other) to prevent breakages, with the more fragile bones (such as the pelvis) on top. Different parts of the skeleton should preferably be stored in separate sealable bags and identified with Tyvek labels recording the site name, context/skeleton number and a description of its contents. Storing a skeleton into several bags protects the bones from being damaged, provides some padding and allows direct access to specific parts of the skeleton. This prevents a whole skeleton being unpacked when a researcher only wishes to study part of the skeleton (e.g. only teeth may be required when studying dental diseases). Ideally, the skull, mandible, vertebrae, ribs, hands, arms (humerus, ulna and radius), pelvis, sacrum, scapulae, legs (femur, tibia, fibula and patella), feet and any loose teeth should be packed separately in sealable bags, separating left and right. When bones are fragmented, each bone should be bagged separately (e.g. the bones of an arm – humerus, radius and ulna – should be separated into three bags).

Unless the bones are fragile and require careful packing, an entire skeleton should ideally be stored in a single box (this does not apply to commingled remains). In order to save space, and as long as bones are carefully arranged to avoid any damage, incomplete or smaller skeletons can be stored together within a shared box, with each individual placed in a clearly identifiable and labelled sub-container (e.g. a larger bag or smaller box). Importantly, recently excavated bones may be damp or contain residual humidity (widespread in British material) and each bag should have small perforations so that the material can slowly dry out, preventing condensation or mould growth. When appropriate, fragile and/or pathological bones should be supported with an inert material (e.g. Plastazote® or acid-free tissue) and bagged separately with a Tyvek label. Fragile bones are often wrapped in acid-free tissue, but this is not an ideal solution as you cannot see – or adapt your

handling of – the fragile part until it has been unwrapped. Creating a supporting 'nest' around and below a fragile bone is often more appropriate as it offers high visibility. Mummified and other well-preserved remains, such as bog bodies, are particularly fragile and often require special storage solutions, as well as guidance from a trained conservator (see Chapters Two and Six, this volume).

Transporting human remains: examples from the Egyptian collection

Additional levels of care are required when human remains are moved, particularly if they need to be transported as part of a loan or an exhibition. This requires careful planning by collection staff in addition to tailor-made solutions that match the specific requirements of the individual remains. As with other parts of the collection, human remains are condition assessed by the Conservation Department at the British Museum before any kind of travel or loan is agreed (see Cassman and Odegaard 2007b; 2007c). Many variables are taken into account, including the transportation mode(s), the length of the journey, the prospective display conditions, as well as the current state of preservation of the remains. If approved for transport, and once any conservation treatments have taken place, conservation and collections staff usually discuss whether the packing needs to accommodate fragile areas with additional support or protection. Articulated bodies, such as mummies, are particularly fragile and should be fully horizontal and supported during travel. For this reason, mummified remains are traditionally placed on a handling board, on which they stay for the duration of travel and display and possibly also whilst in storage at the British Museum (see Chapter Six, this volume). Depending on the purpose and duration of travel, the materials used may differ (e.g. Chapter Six, this volume; Cassman and Odegaard, 2007c). The materials used in long-term displays, transit, loans and storage are tested to determine their chemical stability and level of inertia. Handling boards recently made for mummies on display as part of the international touring exhibitions *Mummy: The Inside Story* and *Journey through the Afterlife: Ancient Egyptian Book of the Dead* were made from an aluminium coated Cellite® board fitted with a 5mm layer of Plastazote and covered with calico and jersey.[3] A layer of

Plate 2 The coffin of Horaawesheb (22nd Dynasty) containing the mummy of an unidentified female of the 26th Dynasty (British Museum, EA 6666) packed for travel to *Journey through the Afterlife: Ancient Egyptian Book of the Dead* at the Western Australian Museum, May 2013

Plate 3 Detail of the coffin and mummy shown in Plate 2 (British Museum, EA 6666)

Melinex® cut to the shape serves as a barrier between the jersey and the linen wrappings of the mummy (**Pl. 1**). Mummies are sometimes permanently stored in their original coffins, and depending on their condition and stability, they do not require a handling board as the coffin itself provides the required support (**Pl. 2**). Alternatively, a handling board may be placed under the coffin to support both the coffin and the mummy. Transporting mummified remains to a local hospital for a CT scan may not require complex support and a simple MDF board covered with a layer of Plastazote or foam with a barrier layer of tissue or Tyvek is usually sufficient.

External packing for transportation should be tailored to the form and nature of the remains and their supporting structures (e.g. handling boards). Any crate or box used should allow a minimum of 10cm of packing space for the addition of foam or similar supportive and cushioning substances around the maximum measurements of the remains (or the coffin in which the remains are stored). Crates are generally painted with gloss enamel paint to ensure they are waterproof if accidentally exposed to rain (or other hazards) whilst being loaded onto trucks or planes. Wrapped mummies are often uniform in shape, but the body itself is not visible and great care must be taken to provide enough support to prevent movement in transit without applying too much pressure on the actual remains or coffin. Mummies will generally travel in treated plywood and timber crates lined with a medium or soft density foam. The handling board is laid in the bottom of the crate, and pads made from foam and covered with Tyvek are cut to size at intervals to fit the negative space and prevent the mummy from moving. These pads are designed to be removed in sections, so that they will not rub against the surface of the object on its removal or insertion into the crate. The pads are also labelled according to their position in the crate to ensure that the person repacking the crate is able to place them in their original positions. Depending on the original material(s) covering the mummy, an extra barrier layer of non-abrasive material (e.g. Tyvek or Melinex) will also be applied. Beaded, heavily painted and fragile areas of linen should, if at all possible, be packed so that they do not come into contact with other materials, and mummies stored in coffins may require extra support to prevent movement

within the coffin (**Pls 2–3**). Unwrapped and naturally mummified remains can prove more challenging due to the variability of positioning and unsupported fragile articulations. The recently CT-scanned Predynastic mummy of Gebelein Man (see Chapter Three, this volume) was laid on a handling board, covered with tissue and packed into a wooden crate. The negative space was then filled with plastic sealed bags loosely filled with polystyrene beads. This was an effective solution in that it allowed a malleable packing material to be used that would fit the complex shape of the body being packed without exerting any pressure. Especially sensitive and fragile areas of the mummy's anatomy, such as an extended hand and fingers, could also remain untouched by careful placement of the packing materials. Contact with the naturally preserved tissues and hair was also avoided. Disarticulated bones and incomplete remains can also be packed in the same way, but are usually transported in acid-free boxes lined with acid-free tissue and placed into crates or protective boxes.

Crates in transit will inevitably travel by several forms of transport until they reach their final destination. To limit vibrations, fragile remains are usually carried by hand and require vehicles with suspension facility (e.g. 'air-ride' trucks) that dampen vibration. Loans are accompanied by a British Museum courier, but crates should also have clear labelling to specify how they should be handled, with arrows indicating the orientation in which they should be kept at all times. Customs and the carrier may need to be notified that human remains are being transported, and the regulations and legislation governing the transport of human remains at the destination must be confirmed before leaving the UK (see Márquez-Grant and Fibiger 2011; Giesen and White 2013; Hall 2013; Sharp and Hall 2013). Loans are condition checked on arrival at the borrowing venue to assess whether any changes have taken place during transport. Representatives from the British Museum and the host institution carefully determine if any damage has occurred and all noticeable changes are photographed and recorded. The environmental conditions in which the remains are to be stored and displayed (e.g. temperature, humidity and light) are also agreed in advance as part of a loan agreement (see Chapters One and Three, this volume). It is the British Museum courier's responsibility to ensure that these conditions are met in accordance with the loan agreement. Human remains, as with all parts of the collection, are also checked after de-installation and once they have returned to the British Museum. It is now possible to monitor the condition of wrapped and encased bodies, such as Peruvian and Egyptian mummies, and determine whether they have suffered adversely from having been transported by comparing old x-rays and CT scans with more recent ones. Such condition checks are an essential part of caring for the collection at the British Museum and help monitor – and in turn limit – any damage that may occur during the transportation of human remains.

Conclusion

Curating human remains is both a privilege and a responsibility. If museums are going to continue to benefit from the public's trust and support, they must make sure that the human remains held in their collections are always handled, stored and transported with great care and in a respectful and dignified way. Such ethical considerations should cover the full spectrum of the curatorial process, from what occurs behind the scenes (e.g. storage and handling) to the display of human remains in museum galleries. This also applies outside the museum and, for example, the sensitivities of hospital staff, patients and visitors should also be considered when CT scanning mummified remains. Collection staff should also be aware of the health and safety implications associated with the human remains in the collection. When appropriate and possible, the handling, storage and transportation of human remains should take into account any cultural preferences and sensitivities of communities that have cultural continuity with the remains, or for whom the remains have cultural importance (see Giesen and White 2013; Chapter One, this volume). The methods used to handle, store and care for the human remains in the British Museum collection endeavour not only to be appropriate and respectful, but they have been developed to ensure the long-term preservation of this unique and important collection for future generations.

Notes

1 The British Museum Human Remains Working Group includes representatives from the Curatorial and Conservation and Scientific Research departments, as well as Collection Services and the Directorate. It acts as an internal forum to discuss the human remains in the British Museum collection in order to maintain best practice and develop guidance documents.
2 A detailed discussion of the health and safety aspects of crypt archaeology, including issues such as exposure to lead oxide, post traumatic stress disorder, infectious disease and personal protective equipment recommendations can be found in Cox 2000.
3 Not recommended for CT scanning as metal interferes with the X-rays. Suitable alternatives include resin-coated Cellite boards and wood.

Bibliography

Arriaza, B. and Pfister, L-A., 2007. 'Working with the dead – health concerns', in Cassman *et al.* 2007, 205–21.

Cassman, V., Odegaard, N. and Powell. J. (eds), 2007. *Human Remains: Guide for Museums and Academic Institutions*. Oxford.

— and Odegaard, N., 2007a. 'Examination and analysis', in Cassman *et al.* 2007, 49–75.

— and Odegaard, N., 2007b. 'Condition assessment of osteological collections', in Cassman *et al.* 2007, 29–47.

— and Odegaard, N., 2007c. 'Storage and transport', in Cassman *et al.* 2007, 103–28.

Cox, M., 2000. *Crypt Archaeology: An Approach* (available at http://www.archaeologists.net/modules/icontent/inPages/docs/pubs/cryptarchaeology.pdf).

Crist, T.A.J., 2001. 'Smallpox and other scourges of the dead', in Poirier and Feder 2001, 79–106. London.

DCMS (Department for Culture, Media and Sport), 2005. *Guidance for the Care of Human Remains in Museums* (available at http://webarchive.nationalarchives.gov.uk/+/http://www.culture.gov.uk/images/publications/GuidanceHumanRemains11Oct.pdf).

Díaz-Jara, M., Kao, A., Ordoqui, E., Zubeldia, J.M. and Baeza, M.L., 2001. 'Allergy to cow bone dust', *Allergy* 56: 1014–15.

English Heritage and the Church of England, 2005. 'Annexe S5 – health and safety aspects specific to human remains', in *Guidance for Best Practice for Treatment of Human Remains Excavated from Christian Burial Grounds in England*, 45 (available at http://www.english-heritage.org.uk/publications/human-remains-excavated-from-christian-burial-grounds-in-england/).

Galloway, A. and Snodgrass, J.J., 1998. 'Biological and chemical hazards of forensic skeletal analysis', *Journal of Forensic Science* 43(5), 940–8.

Giesen, M. (ed.), 2013. *Curating Human Remains – Caring for the Dead in the United Kingdom*. Woodbridge.

— and White, L., 2013. 'International perspectives towards human remains curation', in Giesen 2013, 13–23.

Hall, M.A., 2013. 'The quick and the deid: a Scottish perspective on caring for human remains at the Perth Museum and Art Gallery', in Giesen 2013, 75–86.

Irvin, A.D., Cooper, J.E. and Hedges, S.R., 1972. 'Possible health hazards associated with the collection and handling of post-mortem zoological material', *Mammals Review* 2(2), 43–54.

Kolmodin-Hedman, B., Blomquist, G. and Sikström, E., 1986. 'Mould exposure in museum personnel, *International Archives of Occupational and Environmental Health* 57, 321–3.

Konefes, J.L. and McGee, M.K., 2001. 'Old cemeteries, arsenic, and health safety', in Poirier and Feder 2001, 127–35.

Legendre, M., Bartoli, J., Shmakova, L., Jeudy, S., Labadie, K., Adrait, A., Lescot, M., Poirot, O., Bertaux, L., Bruley, C., Couté, Y., Rivkina, E., Abergel, C. and Claverie, J.-M., 2014. 'Thirty-thousand-year-old distant relative of giant icosahedral DNA viruses with a pandoravirus morphology', *PNAS*.

Márquez-Grant, N. and Fibiger, L. (eds), 2011. *The Routledge Handbook of Archaeological Human Remains and Legislation – An International Guide to Laws and Practice in the Excavation and Treatment of Archaeological Human Remains*. London.

Mays, S., 2013. 'Curation of human remains at St Peter's Church, Barton-upon-Humber, England', in Giesen 2013, 109–21.

McKinley, J.I., 2013. '"No room at the inn"... Contract archaeology and the storage of human remains', in Giesen 2013, 135–45.

Poirier, D.A. and Feder, K.L., 2001. *Dangerous Places – Health, Safety, and Archaeology*. London.

Redfern, R. and Bekvalac, J., 2013. 'The Museum of London: an overview of policy and practice', in Giesen 2013, 87–98.

Roberts, C.A., 2009. *Human Remains in Archaeology: A Handbook*. York.

Roberts, C., 2013. 'Archaeological human remains and laboratories: attaining acceptable standards for curating skeletal remains for teaching and research', in Giesen 2013, 123–34.

Scott, G., 2013. 'Curating human remains in a regional museum: policy and practice at the Great North Museum: Hancock', in Giesen 2013, 99–107.

Sharp, J and Hall, M.A., 2013. 'Tethering time and tide? Human remains guidance and legislation for Scottish museums', in Giesen 2013, 65–74.

Sledzik, P.S., 2001. 'Nasty little things: molds, fungi, and spores', in Poirier and Feder 2001, 71–7.

Trustees of the British Museum 2013. The British Museum Policy on Human Remains (available at http://www.britishmuseum.org/about_us/management/museum_governance.aspx).

Wiszniewska, M., Walusiak-Skorupa, J., Pannenko, I., Draniak, M. and Palczynski, C., 2009. 'Occupational exposure and sensitization to fungi among museum workers', *Occupational Medicine* 59, 237–42.

Chapter 6
Conservation of Human Remains from Archaeological Contexts

Barbara Wills, Clare Ward and Vanessa Sáiz Gómez with contributions by Capucine Korenberg and Julianne Phippard

A wide range of human remains are held in the British Museum collection. These include skeletons, bog bodies, mummies, human remains preserved using other indigenous preservation techniques, spontaneous ('natural') mummies, human tissue such as hair and also fragments of bone or teeth, samples and slide preparations of human tissue. Most surviving human remains consist of skeletal and dental material alone. Mummified remains and bog bodies are less frequently encountered and include the presence of non-bony tissue, thereby offering a different range of potential information about past lives.

Human remains are recovered from a wide range of archaeological contexts. Their degree of preservation depends on several factors including the condition of the body before burial, the success of any preservation techniques, the rituals of deposition, the local climate and the burial environment. When human remains are found during an archaeological excavation or investigation, they require informed and thoughtful retrieval on site and appropriate care in subsequent storage. Additional material found associated with the human remains complements the information offered by the body itself, so any related finds should be treated with equal care and respect.

This chapter describes the condition, recovery, treatment and storage of human material from archaeological sites held in the collection of the British Museum, followed by a discussion of the care of bog bodies, intentionally mummified human remains and spontaneous mummies. The ethos of conservation is also discussed, and case studies are included to help illustrate the care of each type of human preservation. The protocols described in detail for skeletal material, such as conservation assessments and hygiene recommendations, are equally applicable to all human remains.

Conservation of human remains

Conservation has a key role to play in making human remains available and accessible for long-term study. Conservators seek to preserve the past for the future by using a variety of techniques. The aim of treatment is to extend the 'life' of an item so that the information that is intrinsic – the story of the artefact, collection or human remains – continues to be available over an extended period of time. Information relevant to conservation intervention includes the scientific, historical and cultural background. A conservator therefore needs a multifaceted understanding of any item that they are working to preserve, including the range of materials present; how all parts were made and assembled; the present condition; the types of decay and the reasons why it has occurred; the processes which have led to the continued existence of the item as well as those that may threaten its survival; current professional standards regarding treatment and environmental condition recommendations; present (and future) curatorial, study and storage needs; and the intended use and destination (loan, display, study or storage). The fundamental sense of care a conservator develops when working with objects translates easily into treating and caring for human remains, but there are additional considerations namely institutional, national (such as the *Guidance for the Care of Human Remains in Museums* issued by the Department for

Culture, Media and Sport) and international policies, legislation and guidance regarding the care of human remains (see Chapter One, this volume), in addition to the range of scientific analytical processes presently used in the interpretation of the remains, as well as an anticipation of the ones that are likely to be significant in the future.

The process of conservation in itself offers insights concerning the material under study (Coddington and Hickey 2013), and the conservator may discover information that contributes to scholarship in conservation and other disciplines. The aim therefore when working with human remains is both to preserve the body and to maximize present and future opportunities for access to information. Accredited conservators in Britain follow the European Confederation of Conservator-Restorers' Organisations 2003 code of ethics; Article 9 requires conservators to strive to ensure their methods and materials are as reversible and stable as possible. No treatment should fundamentally alter or contaminate the subject of the work, nor should it interfere with present or future analyses. In terms of treating human remains, an approach of minimum intervention is followed. This increases the potential for successful further study and analyses, both now and in the future. It also accords well with the demands and sensitivities of stakeholders such as curators, bioanthropologists, scientists, relevant communities or museum visitors.

During excavation, good procedures are essential in preparing for the recovery of human remains and subsequently in applying strategies for the treatment, packing, later housing and study. There should also be clear, accessible protocols in place before human remains are encountered so that people know what to do and who to approach if a discovery is made. For museums, appropriate protocols should be in place regarding the care, handling and study of human remains (see Chapter One, this volume). These need to be consulted prior to interacting with the human remains. Protocols include international, national and institutional human remains policies, COSHH (Control of Substances Hazardous to Health) assessments, risk assessments (see Appendix 1 for a recent example), adapted where necessary to the individual or collection to be studied, treated or displayed.

Working with human remains can be emotionally sensitive or even difficult (Balachandran 2009). This is especially true of remains that include soft tissue, hair or skin and where the remains are physically discernible and have a clear and recognizable physical presence. Treatment requires not only care, understanding and good handling skills, but also sensitivity on many levels. Even those who are well informed, carefully selected, prepared and acclimatized may become distressed by the presence of the dead. People cannot fully anticipate their own reactions to working with human remains, so special preparation for such tasks is needed in terms of risk assessments and care should continue to be shown throughout the period of work. Working with human remains can also be a fascinating journey, revealing the living aspects of the dead and making their individual stories available to others.

Human skeletal material

This discussion will begin with the most frequently encountered form of human remains from archaeological contexts: skeletons.

Preservation

Human bone includes an organic component (collagen), but mostly consists of a mineral component (hydroxyapatite), which increases the likelihood of preservation when compared with soft tissue. The state of the bones when found depends on their condition at burial and subsequent environment. An alkaline burial environment, such as a chalky soil, will result in the loss of organic component and bone becomes very brittle. An acidic environment, such as a sandy soil, will result in the loss of mineral components. In extreme situations, such as the excavations of Anglo-Saxon burials at Sutton Hoo, the very high acidity of the sandy soil (pH 3–4) resulted in the bodies decaying to such an extent that in some cases they were only present as a dark stain (Hummler and Roe 2013; Evans 2013).

Excavation and recovery

The condition and fragility of materials must be assessed before moving them from the burial context. The presence of cracks, surface crumbling or soft tissue should be assessed. This may differ from bone to bone, for example epiphyses (ends of long bones) and pathological bone (i.e. showing evidence of disease) may be particularly fragile. The bones need to be supported when lifting and any loose or broken pieces must be collected. This can usually be done by appropriate placement of hands beneath and around the bone. The bone can then be eased directly onto a flat, rigid supportive surface such as a tray or even a hand shovel with padding as appropriate. It may be advisable to leave soil in place around bones if this helps to support them during removal from their archaeological context. In some cases supportive materials can be slid underneath the bone to aid lifting; however care must be taken that there is nothing of archaeological significance directly below the bone, as it could be damaged by this approach. Usually a careful lifting technique is sufficient. In the past people have used resins and adhered unnecessary supporting materials, but these can be difficult to remove, can cause damage and also affect future analysis (Cronyn 1990, 5). Where fragile bone is present, advice should be sought from a conservator. If a conservator is not available, it is important to ensure that all pieces are individually supported with inert materials such as acid-free tissue paper or polyethylene foam (Plastazote®) during packing for removal from the site. Any material adhering to the bone also needs to be assessed early in the process of removal from the ground. Conservators and archaeologists alike should question whether such matter is dirt or something that has been deliberately applied to the bone such as red ochre. It is also important to assess how strongly such material is attached or adhering to the bone and to therefore support it where necessary to prevent loss.

Damp, but not waterlogged, robust bones should be left to dry out of direct sunlight post-excavation before any further handling or treatment is carried out. If the bone and teeth are in good condition, and there is no tissue or culturally applied materials present, the following procedure can be carried out. Bones can be gently dry brushed to remove any loose adhering soil using a soft paint brush. Soil may be retained for future scientific analysis, particularly if recovered from the stomach area (e.g. sacrum, spine or ribs). As far as possible, skeletal remains should not be washed on site. If washing is absolutely necessary, the bones should not be saturated and should be cleaned with a soft paint brush and minimal amounts of water. Bones or teeth should never be immersed in water. Soil should not be left inside skulls as it can harden and crush the bones, but equally it should only be removed if it comes out easily. If this is not the case, the skull can be packed in a supportive manner and the advice of a conservator sought. Soil should not be confused with preserved soft tissues (i.e. eyes or brain) or items such as bandages, which should not be removed but retained separately in a sealed polythene bag and packed together with the skull. The ear orifices should only be cleaned out in a controlled environment (as they contain very small ear bones that may otherwise be lost). Teeth can appear strong on the outside, but can be fragile internally. If cleaning is required this should be done very gently to ensure that calculus deposits are not removed and that the surfaces of teeth are not marked. Dry brushing should be avoided as it can damage the surface tissues (enamel) and affect future research (e.g. dental microwear studies). If required, cotton wool buds slightly dampened with deionized water can be used, gently rolled over the soiled area to pick up loose dirt. Bones from lead coffins have additional problems as health and safety personal protective equipment appropriate for lead should be worn. Lead dust should be vacuumed away with a lead appropriate vacuum cleaner. Bones should be stored in sealed packaging, labelled with lead hazard warnings.

Conservation and handling

The treatment of bones to strengthen them during and after excavation has a long history. Materials used in the past include paraffin wax, animal glue, shellac, polyvinyl acetate emulsions, acrylic emulsions and more recently acrylic resins in solvent (Shelton and Johnson 1995). These could have been applied over layers of dirt and may be shiny or discoloured, which makes it difficult to see surface detail of the bone. They can also shrink, causing damage to the bone surface. These materials can also be difficult to remove and a range of solvents may be required depending on their solubility. These solvents are usually applied to the surfaces in small amounts using cotton wool buds. Recently, tests have been carried out to remove these old resins using lasers and preliminary results are promising (Korenberg et al. 2012).

Past reconstructions of bones, particularly skulls, have taken place using a range of inappropriate materials such as Plasticine®, nails and cocktail sticks (Ward 2003). Often the fragile break edges have not been strengthened by consolidation before joining. Therefore the bond is only between fragile porous surfaces and is likely to come apart very easily, leaving a layer of adhesive and a skim of bone on one side of the break edge. If the join is then repeatedly re-adhered in the same manner, this will result in a build-up of layers of bone and glue, making the join unstable and inaccurate (Cook and Ward 2008).

Skeletal remains in the British Museum collection are assessed by conservators in order to determine their condition and any conservation treatment required. Treatments are agreed in consultation with curators and physical anthropologists. Human remains are covered or screened when not being worked on. The conservator assesses how fragile the bone is, whether there is flaking, surface loss, breaks, loss of physical strength or soil present. The bone also needs to be examined for any applied substances that may relate to burial practices.

Hands should be washed before and after handling bone to prevent contamination of the bone and also as a health and safety consideration. Disposable nitrile gloves can be worn if necessary, but this will restrict the ability to determine the condition of the surface through touch. Bones should be examined on a clean padded surface to cushion them. Skulls should be immobilized to prevent movement, for example by using a cut-out ring of polyethylene foam as support. If there are no applied substances or further concerns, and depending on the type of dirt present, cleaning can take place if required. A light brush or swabs dampened with small amounts of deionized water can be used for cleaning. Solvents are usually avoided as these can affect future analysis (see Eklund and Thomas 2010). Decisions about the application of resins for joining or consolidation need to be discussed as these may also affect the potential for future analyses. Treatments are kept to a minimum as conservation practices tend to lean towards supportive storage and good handling techniques. If resins (i.e. adhesives and consolidants) are applied, materials are used which have long-term stability and are reversible.

Principally, a minimalist approach to conservation is desirable. The aim is for the material to be stable with the least intervention in terms of use of chemicals, application of resins and reconstruction. Decisions on treatment are made depending on the intended purpose of the material – research, storage or display. Therefore, compromises sometimes need to be made. For example, in some cases it is not necessary to reconstruct broken skull fragments for storage purposes. For display however, it may be appropriate for skull fragments to be joined and some missing areas filled. This should make the material more suitable, recognizable or understandable in an exhibition.

If joins are required, the porous adjoining bone surfaces require consolidation, otherwise the edges will be softer than the join itself and eventually the join will fail and pull away the surrounding bone. Bones can be held in position while adhesive is drying using various techniques, for example support in sand trays, using a separator of tissue or cling film between the bone and the surrounding material. Masking tape can also be used to hold fragments in position. However, this treatment should only be carried out on robust surfaces and used on a very temporary basis and removed within a few hours or days of application. Fills may be needed to provide support in situations where there are losses in the bones. A range of stable conservation filling materials with different properties is available for use. Very fragile bone may need to be consolidated prior to making adjacent fills and unconsolidated pieces may be kept for analysis.

Case study: Conservation practices required for the display of human skeletal remains from the Wendorf Collection

This case study will discuss the late Palaeolithic human skeletal remains from the Wendorf Collection in the British Museum that were conserved for permanent display. Conservation consisted of reversing a previous reconstruction of the skull, which was unsuitable for exhibition, and making new repairs to preserve its integrity and improve visual appreciation. Treatment was based on current conservation approaches following the protocols described in the British Museum Policy on Human Remains (Trustees of the British Museum 2013) and the *British Museum Guidance for the Care, Study and Display of Human Remains* (British Museum n.d.). The whole process encompassed technical complexity due to the fragile condition of the bones; however, the outcome of conservation was satisfactory both in terms of stability and legibility. It also facilitated the possible re-study of human remains as the new treatment revealed original surface and features previously obscured by extraneous additions such as old fill materials.

Collection history

In 2001 Professor Fred Wendorf, from the Department of Anthropology at Southern Methodist University in Dallas, Texas, donated to the Department of Ancient Egypt and Sudan at the British Museum a collection of artefacts, human skeletal remains and documentary material recovered and produced in the 1960s during his research projects and excavations in the Nubian region of Egypt and Sudan. A large proportion of this collection composed of human skeletal remains recovered from site 117 at the Palaeolithic cemetery in Jebel Sahaba, dating from around 12000 BC (Wendorf 1968, 954). They consisted of 61 individuals, some of which had embedded fragments of flint projectile points and distinct cut marks on bones that were inflicted at the time of death or shortly after (Anderson 1968, 1028). This evidence represents one of the earliest archaeological records of possible organized violence, and manifests the great potential for research of this unique collection.

The osteological material was studied in the 1960s in the laboratory of the Anthropology Research Center at Southern Methodist University in Dallas and involved some reconstruction of bones and infilling of areas of loss to record

Plate 2 Cut marks on right femur of skeleton 21

Plate 3 Embedded lithic on pelvic bone of skeleton 21 observed under magnification (x6)

osteometric and morphological measures, principally on the skulls. The treatment resulted in significant reconstructions, which hampered the observation of some features and the restudy of the skeletal remains. When the collection was donated to the British Museum in 2001, the human remains were inventoried and assessed by bioarchaeologists and conservators (Judd 2002; 2003; Wills and Ward 2002; Ward 2003). Bones were bagged and packed appropriately to ensure a safe storage that could guarantee their long-term preservation, and some of the skeletons that required further conservation treatments were flagged. Two of these skeletons were selected for display in the then recently refurbished Early Egypt gallery at the British Museum, The Raymond

Plate 1 Skeleton 21 in the burial context at Jebel Sahaba, *c.* 12000 BC. British Museum, London (EA 77841)

Plate 4 Ulna bone of skeleton 21 showing oversized numbers

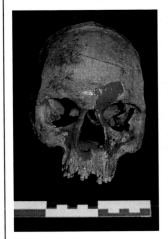
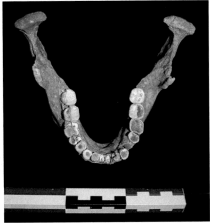
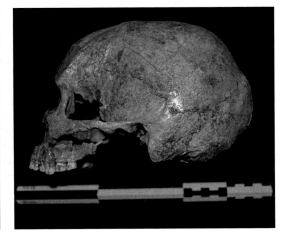

Plate 5 Cranium and mandible of skeleton 21 before conservation

and Beverly Sackler Gallery (Room 64). The human remains discussed here are of skeleton 21 (EA 77841) (**Pl. 1**) belonging to a robust middle-aged adult male. The skeleton presented evidence of trauma with distinct short and deep cuts in long bones and clavicles (**Pl. 2**), and some embedded fragments of lithics in the pelvic bones (**Pl. 3**). The skull was extensively reconstructed and needed to undergo conservation treatment before display.

Condition of human skeletal remains before conservation

The skeleton was fragmentary, with only around 40% of the bones present, while the skull was almost complete, with approximately 90% of the bone preserved (Judd 2003). After excavation, most of the bones from the skeleton were labelled with oversized numbers using a thick, waxy, black paint that had penetrated through the porous surface producing irreversible markings (**Pl. 4**).

The bones were dusty with mixed soil and sand from excavation. They showed patchy white accretions, some loose and powdery, others hard and well attached to the bone surface. Both types were identified as anhydrite ($CaSO_4$), formed as a result of the recrystallization of the sulphate and the calcium from the soil absorbed by the bone (Robinet 2002). Nonetheless, these accretions appeared to be stable and were not damaging the original surface.

Most of the bones of the skeleton were fragmented and showed inappropriate repairs, carried out without previous cleaning of the broken edges. The repairs exhibited soil deposits from the excavation mixed with thick coatings of a rubbery white adhesive identified as polyvinyl acetate (PVA) (Robinet 2002). As a result of this, some of the repairs had failed and others were loose and at risk of breaking. A close examination revealed that the reconstruction of the skull was not completely accurate. There were slight misalignments on joins and some of the infilled areas had been over-interpreted to simulate completeness (**Pl. 5**).

In some cases, integrations were poorly applied and covered the original surface of the bone, which contributed to the unusual morphological appearance of the skull. In addition to this, the materials used as fillers were not of conservation quality. Missing parts of the palatal, nasal and frontal bones had been infilled with a grey modelling material similar to Plasticine composed of kaolinite clay.

The infills were surface-coated with a thick layer of PVA adhesive to increase strength, and some of them were supported on a structure formed of wooden cocktail sticks fixed to the bone with a generous application of the same PVA adhesive (Robinet 2002) (**Pl. 6**). The skull and mandible were covered with a shiny resin similar to cellulose nitrate which was soluble in acetone (Robinet 2002). The resin had discoloured and appeared yellow. The dentition on the skull was vulnerable. Some teeth were loose or, unfortunately, adhered to the maxilla and mandible. Some small fragments of the teeth had not been repositioned and were kept apart inside a small plastic bag.

Rationale for treatment

The skeletal remains could not be displayed in this condition. The bones needed to be stabilized and their appearance improved for display. The skull, which presented a more invasive treatment, was prioritized for conservation together with those bones presenting evidence of cut marks or possible embedded lithics. Considering the fragility of the skeletal remains, the skull in particular, it was initially thought that the previous reconstruction could be maintained by bringing down the shine of the adhesive coating and improving the surface of the infills. This would have minimized any possible damage occurred during re-treatment and significantly reduced the amount of time required for conservation.

Plate 6 Former reconstruction of the palatal bone of skeleton 21 using wooden picks and Plasticine during dismantling

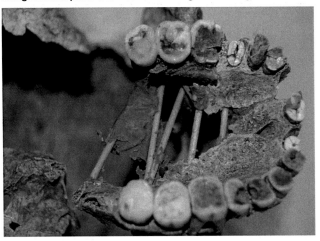

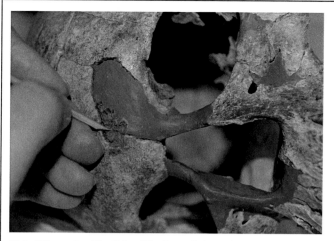

Plate 7 Removing Plasticine filler from skeleton 21

However, after careful examination of the assemblage and an analysis of materials, it was believed that the complete removal of the previous treatment would considerably improve the appearance of the skull. More importantly, this would help to present its morphology in a more accurate way by removing obtrusive fillers, wooden cocktail sticks and Plasticine. Likewise, the removal of oversized excavation numbers would help to avoid the possible perception of human remains on display as mere 'objects'. The level of conservation and quality of the previous treatment was discussed in liaison with the Curator of Physical Anthropology and other conservators specialized in the treatment of human remains. It was finally agreed that conservation had to be based on the principle of minimum intervention regarding the extent of infilling and consolidation, whereas repairs needed to have a certain aesthetic quality in order to not be obtrusive.

Conservation treatment for display

Although the previous reconstruction had been rather invasive and had covered the original surface of the bone, the new treatment tried not to jeopardize residual evidence that could be the subject of future investigations or analysis. Principally, conservation work consisted of the surface cleaning of bones, the removal of aged adhesives, fillers and coatings, the stabilization of friable areas compromised by repairs and the reassembling of the skull. It was a labour-intensive treatment that required careful manipulation and thoughtful planning. Surface cleaning was kept to a minimum. The bones of the skeleton were gently brushed to remove loose deposits of soil and accretions, while hard, calcified accretions were not treated as they seemed stable. Although no new information was revealed, cut marks on bones and embedded lithics were more noticeable after cleaning. Previous joins were undone when they exhibited excess of adhesive, were failing or inappropriate. The adhesive was softened with cotton wool pads of acetone covered with aluminium foil to reduce evaporation. After the removal of aged adhesive, the broken surface was consolidated with Paraloid B72® (ethyl methacrylate, acryl methacrylate copolymer) applied with a fine brush at 5% w/v (weight/volume) in acetone. At this point, the bones were reassembled with the same resin prepared at 20% w/v in acetone.

New conjoins of bones presenting fresh breaks were made with the sole purpose of improving the recognizability of the skeletal elements on display. This was partly successful in the case of the pelvic bones, which were rather fragmented and could be reassembled into larger pieces. The process was carried out with particular care not to compromise possible evidence of trauma. As a general rule, the use of consolidants and adhesives was localized and applied only when strictly necessary. Although these had already been extensively used in the previous treatment, there was a concern that they could compromise future investigations such as DNA analysis or radiocarbon dating (D'Elia *et al.* 2007; Eklund and Thomas 2010; Johnson 1994).

Numbers on bones were mechanically removed under an optical microscope using a scalpel blade to eliminate only superficial layers of the paint. Further cleaning was attempted with cotton wool swabs slightly moistened in acetone. However, part of the paint was anchored to the porous surface of the bone and it was not possible to remove it completely. Nonetheless the result of cleaning was satisfactory as the numbers are now only visible at very close sight. The resin coating on the skull was unsightly and unnecessary and was carefully reduced using acetone applied with cotton wool swabs. The original surface revealed was significantly improved and no additional consolidation was required. Old filler was mechanically removed with a fine scalpel and the application of cotton wool pads of acetone was used to soften the adhesive coating. Sharpened wooden skewers were also used to reveal fragile bone surface along the edges of the infilled areas (**Pl. 7**).

After removal, some of the joins had insufficient or unstable contact surfaces that required additional support for reconstruction. This was the case of the left zygomatic suture, which was reinforced with Paraloid B72 applied at 40% w/v in acetone mixed with glass microballoons. As previously, the areas to be infilled were consolidated with Paraloid B72 at 5% w/v in acetone in order to protect and strengthen the fragile bone surface before the filler was applied. The material used to fill the areas of loss had to be lightweight, but relatively hard and strong to compensate for

Plate 8 Skull of skeleton 21 showing infills before inpainting

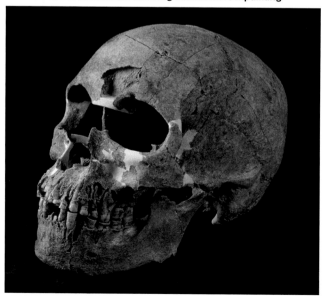

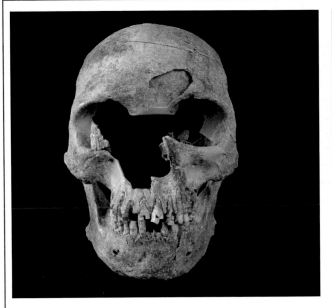

Plate 9 Skull after treatment, front and left sides

the weak structure of the skull. Materials like plaster of Paris and Paraloid B72 bulked with glass microballoons were initially considered for gap-filling; however, they were thought to be excessively hard in comparison to fragile bones, or difficult to apply, which posed a serious problem in areas with limited accessibility. A mock-up infill was made using Flügger® putty. Flügger is a fine paste composed of butyl methacrylate and calcium carbonate. It is a ready made material, and can be easily applied with a spatula. The test showed that some shrinkage occurred after drying; however, the putty could be reapplied as many times as necessary to correct any imperfection. It was therefore decided that this product should be used for gap-filling.

Applied on the bone, the putty provided optimum structural strength and hardness (**Pl. 8**). The final surface was rather smooth and needed minimum improvement after application; a simple rubbing of the surface with a cotton swab moistened in acetone was sufficient to achieve a smooth finishing for colouring. Liquitex® acrylic paints and Schmincke® gouache colours were tested for inpainting and eventually the mixture of both products delivered the best colour effect. The acrylics produced a solid covering film; however, this resulted in a plastic and shiny appearance that could only be reduced in combination with the gouache paints (**Pl. 9**). The colour was applied with a fine brush and toned in with the original surrounding areas using a uniform and neutral colour that made the infills unobtrusive, but clearly distinguishable.

Packing and padding the storage box
Once cleaned and repaired, the bones were repacked inside a lidded rigid cardboard box. Bones were put inside polyethylene zip-lock bags with some folded acid-free tissue paper to prevent further fractures or excessive movement during transport. When possible, bones were bagged individually and the original paper labels were kept with them. As an additional labelling system, bags were marked using small circular stickers to indicate the possible presence of cut marks (green stickers) or embedded lithics (red stickers). A card with a legend was introduced inside the storage box so users could understand the colour code.

The disposition of the bones inside the box was carried out according to the guidelines proposed by the Museum (see Chapter Five, this volume) and taking into consideration the condition of bones. The more robust and larger bones were placed at the bottom, such as bones from the legs and arms. The bones from the pelvis were also placed at the lower level. As they are very fragile they were stored in special clear polystyrene boxes, padded with a Plastazote base and spider tissue (100% mulberry fibres), which created a soft and smooth pillow around them. Smaller bones corresponding to the hands, feet, vertebrae and scapulae were carefully placed on top of them trying to create uniform layers. The skull and mandible were placed at the top of the box together with fragile bones exhibiting various repairs (**Pl. 10**).

These bones were supported on a piece of Plastazote and secured to it with bowknots of cotton tape, in order to prevent movement and the possibility of new breaks occurring during transport or handling (**Pl. 11**). The skull was safely supported during treatment on a circular cushion in the shape of a 'doughnut ring' made out of cotton calico fabric padded inside with polyester wadding. During treatment the cushion was covered with clear plastic wrap (cling film) to avoid soiling, but this was removed and the cushion reused as a handling and storage support (**Pl. 12**).

Plate 10 Bones inside the storage box after treatment

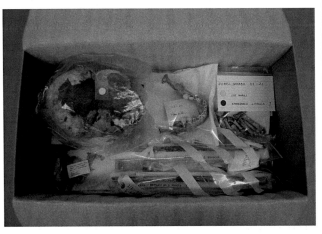

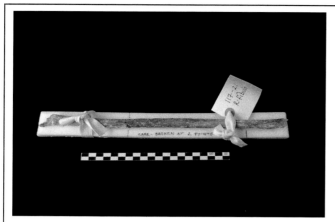

Plate 11 Storage foam support for fragile fibula with various repairs

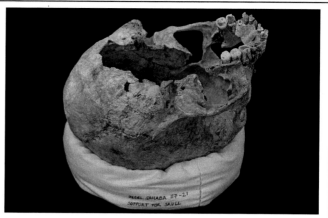

Plate 12 'Doughnut ring' to support the skull in storage or during handling

Conclusions

The new treatment of the human skeletal remains using conservation grade materials ensured their long-term preservation and minimized the need for further intervention in the future. Bones were stabilized successfully and the new repairs and infills helped to strengthen fragile joins and weak areas. The new repairs were sympathetic with the nature of bone and well integrated with the original surfaces, reducing considerably the visual disruption caused by the areas of loss. The treatment reached a good balance between minimal interventive conservation and a more aesthetic approach in order to prepare the human remains for display. The large fragmentation and loss of skeletal remains required an interventive approach to improve the morphological appearance of the bones. It is expected that further conservation work will be carried out on the rest of the skeletons from the Wendorf Collection; however, treatments will follow a remedial approach aimed only at facilitating access and research.

Human remains with preserved soft tissue

The best examples of extensively preserved human remains come from extreme contexts such as wet, arid or frozen environments that inhibit the deterioration of soft tissue. As discussed below, ancient waterlogged bodies from northern European bogs, such as Lindow Man (see Chapter Two, this volume) tend to have exceptional soft tissue preservation although less skeletal survival. Similarly, consistently dry areas such as Egypt, Sudan and the high areas of the Andes can provide examples of exceptionally good soft tissue preservation (an example is a child mummy from Chile in the British Museum; **Pl. 13**), and bodies that are frozen soon after death also survive remarkably well in that state. Perhaps the best known example of this kind is 'Ötzi the Iceman' who lived around 3300 BC (on display at the South Tyrol Museum of Archaeology in Bolzano, Italy). Other bodies or parts have been preserved using a range of indigenous techniques and subsequently entered museum collections (for example, shrunken heads from South America), but are not described here as these are not from an excavated context.

Bog bodies

Preservation

Several examples of well-preserved human remains have been recovered from areas of waterlogged ground such as peat bogs, usually during peat cutting. The environment in a peat bog is anaerobic and decomposition is much reduced (see Chapter Two, this volume). The high pH also contributes to the preservation of the soft tissue, but dissolves the mineral content of the bone, leaving a very fragile bone structure. The humic acids in the bog create a natural tanning of the skin which aids preservation (Painter 1991; Joy 2009; see also Chapter Two, this volume).

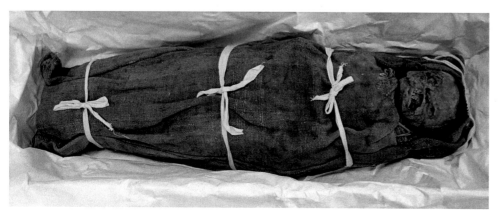

Plate 13 Child mummy from Chile. British Museum, London (Am1832,1208.1)

Excavation and recovery

The ideal scenario is for minimal excavation on site. The body is best lifted together with soil around it for support and to help maintain the acidity of the surrounding environment. Additional support may be required to prevent flexing, for example a wooden box padded with expanded polyurethane foam. The surrounding deposits may provide further archaeological and environmental evidence relating to the context of deposition. Once lifted, the body should be stored in the dark and kept cool to prevent biological activity. X-rays and CT scans can be used to determine the condition of the bones and internal organs. Excavation should be carried out in controlled conditions by curators, conservators and physical anthropologists, working in collaboration with one another. The body should be kept cool and wet throughout this process to prevent drying out, shrinkage and cracking (Omar *et al.* 1989).

The now well-known bog-body Lindow Man (see also Chapter Two, this volume) was lifted resting on a peat block, supported by water-soaked plastic foam and thin plastic sheeting. The block was then placed in a specially constructed box. From the time of initial excavation, the body was kept cool by storage at approximately 4°C, initially in a mortuary fridge and then in a specially constructed cooler at the British Museum. He was monitored during storage and kept wet with cooled, sterilized distilled water.

Conservation and handling

Various treatments have been used to conserve bog bodies (see Asingh and Lynnerup 2007; Omar *et al.* 1989; Chapter Two, this volume), however freeze drying is currently regarded as the standard approach. When recovered from the bog, water fills the deteriorated human tissue and so acts as a support. If left to dry out naturally, shrinkage will occur due to the high surface tension of the receding water which results in drying stresses. In the freeze drying process, the water is removed by sublimation (the water goes directly from a frozen to a vapour phase) and so drying stresses are reduced. The water is first replaced with a solution of water and a water soluble wax, usually polyethylene glycol (PEG). The body is then frozen and placed in a freeze-drying chamber. PEG is a cryoprotectant and so helps to counteract any dimensional changes due to freezing. It also helps to bulk and support the human tissue on a cellular level. This treatment was used on Meenybradden Woman (National Museum of Ireland, Dublin), Lindow Man (British Museum) and, more recently, two excavated Irish bog bodies from Old Croghan (Co. Offaly) and Clonycavan (Co. Meath), now displayed at the National Museum of Ireland (R. Reade pers. comm.). Reassessments of such treatments have been carried out over the years and, overall, they appear to have been successful (Bradley *et al.* 2009).

During the excavation of Lindow Man, various samples of tissue were taken for further analysis. Most of these are now stored in glass vials in sealed polypropylene containers mainly in distilled water (Hacke and Stacey 2008) in a fridge at 4°C and regularly monitored. Recently there has been discussion as to whether to replace the distilled water with 70% ethanol/30% distilled water as recommended for storage of this type of material by English Heritage (English Heritage 2008), but since storage in solvent can affect future DNA analysis, it has been decided to maintain current conditions. Some additional fragments of bog body were excavated from Lindow Moss several years later. At the time it was considered that this material was more valuable if stored for future analysis rather than conserved. Therefore the fragments were individually supported, packed and heat sealed within polyethylene bags, and then placed in a freezer. One small fragment was frozen in nitrogen.

Mummified human remains

Mummies from ancient Egypt

Intentionally preserved mummies from ancient Egypt have survived in remarkable condition due to the expertise of the practitioners' mummification techniques and the favourable, consistently dry burial conditions. As recovery of soft tissue is rare, and when found generally fragile, additional care and preparation is required before moving mummified human remains. Good lifting techniques may be crucial to the survival of the mummified tissue and associated materials such as linen textiles. As with bog bodies (above), the ideal scenario is for minimal intervention on site and the mummy is best lifted en bloc together with any surrounding deposits if present. Such deposits can be used to provide support and may be a source of further archaeological evidence relating to the burial. Additional support, such as an appropriate wooden box lined with temporary padding such as expanded polyethylene foam may be required to prevent flexing. All recently excavated Egyptian archaeological material, including mummies, now stays in Egypt so good communication with Egyptian colleagues and conservators is valuable and mutually beneficial.

Conservation and handling

Ancient Egyptian mummies have been part of museum collections for over a century and some have been exposed to interventions and repairs using materials and techniques that were prevalent at the time. These methods of restoration may have occurred before acquisition in order to enhance sale values. Typical materials used at the end of the 19th and the beginning of the 20th century include plaster of Paris, wooden dowels, animal glue, nails and screws, contemporary paint and textiles. Mummies were unwrapped for both study and entertainment in the West. The surgeon and antiquarian Thomas Pettigrew relished unwrapping mummies before a Victorian audience; however the Trustees of the British Museum refused to allow Pettigrew to unwrap any of the mummies in the British Museum collection as this would 'destroy the integrity of the collection' (Andrews 2004, 13).

At the British Museum, most of the mummies in the collection are still in their wrappings. As these are made from a variety of materials, any conservation treatment or other intervention is designed to take account of the associated materials, structures (such as coffins) and objects with equal consideration (Wills forthcoming). More subtle and evanescent traces may also survive (such as poured libations, flowers laid on the body or residues of mortuary

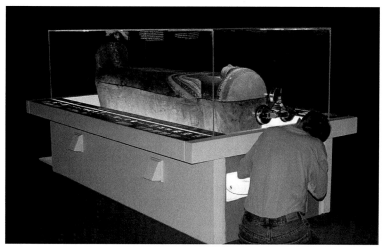

Plate 14 Preparing the mummy of Nesperennub (22nd Dynasty) for display at the British Museum (EA 30720)

practice). This wide range of preserved materials, in addition to the human remains, requires care and a good understanding of the burial practices to conserve and curate.

Conservation treatments of mummies at the British Museum developed significantly over the latter part of the 20th century. In the past, treatments were more interventive, for example adding stable conservation materials to the fragile original material in order to strengthen it. The recent tendency has been to use the minimal amount of conservation materials required with a focus on more

precise, developed and technically adept interventions. Mummies chosen for long-term loan have to be both robust and stable. Mummies stabilized for storage within the collection may benefit from more subtle conservation treatment. The mummies presently on display in the Roxie Walker Galleries, Rooms 62–3, have for example been prepared by conservation for display, but not for loan.

In 2004–5, the British Museum developed an exhibition entitled *Mummy: The Inside Story* which focused on the mummy of Nesperennub, a priest of Khoms at the temple of Karnak during the 22nd Dynasty, *c.* 800 BC (**Pl. 14**). One of

Plate 15 Nesperennub: interior of the wood coffin (left) and the upper and underside of the cartonnage coffin (right)

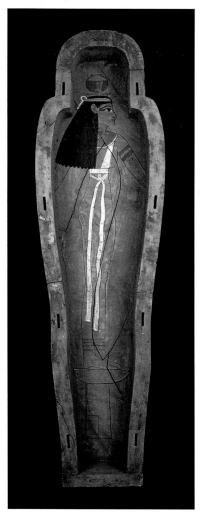
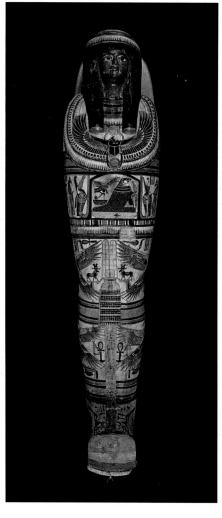
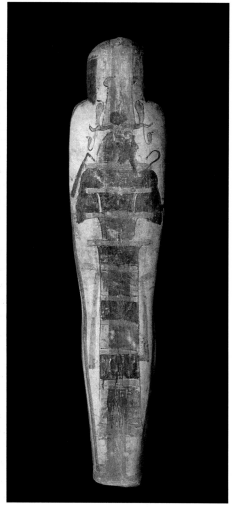

Plate 16 Nesperennub: detail of lid of wooden coffin before treatment (left) and detail of filler and overpaint (right)

the remarkable features of this exhibition was that the mummy could be virtually unwrapped using 3D technology. Non-invasive X-ray and computerized tomography (CT) scanning techniques made it possible to look inside the mummy without disturbing the wrappings.

The conservation treatment of Nesperennub illustrates the variety of materials and objects that can constitute a burial ensemble, which in this case consists of a wood outer coffin enclosing a cartonnage inner coffin which itself encloses the mummified body (**Pl. 15**). Close examination of the painted outer wooden coffin revealed extensive restoration (**Pl. 16**). Filler in the splits of the old wood and modern paint could be seen, confirmed by examination under ultra-violet light, which showed the modern materials clearly fluorescing (**Pl. 17**). Both filler and paint had been crudely applied over the original painted surfaces and this may have been done prior to the mummy entering the collection at the end of the 19th century. After discussion with the curator John Taylor, it was decided that only the non-original brown paint from the main body of the coffin should be removed and fills were retouched in a more visually sympathetic way.

The cartonnage was slightly dirty, the edges friable and there were areas of lifting, delaminating paint. On the foot plate, the linen ties were loose and frayed, making the foot plate liable to detach during handling. The tabs on the leather *stola* (straps placed around the neck of the wrapped mummy) were dirty, distorted and curling, with a sticky surface. One tab had a pinkish addition stitched to the upper end which was found to be attached using a modern rayon thread. After consultation with the curator, the

non-original parts were removed. The tabs were cleaned to remove the sticky, dirty surface and reshaped to recover something closer to the original shape. The cartonnage was cleaned, the paint surface secured and the linen ties strengthened.

Support of the cartonnage was necessary so a mount was made from a 10mm Perspex® sheet, modified to fit the shape of the underside. The mummy case was removed from the old wood support board by gently inserting a sheet of Melinex® (clear polyester film) beneath the cartonnage, then sliding it carefully onto the new Perspex mount. The underside of the cartonnage was visible for the first time and photographs could be taken, completing the documentation of the mummy.

Spontaneous mummies

Preservation
Spontaneous mummies are created through a set of specific circumstances, none of which appear to have been deliberately chosen to produce a mummy. Contributory factors towards the spontaneous preservation of soft tissue and organic materials include the absence of a coffin which allows free air movement around the body and the presence of dry or intensely hot air. Spontaneously

Plate 17 Nesperennub: fluorescence under ultra-violet light. More modern paints and varnish show fluorescence under ultra-violet light

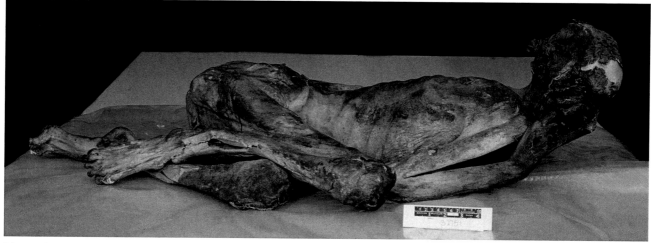

Plate 18 Gebelein Man, late Predynastic, *c.* 3500 BC. British Museum, London (EA 32751)

mummified bodies can show a range of preservation states, from very good – where most of the body remains intact, complete with skin and hair – to partial, where only some of the soft tissue remains. The skeleton, however, usually remains in excellent condition when other tissues have been lost.

The British Museum has in its collection a range of spontaneous mummies originating from the Nile valley. Preservation has been inadvertently achieved primarily through the absence of moisture in the burial context, inhibiting the processes of autolysis (the self-destruction of tissues within the living body) and the decaying action of microorganisms. Examples of this type of mummy include the Predynastic mummies from Gebelein, Upper Egypt (**Pl. 18**), comprising a group of six bodies found in sand. During the Predynastic period (4400–3100 BC), the dead were buried in shallow graves cut into the desert sand, often lined with reed mats. The heat and aridity have preserved the bodies. The collection also includes a number of spontaneous medieval mummies recovered from the area of the Fourth Nile Cataract (Sudan) that have been lifted during salvage excavations (1999–2007) in advance of flooding caused by the Merowe/Hamadab hydroelectric dam (see also Chapter Three, this volume). They were given to the Sudan Archaeological Research Society by the National Corporation for Antiquities and Museums of Sudan, Khartoum, who then donated them to the British Museum (see Chapter Three, this volume). The human remains date from the 6th to 15th centuries AD. Some were interred in grave cuts of dry soil consisting of mixed alluvium and

coarse sand. Lintels made of stone or mud brick may have protected, or partially protected, the body from any destructive action of soil above. However, earth-filled grave cuts also produced mummified bodies (Welsby 2003). The absence of a coffin, the aridity and the salinity of the soil all presumably contributed to the remarkable preservation of the soft tissues as well as a wide range of original wrappings comprising mostly a range of textiles, but also including skin products such as leather (Wills 2013). These 40 natural mummies from the Nile valley have been the subject of a two-year project supported by the Clothworkers' Foundation (*Safeguarding a Body of Evidence: Researching and Conserving a Group of Exceptional Naturally-mummified Nilotic Human Remains*) to clean, stabilize, support and investigate the remains, together with the associated wrappings.

Stabilization and mounting

The mounting and storage system for the 40 natural mummies was designed to support the varied shapes and materials of these fragile specimens in order to keep them stable under conventional storage conditions and during study. The system, recently developed from earlier mounting techniques, is applicable not only to these human remains, but also to a wider range of fragile material. The storage area refurbishment was planned in detail, first surveying the condition of the bodies, then evaluating requirements and calculating space, materials and costs as well as the availability of practical assistance. For each individual body or related group, a stable baseboard was provided from Cellite® 220 aluminium honeycomb panel. All panel surfaces were cleaned thoroughly and rough edges smoothed, then covered with a stable tape such as adhesive-gummed linen tape. Lengths of black Plastazote were stuck beneath the baseboard, two or three according to need. These battens allow the board to be raised from the surface beneath, absorb vibration and provide space for trays (**Pl. 19**). In this instance, Plastazote density LD45 was chosen because of its resilience and ability to absorb vibration. A sheet of Plastazote 3cm thick (the softer LD33) was then cut to fit the baseboard and wrapped with Tyvek® sheeting (spunbonded olefin fibre) with the rough side on the interior. The Tyvek-wrapped 'mattress' was secured to the baseboard using a hot-melt glue. Each specimen, having been

Plate 19 Diagram of mount board

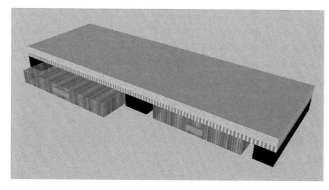

Plate 20 Tissues secured in place with PTFE tape

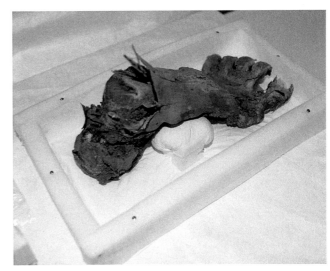

Plate 21 Foot supported by padding and hammock

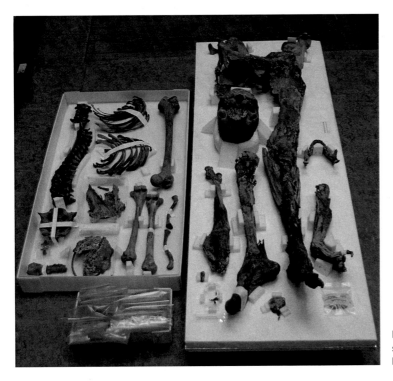

Plate 22 Skeleton 4310 after treatment showing body parts secured on the baseboard with other skeletal elements located in a tray that slides beneath the support board

unpacked, cleaned for study and sampled as necessary, was laid on the wrapped 'mattress' in the most appropriate way following advice from Daniel Antoine, the Curator of Physical Anthropology. Working from the centre outwards, the fragile human remains were stabilized in position by creating side and base supports using wedges of Plastazote. Where necessary to support areas of great fragility, the Plastazote was covered with polyester wadding to provide cushioning, then wrapped with Relic-wrap PTFE™ (a thin, very smooth and stable polytetrafluoroethylene film). Vulnerable detaching tissues were held in place by wrapping with PTFE tape (**Pl. 20**). The locations of the side and base supports were chosen with care to be in contact with the most stable areas of the body. Having estimated the minimum number of supports required, positioning and height, each was shaped to match the adjacent area of the body as closely as possible. A 'hammock' made of Relic-wrap created the softest of supports for the most vulnerable tissue (**Pl. 21**).

The Plastazote supports were held in place by pinning stable stainless steel pins ('Austerlitz' pins) through the support into the Tyvek-covered Plastazote 'mattress' below (**Pl. 22**). This flexible system of movable supports and pads facilitated the positioning of optimal support, and could easily be repositioned later if required. Correx® (twin wall polypropylene sheet) or Tycore® (three-layered archival quality support board) boxes were made to store samples and loose material (**Pl. 22**). These were designed to be slid beneath the baseboard to give additional support and retain the unity of the complete specimen. Finally, all mounted bodies were clearly labelled. All stages of treatment were recorded in report documentation and photographs.

This system of passive conservation using no chemicals, consolidants or adhesives was developed to avoid compromising not only present analytical procedures, but also the potential for future investigation. This method makes each part of the body as accessible as it can be while keeping it stable and secure.

Case study: Rehousing a mummified hand from the Stein Collection

Introduction

This case study will discuss preventive conservation measures to upgrade storage conditions of a mummified hand (British Museum, 1928,1022.121) and an associated wooden cylinder. The project focused on providing a supportive mount and protective box that could guarantee safe long-term storage and would avoid unnecessary handling or exposure. The hand was collected by Sir Marc Aurel Stein, who carried out three expeditions to the western regions of China between 1900 and 1916 in order to conduct archaeological excavations, geographical survey, ethnographic survey and photography. The material dates to the 7th century AD and was found during Stein's third Central Asian Expedition (1913–16) (Stein 1928, 683) in tomb-group I in the Astana cemetery, Xinjiang Uyghur Autonomous Region, north-west China, which is on the north-eastern Silk Route. The cemetery was used from the 4th to 8th century AD and contains in excess of 1,000 tombs. Due to the arid environment, the formation of spontaneous mummified human remains occurred and organic preservation was excellent.

Condition before treatment

Rehousing of the hand was requested after a survey of the Stein Collection in the British Museum's Department of Asia revealed that the existing storage conditions of the mummified hand were unsuitable. The hand seemed fragile, but relatively well preserved. The cohesion of skeletal tissues appeared to be weak and some of the carpal bones (lower hand/wrist) had detached. Despite this, the hand was almost complete and only exhibited a damaged area across the palm. The area had lost part of the soft tissues and was depressed, perhaps as a result of the weight of the associated wooden cylinder that once rested on it. This made the fragile condition of the hand even more vulnerable and considerably limited the possibility of manipulation or access to the back. The wooden cylinder was soiled, but in relatively good condition. In contrast, an original silk fabric,

which was formerly wrapped around the cylinder, had disintegrated and only minute fragments were still resting on the palm of the hand (**Pl. 23**).

Rationale for treatment

The storage solution had to protect the hand and the associated materials from dust and light. Additionally, a safe storage support was required to ensure the long-term preservation of the hand and its integrity, while minimizing the need for handling or the possibility of movement. It was noticed that the wooden cylinder accompanying the hand could be a *vajra*, a Buddhist ritual object representing strong spiritual power. Taking this into consideration, it was initially proposed to relocate the cylinder back into the hand, simulating the original position during burial. This could have been achieved by means of an additional support which would have avoided direct contact with the fragile tissues of the hand and be understood as an expression of respect, intended to return not only the physical position of the *vajra*, but also its spiritual dimension and symbolism (see McGowan and LaRoche 1996; Jones and Harris 1998).

The new storage conditions for the hand and related objects

As with most human material, the hand has potential for future research. Therefore, no interventive treatment such as cleaning or consolidation was carried out. The only action undertaken apart from providing support and protection to the assemblage was the selection and

Plate 24 Hand and wooden cylinder with associated tissues and materials prepared for storage

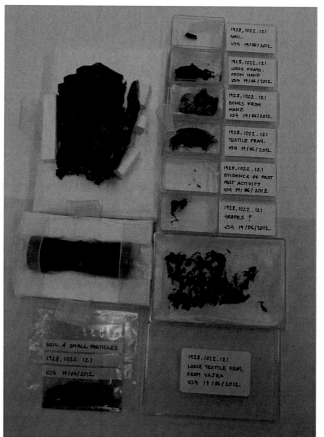

Plate 23 Hand and wooden cylinder before conservation, 7th century AD. British Museum, London (1928,1022.121)

Plate 25 Hand, wooden cylinder and associated materials inside the new storage box

classification of decontextualized materials. Fibres, fragments of textiles and other tissues that could not be repositioned in their original context were classified and put inside small, labelled clear boxes (polystyrene). Loose soil from the burial was double-bagged inside zip-lock polyethylene bags (**Pl. 24**).

Although the idea of reproducing the original position of the wooden cylinder in the hand was received with interest, the device needed to hold the wooden cylinder would have required specialized mounting assistance, not available at the time of treatment. Therefore, the hand and the cylinder had to be mounted on separate supports that were kept inside the same storage box.

The supports were a modified form of fabric-covered museum boards, a storage system commonly used for mounting flat textiles. They were constructed from expanded polyethylene foam bases (Plastazote), lined with a thick layer of cotton domette (100% cotton fabric) to provide some padding, and finally covered with Tyvek. The Tyvek was first secured with double-sided tape adhesive to the back of the foam and then stitched to another layer of Tyvek which covered the back of the base completely. Initially, fine Bondina®, PTFE sheet and fine cotton lawn were tested as fabric covers. Bondina and PTFE sheet were too slick, while the nap of cotton lawn rendered it unsuitable in contact with the friable soft tissues of the hand. The Tyvek provided a smooth and non-slip surface that helped to hold the hand and the wooden cylinder in place. The hand was additionally supported at weak areas by means of small blocks of Plastazote lined with Tyvek and stitched to the main support (**Pl. 25**). For the wooden cylinder, two pieces of Plastazote were placed along both sides of the base to prevent the object from rolling. The cylinder was fastened to the mount with two ties made of fine silk tape (100% silk). This provided a very smooth surface and its high translucency allowed for visibility of the object (**Pl. 25**). A lidded box made of acid-free archival cardboard was made

to contain the supports and the small boxes with the rest of the materials and tissues (**Pl. 25**). Old packing materials were kept in a separate box in case they could serve as reference or provide any evidence for future research.

Environmental recommendations and storage facilities

The environment in the storage room of the Stein Collection had previously been evaluated by preventive conservators (Brierly 2011). The assessment found that the environment was suitable for organic collections; nevertheless, a regular inspection was advised to detect any possible sign of further deterioration. An ambient temperature of 16–25°C and a relative humidity of 35–45% were recommended to maintain a stable condition of the human remains (see below). As a preventive measure, it was suggested to place the storage box containing the hand in a drawer of the cupboard that receives minimal disturbance, together with other objects of the collection that are not frequently consulted or used. Additionally, it was proposed that visible instructions inside the cupboard should be provided to remind users to open and close the drawers carefully to avoid vibrations that could affect the fragile condition of the human remains inside.

Conclusions

The treatment, which involved exclusively preventive conservation measures including the use of inert and stable materials, contributed to an improved condition and ensured the safe storage and long-term preservation of the mummified hand and associated objects. The simple construction and manufacture of the support system can easily be reproduced to be suitable for other items in the British Museum collection. The supports were adapted to the physical needs posed by their condition and also took into account spiritual and religious beliefs as regards to the wooden cylinder. Although these aspirations could not be fully realized, both the hand and the cylinder were finally reunited in the same box.

| Human remains | Desirable conditions | | Acceptable conditions | |
	Relative humidity (%)	Temp (°C)	Relative humidity (%)	Temp (°C)
Ancient Egyptian mummies	35–45 (daily variation < ± 3)	16–20 (daily variation < ± 2)	35–45	16–25
Bog bodies (Lindow Man)	50–60 (daily variation < ± 3)	16–20 (daily variation < ± 2)	50–60	16–25
Skeletal material	40–55 (daily variation < ± 5)	16–20 (daily variation < ± 2)	40–60	16–25

Table 1 An outline of both the desirable and acceptable storage and display conditions for human remains

The importance of condition assessment by survey

A survey of a collection in storage or on display determines its condition and classifies the urgency of conservation care (see Appendix 2 for an example of a survey form). From this a recommendation can be made as to the treatment required and other resources necessary such as available expertise, conservation materials, time and storage requirements. For example, due to the range of materials found in the burial ensembles of ancient Egyptian mummies, assessment of this material requires a broad range of conservation skills, including those relating to human remains, textiles, wood, painted surfaces and metalwork.

For skeletal material, several surveys have been carried out on British Museum material (Ward 2003) and also on material for other museums (see Cook and Ward 2008). Such surveys have demonstrated the range of old adhesives used in the past and problems encountered by their use (Monge and Mann 2005) and in addition, the damage caused by researchers using moulding materials and metal measuring instruments. This may have involved application of a material directly onto or into the bone, or an indirect intervention using a specialized supportive system.

For naturally mummified human remains, the survey of the Fourth Nile Cataract human remains is particularly relevant (Wills *et al.* 2010). The survey aimed to understand the condition of the bodies and the range of materials present so that bodies could be stored appropriately and be made available for study. Those that were suitable for CT scanning were also identified. The survey was able to record the present condition as a benchmark for the future and began to identify material that would benefit from additional research such as textiles, body markings and hair. It also acted as a post-excavation assessment as the material had come almost directly from a rescue excavation. The potential for storage improvements was assessed, offering suggestions for upgrading the support boards, providing good soft supports for vulnerable tissues, removal of loose soil and identifying, bagging and labelling sample material.

Maintaining conditions in storage and on display

The best strategy for the long-term preservation of human remains centres on well-planned storage and display solutions that specifies appropriate housing and materials in addition to the maintenance of stable environmental conditions. A handling protocol for those studying or working with the collection should also be in place and referred to before study or handling (see Chapter One, this volume). At the British Museum, the preservation strategy for all collections, including human remains, is to prevent or slow down damage that may be caused by various factors including inappropriate temperature or relative humidity,

light, dust, pollutants, pests and physical forces such as handling, abrasion and vibration. The recommended environmental conditions for organic material are generally considered to be a relative humidity of 50% (+/-5%) and a temperature range of 16–25°C (Saunders 2006). However, materials that have adapted to environmental conditions different to these and are in good condition should be kept in those conditions. In particular, desiccated material should be kept at lower relative humidity levels (e.g. ancient Egyptian mummies are stored at around 40 +/-5% in the British Museum) otherwise they might deteriorate, whereas bog bodies require a more humid environment (relative humidity 50–60%). Daily variations in environment both in storage and on display should be kept to a minimum. Acceptable and desirable conditions are shown in **Table 1**. Mechanical conditioning units to control humidity levels are employed both in showcases and in stores at the British Museum. Temperature and relative humidity in different locations are monitored using Hanwell telemetric sensors to check that conditioning units are working correctly.

Human remains should be stored in the dark when they are not exhibited. Light levels should, as far as possible, be below 50 lux when such material is on display, with a cumulative light exposure of 150,000 lux.h.year^{-1} (i.e. 1,500,000 lux.h.year^{-1} in any 10 years) and an ultraviolet level of 75 μW.lumen^{-1} or less to minimize the fading of soft tissue when present (Saunders 2006). This is achieved by selection of the appropriate types of lamp, modifying showcases in order to screen out light and by dimming in-case lights. If the remains are skeletal, a maximum of 200 lux is acceptable.

Indoor pollutants such as acidic vapours and sulphur-based gases can be released from some storage and display materials. In enclosed spaces, these pollutants are able to build up to levels that can damage human remains and associated objects. Dust can also damage remains by soiling surfaces and creating hygroscopic layers which are sometimes acidic or alkaline. At the British Museum, these and other vulnerable collections are protected from dust and pollutants by being displayed in well-sealed showcases and packed in appropriate materials for storage or transportation. All materials used for the storage and display of collections are tested prior to use to ensure that they are inert (Thickett and Lee 2004).

Human remains are very vulnerable to damage from insect pests such as clothes moths and carpet beetles. However, different pests can be attracted to the protein and cellulose-based materials found in the human remains collections, and good housekeeping, inspection and monitoring routines are essential. The British Museum has an integrated pest management (IPM) programme to protect collections (British Museum 2010), with high risk materials receiving particular attention.

Packing for transport

Transport of any human remains is required when they are loaned to other institutions for display or moved to facilitate research such as CT scanning. The mummies held within the Department of Ancient Egypt and Sudan are consistently popular with the visiting public and scholars, both on display in London and for loan nationally and internationally. Mummies chosen for long-term loan have to be both robust and stable. The British Museum uses a standard packing system based on wooden crates lined with expanded polyethylene foam padding and Plastazote cut-outs wrapped in Tyvek (see Chapter Five, this volume).

For fragile specimens such as spontaneous mummies however, additional packing is required. The human remains are placed on a 'mattress' created by filling a cushion made from Tyvek with polystyrene balls. Both the mattress and the human remains then rest on a stable baseboard covered with Tyvek. A number of thin polythene bags filled with polystyrene balls are placed around the perimeter and above the body. These can be given different qualities dependent on how much air is expelled. Lots of air within the bag allows the balls to move and flow. Expelling air when sealing results in cushions that are 'mouldable' and hold a given shape. The more air expelled, the harder the cushions. Soft bags are placed against the body; harder, mouldable ones around the edges to keep these in place.

A disadvantage of this packing system is that, as they move, polystyrene balls readily generate static electricity, cling to a variety of surfaces and may therefore adversely affect fragile objects. The charge can be minimized by earthing the bags or using an anti-static gun. High humidity will dissipate any charge, as will a conductor such as metal. Simple handling and leaving the bags for a while will also allow the static charges to fade, or using Tyvek treated with an anti-static agent. In low relative humidity however, all types of Tyvek will build up a static charge, as will polythene bags.

Conclusions

Human remains are often found in a fragile state and therefore may require some kind of physical support during handling. In the past this was often achieved by the use of resins and other materials in order to strengthen the human remains. Incorrect reconstructions also occurred. The materials used can deteriorate and cause damage, while often failing to provide the necessary support and affecting potential analyses. The removal of old resins, adhesives and fills may be important in the survival and proper interpretation of the human remains. This can be a difficult and thoughtful process that requires research to analyse and understand the aged restoration material and and requires sensitivity to implement its removal and replacement.

The current approach adopted by conservators at the British Museum is to support fragile material where possible by the use of external physical supports and to encourage careful handling. When adhesives, consolidants and fills are required, their use is kept to a minimum. Any conservation materials used must have been tested and proved to be stable and reversible or retreatable. All treatments are carried out in close liaison with the appropriate curator or physical anthropologist, which is necessary in both understanding the human material and facilitating study. A record of all conservation treatments is maintained within the Museum's Collection Online database.

The British Museum contains many different types of human remains recovered from a diverse range of cultures, periods and environments. The bodies are an important source of direct information about our ancestors and therefore our approach to conservation is to maximize the survival of these remains and to ensure that they can be accessed safely and with respect.

Bibliography

Anderson, J.E., 1968. 'Late Paleolithic skeletal remains from Nubia', in *The Prehistory of Nubia*, ed. F. Wendorf, vol. 2, 966–1040. Dallas.

Andrews, C., 2004. *Egyptian Mummies*. London.

Asingh, P. and Lynnerup, N., 2007. *Graubolle Man: An Iron Age Bog Body Revisited*. Moesgaard.

Balachandran, S., 2009. 'Among the dead and their possessions: a conservator's role in the death, life, and afterlife of human remains and their associated objects', *Journal of the American Institute for Conservation* 48, no. 3, 199–222.

Bradley, S., Fletcher, P., Korenberg, C., Parker, J. and Ward, C., 2009. 'A review of the colour and condition of Lindow Man 20 years after conservation', *Studies in Conservation* 53, 1–12.

Brierly, L., 2011. *Environmental conditions in the E1021/E1099 Store*, British Museum internal report (unpublished).

British Museum 2010. *Integrated Pest Management Policy* (unpublished).

British Museum n.d. *British Museum Guidance for the Care, Study and Display of Human Remains*. British Museum internal report (unpublished).

Cassman, V. and Odegaard, N., 2004. 'Human remains and the conservator's role', *Studies in Conservation* 49, no. 4, 271–82 (http://www.jstor.org/stable/25487703).

Coddington, J. and Hickey, J., 2013. *MoMA's Jackson Pollock Conservation Project: Insight into the Artist's Process*. The Museum of Modern Art website, New York (http://www.moma.org/explore/inside_out/2013/04/17/momas-jackson-pollock-conservation-project-insight-into-the-artists-process) [accessed 13/8/13].

Cook, J. and Ward, C., 2008. 'Conservation assessment of the Neanderthal human remains from Krapina, Croatia and its implications for the debate on the display and loan of human fossils', *British Museum Technical Bulletin* 2, 39–44.

Cronyn, J., 1990. *The Elements of Archaeological Conservation*. London.

DCMS (Department for Culture, Media and Sport) 2005. *Guidance for the Care of Human Remains in Museums* (see http://webarchive.nationalarchives.gov.uk/+/http://www.culture.gov.uk/images/publications/GuidanceHumanRemains11Oct.pdf).

D'Elia, M., Gianfrate G., Quarta, G., Giotta, L., Giancane, G. and Calcagnile, L., 2007. 'Evaluation of possible contamination sources in the ¹⁴C analysis of bone samples by FTIR spectroscopy', *Radiocarbon* 49, 2, 201–10.

Eklund, J.A. and Thomas, M.G., 2010. 'Assessing the effects of conservation treatments on short sequences of DNA in vitro', *Journal of Archaeological Science* 37, 2831–41.

English Heritage 2008. *Guidelines for the Curation of Waterlogged Macroscopic Plant and Invertebrate Remains*. Swindon.

Evans, A. C., 2013. https://artserve.anu.edu.au/raid1/student_projects/hoo2/cenotaph.html [accessed August 2013].

Hacke, M. and Stacey, R., 2008. 'Identification of the fluids used for storage of tissue specimens from Lindow Man (1984,1002.1)', Department of Conservation, Documentation and Science. CDS Analytical Request No. AR2008/03, British Museum (unpublished).

Hummler, M. and Roe, A., 2013. *Sutton Hoo Burials: Reconstructing the Sequence of Events* (www.york.ac.uk/archaeology/strat/pastpub/96ch6.pdf) [accessed August 2013].

Johnson, J.S., 1994. 'Consolidation of archaeological bone. A conservation perspective', *Journal of Field Archaeology* 21, 2 (13), 221–33.

Johnson, C. and Wills, B., 1988. 'The conservation of two pre-dynastic Egyptian bodies', in *Conservation of Ancient Egyptian Materials*, ed. S. Watkins and C. Brown, 79–84. London.

—, Wills, B., Peacock, T. and Bott, G., 1995. 'The conservation of an Egyptian mummy, cartonnage cover and mask', in *Conservation in Ancient Egyptian Collections Conference*, ed. C. Brown, F. Macalister and M. Wright, 47–56. London.

Jones, D.G. and Harris, R.J., 1998. 'Archaeological human remains, scientific, cultural and ethical considerations', *Current Anthropology*, 39 (2), 253–64.

Joy, J., 2009. *Lindow Man*. London.

Judd, M.A., 2002. *Osteological Assessment – Sahaba Site 117*. Department of Ancient Egypt and Sudan, British Museum internal report (unpublished).

—, 2003. *The Wendorf Collection Skeletal Catalogue*. Department of Ancient Egypt and Sudan, British Museum internal report (unpublished).

Korenberg, C., Ward, C. and Delaunay, H., 2012. 'An initial investigation into the use of the Nd:YAG laser to remove resins from archaeological bone', in *Lasers in the Conservation of Artworks IX*, ed. D. Saunders, M. Strlic, C. Korenberg, N. Luxford and K. Birkholzer, 216–18. London.

McGowan, G.S. and LaRoche, C.J., 1996. 'The ethical dilemma facing conservation: care and treatment of human skeletal remains and mortuary objects', *Journal of the American Institute for Conservation*, 35(2), 109–21.

Monge, J. and Mann, A., 2005. 'Ethical issues in the moulding and casting of fossil specimens', in *Biological Anthropology and Ethics: From Repatriation to Genetic Identity*, ed. T. Turner, 91–110. New York.

Oddy, A., 1992. *The Art of the Conservator*. London.

Omar, S., McCord, M. and Daniels, V., 1989. 'The conservation of bog bodies by freeze-drying', *Studies in Conservation* 34 (3), 101–9.

Painter, T., 1991. 'Lindow Man, Tollund Man and other peat-bog bodies: the preservative and anti-microbial action of spagnan, a reactive glycuronoglycan with tanning and sequestering properties', *Carbohydrate Polymers* 15, 123–42.

Robinet, L., 2002. *Analysis of Bones from the Wendorf Collection*, British Museum internal report (unpublished).

Saunders, D., 2006. *Lighting and Climatic Criteria for the British Museum Collections*, British Museum internal report (unpublished).

Shelton, S.Y. and Johnson, J., 1995. 'Conservation of subfossil bone', in *The Care and Conservation of Palaeontological Material*, ed. C. Collins, 59–71. Boston.

Stein, M.A., 1928. *Innermost Asia: Detailed Report of Explorations in Central Asia, Kan-su and Eastern Iran*. Oxford.

Thickett D. and Lee, L.R., 2004. *Selection of Materials for the Storage or Display of Museum Objects*. London (The British Museum Occasional Paper Number 111) (available at http://www.britishmuseum.org/research/publications/research_publications_series/2004/selection_of_materials.aspx).

Trustees of the British Museum 2013. The British Museum Policy on Human Remains (available online at http://www.britishmuseum.org/about_us/management/museum_governance.aspx).

Veiga, P., 2012. 'Studying mummies and human remains: some current developments and issues', *Journal of the Washington Academy of Sciences* 98 (2), 1–22.

Ward, C., 2003. *Conservation Survey of the Human Skeletal Material in the Wendorf Collection, Department of Ancient Egypt and Sudan*. Department of Conservation Report number: 2003/11/0/7, British Museum (unpublished).

Welsby, D.A., 2003. 'The Amri to Kirbekan survey: the 2002–2003 season', *Sudan and Nubia* 7, 26–32.

Wendorf, F., 1968. 'Site 117: a Nubian final Palaeolithic graveyard near Jebel Sahaba, Sudan' in *The Prehistory of Nubia*, ed. F. Wendorf, vol. 2, 954–87. Dallas.

Wills, B., forthcoming. 'Wrapping the wrapped; development of minimal conservation of ancient Egyptian human wrapped mummies', in *Wrapping Material Culture, Archaeological and Anthropological Approaches*, ed. L. Douny and S. Harris. London.

—, Aboe, G. and Genbrugge, S., 2010. *Conservation Survey of Human Skeletal and Mummified Tissue Material from the Fourth Cataract Merowe Dam Archaeological Salvage Project in Sudan (Department of AES)*. Department of Conservation Report number: 2010/27/0/4, British Museum (unpublished).

— and Ward, C., 2002. *The Wendorf Collection: Proposals for Conservation and Storage*, British Museum internal report (unpublished).

Additional references

Hatchfield, P., 2002. *Pollutants in the Museum Environment: Practical Strategies for Problem Solving in Design, Exhibition and Storage*. London.

Payton, R., 1992. 'On-site conservation techniques: lifting techniques', in *Retrieval of Objects from Archaeological Sites*, ed. R. Payton, 1–26. London.

Williams, E., 2001. *Human Remains: Conservation, Retrieval and Analysis, Proceedings of a Conference held in Williamsburg, VA, 7–11 Nov 1999*. Oxford (BAR International Series 934).

Appendix 1 Example of a British Museum Risk Assessment Form

Severity

Likelihood	Low	Medium	High
Low	Low	Low	Low
Medium	Low	Medium	Medium
High	Low	Medium	High

Likelihood (L) x Severity (S) = Risk (R) (high, medium, low)

This RA is specifically designed for the Senior Clothworkers Fellowship Project: Safeguarding a body of evidence: researching and conserving a group of exceptional naturally mummified Nilotic human remains. It is adapted from the General / Job or / Area specific Assessment for controlling the risks of infection at work from human remains, carried out by Claire Messenger and Tania Watkins (AES) with specific advice from Betina Jakob, Physical Anthropologist, University of Durham. A 2007 review carried out by Sherry Doyal and Clare Ward based on advice sought from: Bill White, Curator Centre for Human Bioarchaeology MOL; Natasha Powers, Head of Osteology, MoLA; Martyn Cooke, Head of Conservation, the Royal College of Surgeons of England; Pat Potter, British School of Leather Technology, 2004. Also referencing 'Controlling the risks of infection at work from human remains' HSE 2005; 'Anthrax and historic plaster-technical advice note' English Heritage 1999 *Crypt Archaeology: an Approach*: Institute of Field Archaeologists Paper no. 3; www.bt.cdc.gov/agent/smallpox/vaccination/faq. asp. Further information is derived from attending a Hazards in Museum Collections course 17/11/11. Advisor was Else Bourguignon, H&S specialist, Conservation and Scientific Research. Also http://www.who.int/csr/resources/publications/ anthrax_webs.pdf, chapter 4.2 Susceptibility: data for risk assessments; WHO publication 2008, p37. Also http://www.hse.gov. uk/pubns/web01.pdf: Controlling the risks of infection at work from Human Remains (Health and Safety executive).

TASK/ ACTIVITY AREA	HAZARDS	WHO'S AT RISK	CONTROLS IN PLACE	L	S	R	FURTHER CONTROLS NEEDED	WHO TO ACTION	COMPLETION DATE
The cleaning, support, sampling and study of c. 40 desiccated, recently excavated and naturally-mummified bodies from the Fourth Cataract region of the Nile. Housed in room 60. Fellowship runs over a period of 2 years (part time). Date range 6th to 15th C AD	Infectious disease (microbial agents or bacterial) from bodies. Risks posed by anthrax and smallpox Soil and other material (textiles, jewellery etc.) associated with bodies.	All staff in contact with material; primarily B Wills and any co-workers.	Likelihood of disease very small ('very remote risk') because spores or infectious agents are unlikely to remain viable after 100 years, and less so in a desiccated context. People in contact should be advised of the degree of danger from infection. Personal hygiene of great importance. Keep hands and fingernails clean, avoid hand-to-mouth contact. Wash hands and face after each episode of contact. No consumption of food and drink in proximity. Cover any cuts, wounds and abrasions with waterproof dressings. Personal protective clothing should be routinely worn such as disposable apron, and Tyvec sleeves. Suggest disposable nitrile gloves, dust mask type FFP3. Remove any contaminated PPE when leaving the area. Keep surrounding areas clean and dust free. Waste, including PPE and vacuum bags, should be disposed of correctly by incineration. Ensure that relevant personnel are informed of the risk and risk management strategy.	L	H	L			

TASK/ ACTIVITY AREA	HAZARDS	WHO'S AT RISK	CONTROLS IN PLACE	L	S	R	FURTHER CONTROLS NEEDED	WHO TO ACTION	COMPLETION DATE
As above, focusing on removal of small area of mould on arm of skeleton 353 (3-J-23 Gr 120)	Fungal growth and spores; may be aerated by process of cleaning/ removal.	As above	Refer to mould removal RA. PPE and disposal as above. Minimise aerosol mould: experiment with the use of Groomstick (molecular trap putty) and compare with brush/vacuum cleaner removal.

Fluctuations of humidity in storage/work area have been reduced by boarding up windows that had failed to close. This reduces risk of future mould outbreaks | L | H | L | Check environmental conditions on a regular basis. | | |
| Removing dust and soil. | Inhalation of particles while removing dust from remains. | All staff in contact area. | Raised dust (with brush or photographers bulb puff ball) should be caught with a vacuum fitted with a high efficiency particulate air filter (HEPA filter).

As above PPE and disposal. Clean area regularly. | L | H | L | Be aware it is important to ensure that work areas are also kept clean. While removing dust from the find please be aware of where it is going in case it could pose a risk to others. | | |
| Removing dust and soil.

Treating bodies as above | Note that at greater risk are those with compromised immunity such as pregnant women, HIV positives and those receiving chemotherapy. | All staff in contact areas who are identified as at higher risk. | All staff have a responsibility to either identify themselves as at risk or to absent themselves from the project.

As above regarding PPE and disposal. Clean area regularly. Check health status of any co-workers/students. | L | H | L | No one should assume that colleagues wish to make personal medical detail public. Make sure the risk is clearly posted to allow colleagues to absent themselves. | | |
| Observing physical work with and on human remains | Psychological stress | Staff passing through room 60.

Staff in OIII. | Work area is screened off and not easily visible. The entrance to the work area clearly warns those entering, denoting the nature of the work and presence of human material.

Issues (ethical and practical) should be fully discussed if requested.

Persons should be sure to treat any excavated human remains with appropriate respect, and take steps to ensure other staff or visitors to the department are not offended | M | H | M | Check regularly with staff in OIII that controls are working. | | |
| Physical work with and on human remains | Psychological stress | B Wills | Regular breaks, including informal discussion, should be taken to allow human responses to emotive situations. Human remains treated with respect as above. | M | H | M | | | |

TASK/ ACTIVITY AREA	HAZARDS	WHO'S AT RISK	CONTROLS IN PLACE	L	S	R	FURTHER CONTROLS NEEDED	WHO TO ACTION	COMPLETION DATE
Physical work with and on human remains		Students/ co-workers	All students etc. to be to be fully briefed on the overall project rationale and recruited carefully. To be made fully aware of the task they will be expected to undertake. Human remains treated with respect as above. Issues (ethical and practical) should be fully discussed if requested. Regular breaks and discussions as above.	M	H	M			

Human Remains Conservation Survey

Identification

Reg./Spec. number [   ]   Location [   ]

Other numbers [   ]

Surveyor(s) [   ]   Date of Survey [   ]

Object description [   ]

Dimensions	Length	Width	Depth	Weight

Provenance [   ]   Period [   ]

Photograph   (including date and registration number)

Photo sequence number [   ]

Description

Body state   ☐ skeleton   ☐ mummified   ☐ other... [   ]

Mummification type   ☐ natural   ☐ artificial   ☐ other... [   ]

Sex   ☐ M ☐ F   ☐ Unknown   Age at death   ☐ child   ☐ teenager   ☐ adult

Position   ☐ straight   ☐ foetal   ☐ other

Body   ☐ complete   ☐ incomplete   ☐ body part   ☐ body parts   ☐ other...

No. of bones [   ]   No. of parts [   ]   No. of bags/boxes [   ]

Human tissue/organs [   ]

Tattoos/Scarification/Piercings [   ]

Hair Visible   ☐ Yes   ☐ No

Hair Location [   ]

Hair Colour [   ]

Teeth Visible   ☐ Yes   ☐ No   Comments [   ]

Associated objects [   ]

Human Remains Conservation Survey

Sketch of the body/ part

Direction
- [ ] Lying on back
- [ ] Lying on front
- [ ] Lying on L side
- [ ] Lying on R side
- [ ] Other..

If other:

Wrappings
- [ ] none
- [ ] leather
- [ ] skin
- [ ] other...
- [ ] fur
- [ ] textile
- [ ] rope/string

weave

fiber [ ] plant [ ] animal [ ] human [ ] unknown

Comment wrappings   e.g., location

Condition

General condition
- [ ] A – no work needed
- [ ] B – low conservation priority
- [ ] C – medium conservation priority
- [ ] D – high conservation priority
- [ ] E – beyond repair

Previous repairs/treatments [ ] yes [ ] no [ ] not known   [ ] stable   [ ] unstable

Comments on previous treatments

Condition Diagram

Please mark the diagram with condition code keys for bone/skin/hair/wrapping.

State of Preservation - Bone: [ ] 1 = < 25%   [ ] 2 = ~ 50%   [ ] 3 = > 75%

State of Preservation - Skin: [ ] 1 = < 25%   [ ] 2 = ~ 50%   [ ] 3 = > 75%

Human Remains Conservation Survey

Bone Condition

Physical damage
- ☐ b01 – break
- ☐ b02 – brittle
- ☐ b03 – crack
- ☐ b04 – cut mark
- ☐ b05 – disarticulated
- ☐ b06 – displaced
- ☐ b07 – holes
- ☐ b08 – missing parts
- ☐ b09 – soil

Comments

Skin Condition

Physical damage
- ☐ s01 – bloom
- ☐ s02 – crack
- ☐ s03 – cut marks
- ☐ s04 – delamination
- ☐ s05 – distortion
- ☐ s06 – efflorescence
- ☐ s07 – loss
- ☐ s08 – metal stain
- ☐ s09 – soil

Biological damage
- ☐ s10 – fungae
- ☐ s11 – insect frass
- ☐ s12 – insect carcasses
- ☐ s13 – mould stain
- ☐ s14 – pest damage
- ☐ s15 – other…

Comments

Hair Condition

Physical damage
- ☐ h01 – loss of hair
- ☐ h02 – slippage
- ☐ h03 – breakage
- ☐ h04 – other…

Comments

Wrapping Condition

Physical damage
- ☐ w01 – torn
- ☐ w02 – stained
- ☐ w03 – other…

Comments

Overall Anomalies

Action Priority List

Please prioritise in numerical order (1 = needing most urgent attention)

- ☐ intervention (please specify)
- ☐ cleaning
- ☐ support / secure fragile parts
- ☐ new storage
- ☐ other…

Human Remains Conservation Survey

Current Storage

Description

Proposed Storage

Room

Temperature	
RH	
Lux	

Box

Size   ☐ Small   ☐ Medium   ☐ Large   ☐ Other...

Shape   ☐ Square   ☐ Rectangular ☐ Oval   ☐ Round   ☐ Other...

Material   ☐ Wood   ☐ Foam board   ☐ Acid free card   ☐ Other...
   ☐ Metal   ☐ Coroplast (polypropylene)   ☐ Polystyrene foam board

Cover Material   ☐ Lid in same material as box   ☐ Acid free tissue
   ☐ Tyvek (Polyolefin)   ☐ Teflon
   ☐ Cotton   ☐ Bonina
   ☐ Polyethylene   ☐ Hollitex (Polyster tissue)
   ☐ Melinex (Polyester)   ☐ Other...

Comments

Support

Material   ☐ Plastozote   ☐ Polyester batting   ☐ Polyethylene foam (etafoam)

Cover Material   ☐ Acid free tissue   ☐ Tyvek (Polyolefin)
   ☐ Teflon   ☐ Cotton
   ☐ Bonina   ☐ Polyethylene
   ☐ Hollitex (Polyster tissue)   ☐ Melinex (Polyester)
   ☐ Other...

Comments

Location of support needed

Microclimate

Part 3
Researching the British Museum Collection

Introduction

Clark Spencer Larsen

In the opening paragraph to Chapter Nine in this volume, John Taylor notes that 'a consistent research strategy for this important collection is … needed'. Be they bones or mummies collected in the 19th century by amateur archaeologists or by leading professionals in the 20th and 21st centuries, the human remains housed in the British Museum's vast collection represents an important resource for documenting life conditions in past societies. The remains discussed in the following five chapters underscore the critical importance of the long-term curation of an irreplaceable resource in telling the story of humankind.

Some of the Museum's best-represented collections and those with the longest history of acquisition, curation and study are from the Middle East, arguably one of the most interesting regions of the globe as pertaining to major adaptive transitions (e.g. foraging-to-farming) and significant social and political developments involving the rise and fall of complex societies. These five chapters reflect the wealth of data from a wide range of settings and collection circumstances. St John Simpson and Theya Molleson provide a preliminary, yet fascinating overview of largely unstudied mortuary sites from the Sasanian Empire, a vast landscape extending from Syria to Central Asia and Azerbaijan to the Persian Gulf, which encompassed many cultures, religions and lifeways spanning four centuries from the early 3rd century AD onwards. Simpson and Molleson acknowledge the difficulty of studying such a complex cultural landscape, but nonetheless make the argument that the mortuary context and human remains provides an important perspective on body treatment. The case studies for two settings, Bushehr (Iran) and Merv (Turkmenistan), show the complexity of mortuary treatments, including evidence of purposeful defleshing prior to interment and placement in specially prepared burial containers. While preliminary, the paper provides a framework for future studies in an understudied region.

Among the most famous archaeological discoveries of the 20th century are the seven plastered human skulls recovered by Kathleen Kenyon in her 1953 excavations of Jericho, dating to the Middle Pre-pottery Neolithic B. In the years since the discovery, there has been an ongoing discussion of the origin of the skulls, who they represent and why they received such special treatment. The fascinating results of the study of the single skull in the British Museum collection by Alexandra Fletcher and collaborators reveal important information about a single person. Owing to the fact that much of the cranium is covered in dense plaster, basic details about the person are initially inaccessible. However, through the use of computerized tomographic (CT) scanning technology, new details about the person are revealed, including age (mature adult), sex (likely male), health (worn and diseased teeth), rare genetic conditions (agenesis of teeth) and body treatment in life (artificial cranial deformation). In addition, this new research shows that key steps were taken to prepare the skull prior to the creation of the plaster face, including filling the skull and eye orbits with soil. This study makes clear the benefits of long-term curation, namely that new technology provides fresh avenues of investigation for addressing old questions.

Like many of my colleagues in the field of anthropology, I was attracted to the discipline as a course of study and professional career in no small part by the accounts in the mainstream media of mummies from Egypt and elsewhere. One of the most famous collections in the world pertaining to ancient Egypt is in the British Museum. Indeed, an Egyptian mummy was part of Hans Sloane's personal collection of artefacts donated for the founding of the institution in the mid-18th century. The chapter by John Taylor provides a concise history of acquisitions and the Museum's collection of mummies, which now numbers some 87 bodies and various parts of bodies, including their provenance and chronology (4,000 years from approximately mid-4th millennium BC to 2nd century AD). This is an important public record of an amazing collection. The scientific importance of the collection, while limited by poor dating and provenance for most mummies, especially those collected in the 18th and 19th centuries, continues to the present day. In the last several decades, CT scanning technology has provided a new understanding of the health, age and sex of the mummies in addition to mummification procedures. Among the most important discoveries are some of the earliest records of health conditions that still affect humans in Egypt and elsewhere today, including schistosomiasis, tuberculosis, eczema and head-lice infestation.

The British Museum's bioarchaeology programme is far more than just the curation of remains collected long ago. Rather, it is a vibrant community of collaborating scholars and scientists intent on understanding significant settings in world history and prehistory. In this vein, Jonathan Tubb and Caroline Cartwright in Chapter Ten describe their research and curation goals for the human remains recovered from the biblical city of Zarethan, known to archaeologists today as Tell es-Sa'idiyeh, located in the central Jordan Valley. This setting witnessed a sequence of Egyptian control and loss of control. Spanning the history of the site is a rich and diverse mortuary record and its archaeological and historical contexts, which have been studied by a team of human bioarchaeologists, archaeobotanists, archaeozoologists and students. The study of the human remains in particular provides the opportunity to document changing patterns of demography and health in relation to gender, status and society in the Late Bronze Age to Early Iron Age transitions. The great underlying story about the project is the collaboration between professional archaeologists and the local community, through the training of local teams of workmen and the sharing of information about their discipline.

Like the Jordan Valley during the Bronze Age, much of the Nile valley in Sudanese Nubia was under the control of Egypt during its New Kingdom period (c. 1550–1070 BC) and then reverted to local control. Bioarchaeology of the town of Amara West, founded on an island in the Nile River around 1300 BC at the height of Egyptian control, provides a record of human impacts involving Egyptian–Nubian interactions and increasing climatic instability during the colonial and post-colonial periods. Like the project at Tell es-Sa'idiyeh, this investigation is emblematic of modern archaeology, which involves a comprehensive study of context (foods eaten, settlement and environment) in order to develop a broader picture of health and lifestyle in a highly dynamic period. Testing the hypothesis that sociopolitical and environmental circumstances led to changes in living conditions, Michaela Binder and Neal Spencer document patterns of health from their diachronic study of the human remains from Amara West. Per their hypothesis, the skeletal records strongly suggest a setting involving a deteriorating quality of life, including increases in *cribra orbitalia* (pathology representing iron deficiency anaemia) and elevated levels of infection, scurvy, dental disease, growth stress and trauma, especially during the post-colonial era.

In addition to providing details about the collection and its history, this set of chapters underscores the centrality and continuing potential of the British Museum's human remains collection in the study of the past. Certainly, it is the more recent collections with their enhanced context that provide some of the more detailed findings. However, the chapters also make clear that collections going back to the 18th century provide important details, in part owing to the development of new methods and technologies for addressing age-old questions about human history. The chapters present a kind of microcosm of changing patterns of museum practice, from acquisition of bones and mummies by amateurs in the 18th, 19th and into the 20th centuries to the full scientific excavation and study involving interdisciplinary teams of collaborators and specialists working in the 21st century, all focused on addressing questions and hypotheses about past societies. The chapters in this section are testimony to the fact that the ancient remains housed in the British Museum provide a fundamental record of life conditions among past societies. They also make clear that this record of skeletons and bodies is not an unlimited resource. It is the mission of the Museum to continue to make strides in the long-term curation and protection of their physical integrity and to develop the kinds of strong research programmes that are so eloquently presented in the following chapters.

Chapter 7
Old Bones Overturned
New Evidence for Funerary Practices from the Sasanian Empire

St John Simpson and Theya Molleson

When the body is properly eaten away, the bones should be carried to an *astodan*, which should be so elevated from the ground and be so [constructed] with a roof [or cover] that the rain shall in no way fall over the dead substance, and that water shall not remain over it from above, and that not a drop shall fall over it from above, and that a dog or a fox shall not have access to it, and holes be made into it for the admission of light. It is further enjoined on this point that the *astodan* shall be prepared of a single stone and its cover be made of a single well-prepared perforated stone, and that it be set with stone and mortar all round (*Dadistan-i-dinik* Question XVII).

Introduction: the variation in funerary practices

The Sasanian Empire was founded in the early 3rd century AD, lasted for over four centuries and encompassed a wide range of peoples and faiths over a large and disparate region stretching from north-east Syria to Central Asia and Azerbaijan to the Persian Gulf. The official religion was Zoroastrianism, but there were substantial and economically important populations of Christians and Jews, particularly in Mesopotamia (modern Iraq and northern Syria), as well as Buddhists in the eastern provinces and numerous minor sects. There are periodic reports of the persecution of non-Zoroastrian communities, violation of their dead and proclamations concerning the exposure of bodies during the reigns of Varahran V (421–39), Yazdgird II (439–57), Peroz (459–84) and Kavad (488–531), but these appear to have been exceptional events and local communities were normally tolerated where they integrated into society. Different faiths have different burial practices and, as the archaeology of Muslim graves shows very clearly, these are often subject to local conditions and customs (Simpson 1995; 2007b, 110–14, 118–20; Insoll 1999, 166–200). Identifying the faith of the deceased is therefore not an easy task on the basis of archaeological evidence alone, and the archaeological evidence for funerary practices in the Sasanian Empire is particularly complex to interpret.

Within Iranian archaeology, much attention has been paid to the interpretation of certain types of rock-cut installations which are particularly numerous on the slopes of Kūh-i Rahmat and Kūh-i Husain above the city of Istakhr (Gotch 1972; Huff 1991; Gotch, Simpson and Taylor forthcoming). A systematic survey of these is long overdue, but the Pahlavi inscriptions engraved next to a small number of these installations or on free-standing column-*dakhmas* and trough-*dakhma* covers (see below) confirm that they were intended as the resting-place for individuals of both genders and in a few cases even give the name of the family members and the date (Frye 1970; Gropp and Nadjmabadi 1970; Nasrollah Zadeh 2007; Tafazzoli 1991; Tafazzoli and Sheikh-al-Hokamayi 1994). The financial status of these individuals is hinted at in an inscription from Iqlīd which refers to payment in silver (Frye 1970, 155–6), and the size and clustering of the tombs around Istakhr strongly suggests that they were used by urban families.

Burials within rock cairns are also attested across southern Iran during this period and represent a widespread 1st millennium AD tradition stretching from Fars to Baluchistan (Stein 1937; Lamberg-Karlovsky 1972; Lamberg-Karlovsky and Humphries 1968; Azarpay 1981; Boucharlat 1989). Pottery, personal ornaments, a spear-head and coins provisionally identified as dating to around AD 100 were found inside a cluster of cairns on a ridge above Qasr-i Abu Nasr, near Shiraz (Whitcomb 1985, 210–16); a Parthian glazed 'pilgrim flask' was found in a cairn tomb excavated south of Tang-i Bulaghi in the Marv Dasht (Stronach 1978, 167, fig. 115: 8, pl. 145a–b), and a lugged plainware pot, four large tanged trilobate iron arrow-heads, a tanged iron knife or short sword, an iron dagger in a silver-studded copper alloy scabbard and a silver coin identified as belonging to Yazdgard III (632–51) found among a group of 24 cairns excavated by Aurel Stein near Bishezard confirm that they remained in use as late as the 7th century AD (Stein 1936, 157–9, fig. 13, pl. XXIX: 5–12, 15, 18, 20, 23–4, 26, 38, 40, 43, 50). The location of these cairns on rocky ridges and along routes ensured that they were easily visible yet situated away from the fertile valley floor. Whether this reflects their construction by nomads, as originally suggested, is unconfirmed and the occasional presence of glazed pottery vessels within the tombs might suggest otherwise. Moreover, the absence or at best highly fragmented state of the human remains within cairns has been interpreted that they either represent cenotaphs or fractional secondary burials.

Elsewhere in the Persian Gulf there is evidence for the secondary interment of multiple individuals placed within shallow cists cut into flat rocky outcrops on Kharg Island (Steve *et al.* 2003, 69–77). Some of the human remains were placed inside pottery jars or bitumen-lined baskets whereas others appear to have been placed directly into the cavities; the accompanying coin of Honorius (395–423), personal seals, glass and pottery all suggest a Sasanian and possibly early Islamic date. The cists are said to have been originally covered with gabled roofs formed by pairs of large flat stones erected over the top, although this is not certain and they may simply have been capped with flat slabs. There is evidence for both Jewish and Christian populations on the island during the 7th to early 9th centuries AD and these had their own cemeteries which differ again in style of interment. Despite the proposal in the final report that the secondary interments may reflect a transfer of remains from the rock-cut niches used by the Christian community (Steve *et al.* 2003), the possibility that they instead represent a local form of *dakhma* seems more likely.

Burial mounds and cairn burials have an even longer history on the western side of the Persian Gulf and there is archaeological evidence for the reuse of a small number of these during this period in parts of eastern Saudi Arabia, Bahrain and the United Arab Emirates (UAE). These late occurrences are datable through associated finds which include Sasanian facet-cut glass, personal seals and weapons placed with articulated skeletal remains in a flexed position (Zarins, Mughannam and Kamal 1984, 42, pl. 50.10; Andersen 2007; Kästner 1987). The identity of the individuals is unclear, but the presence of fragile glass tablewares and seals imply that they belong to sedentized individuals rather than transient Bedouin. Moreover, two burials excavated at Jabal al-Emalah in Sharjah (UAE) were radiocarbon dated to between the late 5th and 8th centuries AD and were found accompanied by a long sword in one case and a heavy thrusting spear in the second. Anthropological analysis of the human remains by Professor D.L. Martin

(Hampshire College) and P.K. Stone (University of Massachusetts) indicates that they belonged to well-built mature male adults aged 35–9 and 25–30 years respectively; the first had osteoarthritis, possibly arising from pulled ligaments or muscles, as well as healed injuries to the left clavicle and left ribs, and the second had well-developed muscles in the lower arm bones (Potts 1997, 135–6). In both cases the findings of healed trauma are consistent with their grave-goods and suggest they may have been warriors, either professional soldiers or client tribesmen, although the radiocarbon dates imply that they may be early Islamic rather than Sasanian (King 2001, 76).

Within Iraq a large number of Sasanian graves have been excavated, either individually or as part of cemeteries. They include extended or flexed burials placed within brick-built or stone-lined cists or shaft graves with undercut side-chambers. They have been broadly dated through associated grave-offerings of pottery, glass and occasionally coins and seals (e.g. Ehrich 1939; Negro Ponzi 1968/9; 2005; Roaf 1984; Kamada and Ohtsu 1988; Simpson 1987; al-Shams 1987/8; al-Haditti 1995). Jar burials have been found at several sites, but the discovery of a cremation urn in what appears to have been a more extensive jar cemetery at Ḥabl as-Sakhr is exceptional (Simon 1989). Most of these sites are set within rural landscapes and probably belong to agricultural villagers, although some may belong to transient groups and the isolated burial of an adult man with an oval bronze drinking-bowl and glass bottle on the summit of the mound of Tell Razuk in the Hamrin basin of east central Iraq (Gibson 1981, 81, pl. 101) may reflect the personal grave location choice of a local late or post-Sasanian landlord, equivalent to the inscribed column-*dakhma* at Tang-i Karam in Fars (Huff 2004, 612). In any case, the location of these excavated finds largely reflects the chances involved in archaeological research as in most cases they were discovered by accident during the excavation of sites from much earlier periods. Urban cemeteries must have also existed, although none have yet been excavated. A possible exception is the site of Umm Kheshm, south of modern Najaf, where the number and density of graves were interpreted by the excavator as evidence that they belonged to the nearby city of al-Hira (al-Haditti 1995).

Despite these finds from Iraq, the extent to which inhumation burial was practised across other parts of the Sasanian Empire has attracted some criticism as it challenges the assumption that the population was exclusively Zoroastrian. However, part of a cemetery containing flexed burials accompanied by similar object categories was excavated on the summit of the site of Haftavan Tepe in western Iran (Burney 1970, 169–71, figs 7–9, pls VIIc–d, VIIIb–c; 1973, 172, pl. VIIId), and Bivar (1970, 157) suggested that they might belong to a local Christian population. Additional graves found at Susa (Boucharlat 1991, 72), Tal-i Malyan in Fars (Balcer 1978), and Kangelou and Pahlauj in Mazanderan (CAIS 2007; 2008) confirm that this practice did extend deeper into Iran and was probably more widespread than currently recognized. The large numbers of complete facet-cut glasswares, high-tin bronzes, occasional skeuomorphic painted pottery pitchers and high-value weapons reportedly found in commercial excavations in the Dailaman region of north-west Iran during the late 1950s and 1960s indicate that these Sasanian and post-Sasanian objects were buried as grave-goods and Japanese investigations confirm the existence of Sasanian (and earlier) cemeteries containing flexed articulated bodies placed at the feet of shaft graves (Sono and Fukai 1968; see also Akira 1981; Simpson 1998). Little is yet known about equivalent funerary practices in north-east Iran, but the density and organization of military as well as civilian and agricultural infrastructure on the Gorgan plain implies that careful thought must have been put into the disposal of the dead (cf. Omrani Rekavandi, Sauer and Wilkinson *et al.* 2008). South of the Elburz mountains, a large ruined Parthian structure at Shahr-i Qumis in the Damghan plain was found to have been reused as a repository in the late 6th century AD judging by an associated coin of Hormizd IV (Bivar 1970). Much further to the south-east, a Kushano-Sasanian cemetery containing adults buried in an extended position within shaft graves and accompanied by items of personal adornment and weapons was excavated at Said Qala Tepe, approximately 25km west of Kandahar (Shaffer and Hoffman 1976) and another cemetery was explored at Shamshir Ghar cave (Dupree 1958). In several instances, the deceased was also accompanied by a coin placed either in the hand or the mouth, and there is additional evidence for this from slightly later Hephthalite burials excavated at Old Kandahar (McNicoll 1996, 235–6, figs 184–6), Kara Tepe (Stavisky 1988, 1403) and Dal'verzin (Turgunov 2006, 58–62).

The archaeological evidence therefore clearly demonstrates a wide variety of local customs and practices pertaining to the disposal of the dead across the Sasanian Empire. Some of these individuals were undoubtedly Zoroastrian, others were clearly not and in some cases the evidence is ambiguous. In the case of highland Iran, it was a relatively easy matter to select accessible rocky outcrops for the exposure and disposal of members of the Zoroastrian community. In lowland areas, particularly with intensive agriculture and pressure on land, other options must have been explored.

The description of Zoroastrian funerary practice quoted at the beginning of this paper comes from a book of religious opinions composed by Manuchihir, the high priest of Fars and Kirman in the 9th century AD. It is very explicit in its description, yet the physical identification of such practices from antiquity has had a mixed history of success within Iranian studies (Casartelli 1890; Boyce 1987, 12–16, 120–1, 157–8; Grenet 1984; Trümpelmann 1984; Meitarchiyan 1990; Huff 2004). The traditional view that the Zoroastrian dead were exposed on the summits of large constructed *dakhmas* (today referred to as 'Towers of Silence') is based on post-medieval Parsi practice in the urban environment of Bombay and there is no evidence that such monuments existed in pre-Islamic Iran. Trümpelmann (1984, 317–18) attempted to identify a circular rampart at Tal-e Khandagh near Sar Mashhad as an exposure *dakhma* founded by the priest Kirder. However, it is more likely to simply be a fortified complex, particularly as it is surrounded by a ditch or moat, and this and other monuments of the type have

been recently discussed by Ghasemi (2012). Moreover, the identification of a recently excavated structure at Bandiyan as a *dakhma* attached to a fire-temple (Rahbar 2004: 13–14; 2007) has also been challenged and the complex instead reinterpreted as a funerary complex associated with a large residence (Gignoux 2008).

There has also been some confusion over the meaning in antiquity of the words *dakhma* and *astodan*. It is now clear, however, that the word *dakhma* was formerly used in the wider sense of tomb whereas *astodan* was used to refer more narrowly to a bone receptacle or ossuary. In the absence of evidence for monuments constructed for this purpose, the place of exposure must have occurred in the open and the carefully levelled rock-cut platforms found above the Sasanian city of Bishapur quite likely represent the remains of open-air exposure platforms (Huff 2004, 595–6). Within southern Iran, several different types of rock-cut *dakhma* have been found. The cliffs around Istakhr and Naqsh-i Rustam contain many small carved niches or chamber-*dakhmas* with a groove along the front indicating that they were originally sealed with a single stone slab (Huff 2004, 596–602). A second type which is found in very large numbers on the nearby mountain known as Kuh-i Rahmat consists of a rock-cut trough-*dakhma* which was originally sealed with a long domed stone lid (Huff 2004, 603–8). The lids of several of these have also been found at other sites, notably in the Qazeroun area, and these are engraved with formulaic Pahlavi inscriptions stating that they were constructed as the *dakhmas* for named individuals (Gignoux 1975, 221–4; Nasrollah Zadeh 2007; Tafazzoli 1991; Tafazzoli and Sheikh-al-Hokamayi 1994). A third type was long regarded as evidence for open-air fire altars, but these are simply free-standing *dakhmas* which have lost their domed covers (Huff 2004, 609–18; cf. Stronach 1966). Some of these are in the form of a pillar and their reidentification is confirmed by Pahlavi inscriptions which again refer to them as *dakhmas* and also give the name of the deceased and/or builder and occasionally a date (Huff 1992a; 1998; Frye 1970). All of these *dakhmas* must have been opened in the past and no traces of human remains are preserved.

Elsewhere in Iran, let alone in other parts of the Sasanian Empire, there appears to have been considerable variation in funerary practices, but the extent to which this reflects local custom or different religious faiths is unclear and in very few cases have detailed analyses been carried out on the human remains themselves. Finally, it might be added that the identification of religious practice either from archaeological evidence or the human remains alone is always challenging.

The following paper offers two case studies, one based on 19th-century antiquarian exploration of Sasanian cemeteries on the Bushehr peninsula of the Persian Gulf coast of southern Iran and the second from more recent excavations between 1992 and 2000 at the city site of Merv in present-day Turkmenistan, both formerly within the Sasanian Empire (**Pl. 1**). The human remains from these sites are part of the registered collection in the British Museum and were the subject of a detailed study by Theya Molleson as part of the project to publish and pursue new research questions arising from the Merv excavation project.[1]

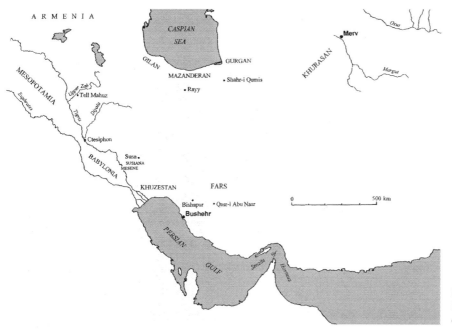

Plate 1 Map showing the location of Bushehr and Merv in relation to selected other Sasanian sites

The archaeological evidence from Bushehr

Bushehr is technically a peninsula, but for much of the year is effectively an island as the landward side of the low rocky outcrop is marshy and prone to regular flooding. An archaeological surface survey carried out in the 1970s prior to the extensive modern urban and industrial sprawl shows that it was densely occupied during the Sasanian period (3rd to 7th centuries AD), with a major settlement located midway along the coast at Rishahr and extensive rural settlement in the hinterland (Whitehouse and Williamson 1973, 36). A total of nine archaeological sites have also provided evidence for the careful disposal of human remains (Simpson 2007a, 153–7; Simpson forthcoming). Broadly datable to the Sasanian period, these remains were found to have been interred in reused and modified pottery jars and purpose-made lidded ossuaries carved from limestone. Most of these sites were discovered in the 19th century, but in recent years further remains have been investigated by the Iranian Cultural Heritage Organisation at the sites of Shoqab, Bahmani and Bagh-e-Zahra, although none have yet been published in detail (Mir Fattah 1374/1996; Curtis and Simpson 1997, 139; Yamauchi 1997, 241–2; Rahbar 2007, 468, figs 19–21; 2008; Tofighian, Nadooshan and Mousavi 2011, 3–4).

Despite periodic flurries of interest throughout the 19th century, relatively little attention has been paid since then to the significance of these finds and one modern writer without access to the original publications went so far as to suggest that the rows of pottery jars were a description of water-channel linings (Whitcomb 1987, 315). Nevertheless, several conclusions can be drawn. The pottery jars were reused as containers for human remains and were modified for this purpose either through being broken in half and secured with metal bands or being cut down at the shoulder and then sealed with an ad hoc lid of pottery or stone (Morier 1818, 44–5; Modi 1889, 3; Rahbar 2008; Tofighian, Nadooshan and Mousavi 2011, 4). The jars were often interred in groups and/or in rows (Alexander 1827, 92; Erskine 1819; Tofighian, Nadooshan and Mousavi 2011, fig.

6), sometimes in proximity to architecture (Modi 1889, 2–3; Rahbar 2008), and in at least two cases were specifically described as being orientated east–west (Johnson 1818, 19; Morier 1818, 44–5; Curzon 1892, vol. II, 235). The jars vary in size, possibly inferring a process of selection for different ages of deceased (Morier 1818, 44–5; Erskine 1819), and human remains previously reported from them include a child, an adult female (Morier 1818, 44–5) and an adult male (Modi 1889, 1–2). Nevertheless, the size of the jars prevented them accepting a fully articulated body, at least that of an adult, and it has generally been accepted that they must contain secondary burials and were places of deposition after burial, exposure or excarnation elsewhere. Where described in the earlier literature, these remains were found disarticulated and the bones contained within a sandy matrix which appears to be different to the surrounding soil (Erskine 1819; Johnson 1818, 19). Although these remains are sometimes described as fragmented and bleached (Erskine 1819), two independent accounts remarked on the quality of the preservation of the teeth (Morier 1818, 44–5; Dickson 1938). The jar burials have been found in proximity to purpose-made lidded limestone ossuaries at three sites (Johnson 1818, 19; Curzon 1892, vol. II, 235; Rahbar 2008). The separate perforated lids of these imply that they were also originally secured (Modi 1889, 1). The remains inside one of these were said to be burnt, but this may be a misidentification based on natural brown staining as will be discussed below (Budge 1920, vol. I, 331) and another was said to contain the remains of a single male individual estimated as about 60 years of age at death, but without the use of modern anthropological methods this estimate is unlikely to have been accurate (Modi 1889, 1–2). Associated finds with any of the interments appear to be scarce, but include beads (Dickson 1938; Rahbar 2008), personal seals (Dickson 1938), a silver crucifix (Rahbar 2008) and occasional coins (Rahbar 2008). Plant seeds were reportedly associated with two of the sites (Ouseley 1819, 215–20, 404, pl. XXIII; Modi 1889, 3); in one case a

Plate 2 Reused torpedo jar ossuary from Sabzabad, 3rd–7th century AD, presented by Captain J.A. Maude, British Museum, London (1823,0614.1 = BM 91952). Munsell pale yellow 5Y 8/2 surfaces with more heavily oxidized fabric; asphalt-lined. Length as preserved 76cm, maximum width 22cm, circular hole 1.5cm across, drilled through the wall at a height of 70cm above the base

Plate 3 Limestone ossuary from Sabzabad, 3rd–7th century AD, presented by Mr T.J. Malcolm, British Museum, London (1888,0714.1 = BM 91933/134691). Length 59.7cm, width 36.6cm, height 24.5cm. Lid length 59.5cm, width 36cm, thickness 3cm

Reanalysing the human remains from Bushehr in the British Museum

There are four complete or semi-complete 'torpedo jars' and two stone ossuaries registered from Bushehr in the British Museum (**Pls 2–3**). Two jars and one stone ossuary are currently on display in galleries 1 (Enlightenment Gallery) and 52 (Rahim Irvani Gallery for Ancient Iran) and both of the stone ossuaries were previously exhibited during the late 19th and early 20th centuries (cf. Simpson 2007a, 156).[2] The jars belong to a well-known class of Mesopotamian transport amphora known as a torpedo jar because of its streamlined shape. There are several different forms and fabrics and, although typically regarded as Sasanian, they date slightly more broadly to span the period between approximately the 2nd and 9th centuries AD, i.e. late Parthian, Sasanian and early Islamic periods (Adams 1965, 132, fig. 14 = Types (k)–(l); 1981, 234; Gibson 1972, 167 = Types K–L; Northedge 1985, 122, 126, fig. 6.2). They are usually lined with asphalt and were probably used for transporting wine (Simpson 2003, 354–5). They were widely distributed in Mesopotamia, most probably through use of the integrated river and canal network, and thence along the Persian Gulf and into the western Indian Ocean as far as Mantai and Anuradhapura in Sri Lanka (Coningham *et al.* 2006, 107–11, fig. 5.2; Tomber 2007) and Qana in Yemen (Salles and Sedov 2010, 42–6, fig. 16: nos 149–55; 154–9, fig. 68: nos 608–11). Rows of them have been observed on the Persian Gulf seabed near the Iranian port of Rig and these clearly belong to the remains of a shipwreck, while additional examples have been dredged up near the Bushehr coastline at Radar and Jalali or excavated at the inland sites of Botol and Bisitun (Tofighian, Nadooshan and Mousavi 2011). Within Arabia they have also been found inland at places such as the silver mines of al-Radrad in the Yemeni highlands (Peli and Téreygeol 2007, 192–3, fig. 4.1–4) and al-Ain oasis in present-day United Arab Emirates (Mouton 2008, fig. 129.4–7). Once empty these jars had limited use and at Coche/Veh Ardashir, they were often reused as drain covers or modified to serve as vertical supports for internal doorposts or low raised benches (Cavallero 1966, 66–7, 78, pl. VI). At many other sites they were used as grave-covers and were laid horizontally, either lengthways above the body or in a transverse row across the backfilled shaft, in both

nearby area of eroding bones was interpreted as a place of open exposure (Modi 1889: 4).

The consensus in 19th-century literature was that these remains from Bushehr belonged to ancient Zoroastrian communities and were assumed to be Sasanian in date (Malcolm 1815, vol. I, 198, n.*; Johnson 1818, 19–20; Curzon 1892, vol. II, 235). Modi (1889) cites K.R. Cama's *Zarthoshti Abhyas [Zoroastrian Studies]* by stating: 'Sir John Malcolm ... brought with him from Persia a jar of this kind, which had some inscriptions on it, and had showed it to the late learned Dustoors Moola Feroze and Edaljee Sanjana. On inquiring from the successors of these learned Dustors, I find that no notes have been left of the decipherment, if any, of these inscriptions' (Modi 1889, 4); this is the only published reference to inscriptions being associated with these ossuaries. Modi went on to draw attention to a passage in the *Vendidad* (VI. 49–51) which stated that the dead ought to be placed in:

> an edifice ... above the reach of a dog, above the reach of a fox, above the reach of a wolf, inaccessible to rain water from above. If the azdayasnans can afford it [they may place the bones] in an *astodan* of stone, or in that of mortar, or in that of an inferior material. If the Mazdayasnans cannot afford to do so, they may place them on their beddings and expose them on the earth to the rays of the sun.

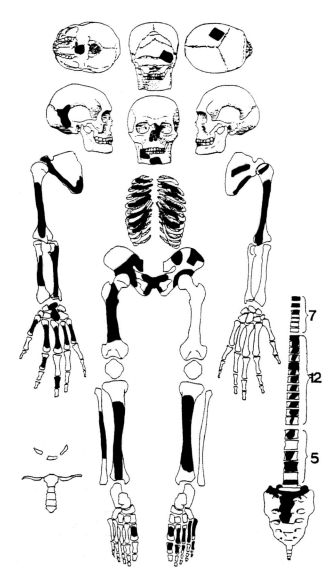

Figure 1 Individual from torpedo jar ossuary from Liyan (BM 91952)

sunlight as recommended in the *Dadistan-i Dilik* (quoted at the start of this chapter) as the holes are not a universal feature and they would otherwise have also admitted water which would not have been acceptable. Incidentally, the shaping marks of an adze are very clear on both the ossuaries and lids in the British Museum.

One of the British Museum torpedo jars (BM 91952) and one of the stone ossuaries (BM 91933) still contained human remains when the present analyses began in 2009, although they are now stored separately for practical and ethical reasons. A detailed taphonomic study of the Bushehr remains has been published elsewhere (Molleson 2009), but is summarized below.

Contents of a torpedo jar ossuary from Liyan (BM 91952)

The associated human remains are fragmented and weathered and belong to a single individual (**Fig. 1**). All parts of the skeleton are represented, although they are incomplete. The bones are not stained and lack surface cracking of sub-aerial weathering, but are extensively damaged from attacks by insects or decay. The skull is represented by a few small fragments that are extremely eroded on the inner surface. The pelvis, which is reasonably complete although fragmented, has a typically female form together with a number of traits that can develop during pregnancy.

The conclusion is that the human remains associated with this jar belong to an adult female who may have undergone pregnancy, was accustomed to carrying loads and was possibly used to working on the ground. The bones are generally fragmented, but do not appear to have been broken up deliberately as often happens with cremations where the bones are subsequently placed in an urn. In support of this argument, the shafts of many of the long bones are fairly complete, measuring up to 190mm in length, although all the ends are damaged. Very few of the cranial bones survive. The few fragments are deeply corroded or etched on the inner surfaces. In some pieces the diploe (the area between the inner and outer surface of the cranial bones) is channelled and tunnelled, presumably by insects and attack by maggots could account for much of the superficial erosion of the bones of both the skull and body. The edges of the ribs have been damaged, especially along the lower border. Some are also penetrated and channelled. Some ribs have a diagenetic crystalline deposit on the ventral ends, possibly where the ribs were in contact with some artefact. The minerals brushite and gypsum will both form within bone in a space consuming way. The inner surfaces of the pelvis are more eroded than the outer surfaces, suggesting that insects were attracted to this area. The long bone ends (epiphyses) have mostly been broken off. The epiphyseal surfaces in general have been preferentially attacked by insects which were able to get to the fat or marrow-rich material within the ends of the big toe bone (first metatarsal).

The widespread evidence for superficial damage to the bones of this individual indicates that the body was not interred beyond the reach of carnivores, but was left exposed on the surface. The evidence is that the most recent stage of

cases probably to deter animals from disturbing the body (e.g. Baqir 1945; al-Haditti 1995, 217–21). It is unsurprising to therefore find evidence from several sites across the Bushehr peninsula for other forms of reuse.

The stone ossuaries belong to a class so far unique to Bushehr and the sizes and shapes of the two examples in the British Museum compare favourably with those described by Modi and more recent authors, and range from 48–60cm in length, 33–6cm in width and 24–7cm in height and the capacities of the two examples in the British Museum are 18,000 and 25,600ml respectively.[3] Each is carved from a single piece of stone, squared off at one end and rounded at the other and has a stepped rim in order to facilitate the secure fitting of a separate flat lid which was carved from the same type of stone. The distinctive shape of the ossuaries resembles the outline of the facades of some of the niche-*dakhmas* found near Istakhr in Fars (cf. Huff 2004, 596–7) and the stepped rim also resembles a feature of the rock-cut trough-*dakhmas* from the same region (cf. Huff 2004, 603), suggesting that there was a connection between these different local traditions.[4] Some lids have a single hole drilled through either end: this was probably in order to secure them tightly rather than as a means of admitting

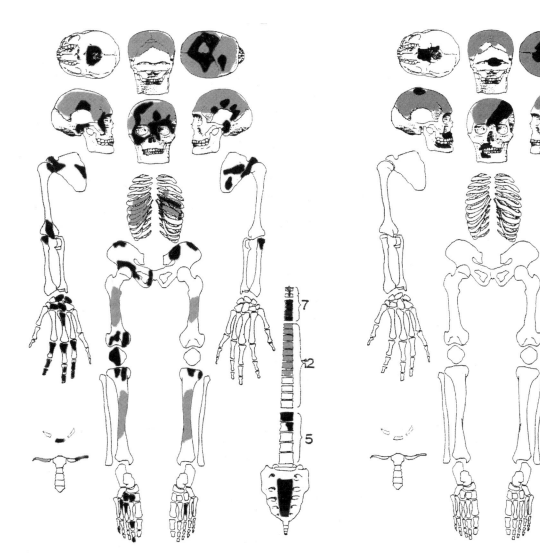

Figure 2 Individual 1 from stone ossuary from Liyan (BM 91933)

Figure 3 Individual 2 from stone ossuary from Liyan (BM 91933)

soft tissue removal was by the maggots of insects. The general loss of ends of the bones, most of the spine and even the left forearm could be due to carnivore scavenging. Any puncture marks are ambivalent: there are two on either side (10.5mm apart) of the little toe bone (fifth metatarsal) and two on the lateral side (38.7mm apart) of the lower leg bone (fibula). No tooth marks were observed which might exclude a dog as the carnivore, but these may not show on human bone that is so weathered. The lack of cracking along the length of the long bone shafts indicates that the bones, although exposed, were sheltered from periodic wetting and drying. Some of the bones (forearm, right pelvis and a few of the ribs) have dark soil staining in patches.

Contents of a stone ossuary from Liyan (BM 91933)

The human remains of this ossuary were contained within a sandy matrix which was otherwise clean and devoid of sediment. They belong to the fragmented and incomplete skeleton of a mature or elderly adult male (Individual 1 = **Fig. 2**) and there was also the isolated cranium of a younger individual (Individual 2 = **Fig. 3**). The limited size range of the cranial fragments of Individual 1 suggests deliberate fragmentation. No cut marks were observed.

The ages at death of the two individuals are quite different. Individual 1 was a mature adult male and the

post-cranial bones have been attributed to this person. All parts of the skeleton are represented. There are some degenerative changes to the vertebrae, notably the fifth bone of the neck, possibly suggesting whiplash strain. There is also some degenerative change to the back and hip joint. The hand bones display a systemic wasting condition, possibly rheumatoid arthritis. The remains of the second individual belong to a late adolescent or young adult and are represented by the cranium and teeth. The bones are not stained except for the jaw fragments. The cranial bones are thick, possibly due to anaemia or other nutritional deficiencies. The teeth show very little wear, suggesting a non-abrasive diet (i.e. of cooked and processed food) and/or a young age.

The bone of Individual 1 has been subjected to exposure and become superficially stained. It has probably not been burnt as the staining does not penetrate the bone. There is possible insect erosion. The superficial weathering and fragmentation of the bones indicate that the body had been exposed on the surface and not buried. The differential survival of bones of the torso and loss of most of the long bones is consistent with scavenging by carrion feeders. The lower border of the mandible ramus is missing. This bone has been typically damaged in this way by canid scavengers (Binford 1981, 63). The bone is too abraded to determine whether there are any tooth marks. The few puncture marks have been noted, but evidence that these may be due to carnivore activity is weak. Some fragments of both skulls have a fine deposit of greenish grey silt that is water laid, but does not extend within the cranium which implies that it may have been complete when it was partially immersed.

Conclusions

The analyses of these human remains from Bushehr are the first to be published. They indicate de-fleshing of the corpses and this is the first occasion that this has been demonstrated archaeologically from Iran. The physical anthropological evidence indicates that the stone ossuary contained the remains of two individuals of different ages, a mature adult male and an adolescent or young adult. The torpedo jar contained the bones of a woman who may have undergone pregnancy. There is no evidence of cut marks on any of the skeletons. All three individuals were exposed to natural decomposition in the open air, hence the indication of fly-laid eggs developing into maggots. However, the local environments were different as the woman was exposed in a dry area, whereas the other two individuals appear to have been subjected to periodic flooding. The dark brown staining noted on many of the bones from the stone ossuary is presumed to be the reason why these remains were initially reported as being cremated, but is more likely to result from discoloration due to wet humic conditions. The repeated deposition of fine grey green sediment on the bones confirms that both sets of remains had been in contact with water. It is uncertain whether this was inside the ossuary after the lid became dislodged, or was prior to being scooped up, but there is evidence for maggot damage on two sets of human remains which is consistent with exposure and the differential preservation of the third set is consistent with scavenging. Decomposition was followed by deliberate fragmentation of the long bones when they were inserted into the relatively short stone ossuaries, but the heights of these seem to have been designed to potentially accommodate a complete cranium as only one of these crania exhibited signs of deliberate breakage. This evidence for deliberate breakage appears to be new in the archaeological record, at least from Iran. However, it is uncertain whether the two sets of human remains were swept up and interred as a single action or whether the second (more complete) set was placed in a reused ossuary which previously only contained the cranium of Individual 2. The fragmentation of bones was not necessary where torpedo jars were used, and the typical removal of the constricted mouth of these jars that is a feature of many of the reported discoveries is best explained by the need to insert complete or semi-complete human crania inside. The bones analysed from within the torpedo jar nevertheless indicate prior exposure and de-fleshing, thus these were also a form of *astodan* or 'bone receptacle', rather than simply representing a novel form of coffin.

It seems unlikely that the place of exposure would have taken place in immediate proximity to settlement, but it need not have been further removed than the equivalent of an extramural cemetery. O'Shea's description (1947, 14) of the situation as late as the 1940s at Sharjah, on the opposite side of the Persian Gulf, offers a possibly equivalent scenario although admittedly in this case of refuse and dead livestock:

> The villages have no drainage or sanitation; garbage and offal are thrown on a heap outside the houses, or on the sea-shore, there to be removed in time by those voracious scavengers, the vultures and kites. It is a common experience to see the carcases of donkeys and other livestock lying on the shore, swollen and covered with flies, decaying under the hot sun. The stench within half a mile ... is simply appalling.

This type of situation was doubtless normal in most ancient societies and archaeological data from a Sasanian residential quarter excavated at Merv confirm the tipping of domestic refuse and coprolites into open drains running between properties. However, larger volumes of refuse were presumably collected and either deposited in municipal dumps or spread as muck on nearby fields (Simpson 2005; 2008).

So who were the individuals placed in these different forms of ossuary? In a few cases, objects have been found associated with the bones inside torpedo jars, although not in the case of those in the British Museum. The addition of objects such as beads, coins, a crucifix and a Sasanian seal bearing Christian iconography in other examples suggest the ancient desire to inter items of personal adornment, currency and evidence of personal ownership or religious belief. The reported occasional presence of coin is particularly evocative as there is archaeological evidence from this period, as well as from more recent periods, for the placing of single coins with inhumation burials as an eastern equivalent of the classical Greek custom of offering payment for services in the afterlife (e.g. Burney 1970, 169, pl. VIII.a; see also Simpson 1995, 245–6). However, as the jar burials were secondary rather than primary, the grave-goods may have been selected by relatives, local communities or professional mourners rather than being the personal possessions of the deceased and in no case is the reported context very specific.

The evidence from Merv

The site of Merv is located in the oasis of the same name in southern Turkmenistan, which was created by the delta of the river Murghab as it fans northwards from Afghanistan before draining into the sands of the Karakum desert. In antiquity it was a major frontier gateway controlling movement both along the Murghab to and from north-west Afghanistan and between north-east Iran and Transoxiana. Moreover, the oasis was extremely fertile and supported a large population and thriving agricultural economy (Simpson *et al.* forthcoming). Consequently, Merv was considered an important part of the region of Khurasan during the period of the Sasanian Empire and the sequence of coins struck and found at Merv proves that its mint functioned continuously throughout the 400 year period of the empire (Loginov and Nikitin 1993).

The city has attracted archaeological attention for over 120 years and between 1992 and 2000 the British Museum was part of a joint project with UCL and the former Academy of Sciences of Turkmenistan to explore the site. Human remains were identified in three areas of the city.

Plate 4 Human remains as discovered during excavations in Gyaur Kala Trench 6 at Merv

Plate 5 Human remains as discovered during excavations in Gyaur Kala Trench 6 at Merv

In two cases, these were isolated stray finds found in infilling contexts and therefore represent redeposited remains, possibly of considerably older age than the 4th to 5th and 6th to early 7th-century AD occupation deposits under investigation. The third area was a section through the fortifications next to the south-west corner bastion of the city (Zavyalov 2007). The fourth major phase of these regularly rebuilt massive defences consisted of a hollow curtain with two levels of galleries raised on a solid platform with a low outer wall (*proteichisma*). This phase is provisionally dated to the Middle Parthian period on the basis of two Parthian-Margiana coins of the late 1st century BC or 1st century AD which were found between bricks. Subsequently, these defences underwent serious reconstruction. The arrow-slits of the lower gallery were blocked and the gallery itself was filled with very clean compacted sand. The *proteichisma* was cut down and a sloping berm constructed over its remains which sealed the blocked arrow-slits. The top of the berm was aligned with the bottom of the upper gallery proving that the actions were directly connected. Coins stratified within deposits inside the upper gallery belong to Shapur II (309–79) and Varahran IV (388–9) or Kavad (488–531). Although these dates are not yet confirmed by radiocarbon, they are sufficient to suggest that any finds made within the infilled lower gallery of the Phase 3 wall date to the early Sasanian period. There were no artefacts found in this gallery and the floor had been kept very clean. The surprising discovery was that of several concentrations of isolated and disarticulated human remains midway up the sandy infilling (**Pls 4–5**). These remains were exported with permission and after cleaning under the supervision of Professor Simon Hillson at the Institute of Archaeology (UCL) were transferred back to the British Museum where they were analysed by Theya Molleson. The section which follows is based on her contribution to the final report (Molleson forthcoming).

The human remains from the fortifications

The first set of remains consists of the partial skeleton of a young child, probably aged three to four years judging by the dental development (The London Atlas 2008). The bones are in good condition and the skull is almost complete (**Fig. 4**). The only long bone – the thigh bone – was incomplete and it is not possible to estimate the original stature of the individual. There is loss of enamel on the lower right deciduous molars with distortion and discoloration of the underlying dentine which might be the result of trauma or an enamel dysplasia. There are several indications of deficiency conditions on the cranium and jaw bone. The thigh bone is bowed possibly due to rickets. Rickets can develop temporally in children who learn to walk in the spring months after a hard winter lacking in exposure to sunlight, especially where the weaning food is cereal based.

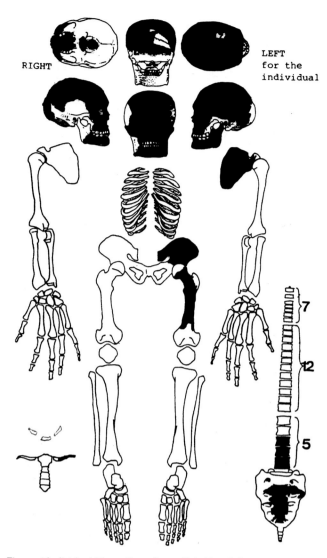

RIGHT

LEFT
for the
individual

Figure 4 Individual 1 from Merv, Gyaur Kala Trench 6

A child of the age indicated by the dental development would normally be weaned, while the lack of wear on the teeth indicates a soft diet such as cooked cereal. None of the deficiency conditions would have been life threatening, but could have lowered the child's resistance to many pathogens.

The second individual was an adult male, represented by a nearly intact cranium (**Fig. 5**). The bones of the face were broken probably post-mortem and there is further damage to the base of the skull. These two areas of damage are not new and could be associated with the deliberate removal of the head. There is a small impact perforation on the back of the upper jaw. Dental attrition is extreme but probably not indicative of age; it is greater than would be developed by normal dietary chewing. Pitting of the palate is likely to be an inflammatory response to the infections of the incisor and molars. The bone around the posterior part of the cranial base has a rough surface, a failure of the bone to grow which may be due to Vitamin A deficiency during childhood (Barnicot 1950; Barasi and Mottram 1987, 78; See *et al.* 2008).

The third individual was a young adult and represented by the cranium, left clavicle and some limb bones (**Fig. 6**). Dentition indicates an age of around 19 to 20 years (The London Atlas). The cranial bones are fragile and lightly stained to a dark pink appearance on the inside. The left side is almost intact; the right has broken into large pieces. The

mandible is in two halves but complete. The long bones of the arms and lower limbs all lack articular ends.

Conclusions

The combination of secure archaeological context, reasonably good dating and physical anthropological analysis of the human remains underline the significance of this data set. The remains belong to three individuals of different ages whose bodies had been placed elsewhere prior to the careful gathering of the disarticulated remains and reinterring them in a new location which was well drained and considered to be free of further disturbance. The sandy deposit in which they were found was completely devoid of other finds and had been deliberately brought in for the purpose of infilling, and it seems most unlikely that the human remains were originally buried in this sand and brought there by accident. The time and choice of place of burial was closely tied to a rebuilding of the urban defences. The choice of such a spot is not as strange as it might first appear and a closely parallel situation from Shahr-i Qumis is discussed below.

General discussion: an insight into funerary practices

The archaeological evidence indicates a Sasanian date for both data sets discussed here. Despite their widely separated locations at almost opposite ends of the Sasanian Empire and the very different circumstances of interment and recovery, they offer important clues into funerary practices of this period.

The evidence discussed above from Bushehr and Merv suggest local solutions. The presence of multiple clusters of jar and stone ossuaries across the Bushehr peninsula is consistent with the archaeological survey evidence that indicates a high density of Sasanian settlement, with the discovery of more than one disarticulated individual in one of the jar ossuaries suggesting that bones were gathered at intervals for ritual reinterment within sealed containers. Whether these individual ossuaries belonged to particular families is unknown. The choice of stone or pottery may have been an economic one, but the capacity of the stone ossuaries was smaller and more suited as the receptacle for the bones of a single individual.

Theya Molleson's analysis of the human remains from Bushehr strongly suggests that the place of exposure was one in the open air and in one case was periodically liable to waterlogging: whereas the former is to be expected, the latter is at odds with strict Zoroastrian belief. One possibility is that this reflects an unusual unexpected event of localized flooding, as areas of the peninsula are liable to, and the place of exposure was perhaps a fenced or walled open-air liminal zone beyond the main area(s) of settlement or farming. This raises a possible solution as to the location and management of Zoroastrian places of exposure in other densely occupied regions such as southern Iraq or the Merv oasis. Tells offer naturally well-drained locations of low agricultural worth which were, and still are, popular places of interment across the Middle East. In the case of the city of Veh Ardashir, opposite Ctesiphon in present-day southern Iraq, it seems likely that the neighbouring site of Seleucia, then known as *deserta civitas* or 'Sliq Kharawta' ('Deserted Seleucia'), offered

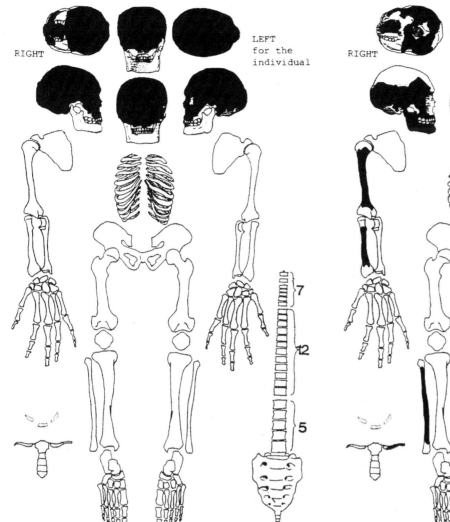

Figure 5 Individual 2 from Merv, Gyaur Kala Trench 6

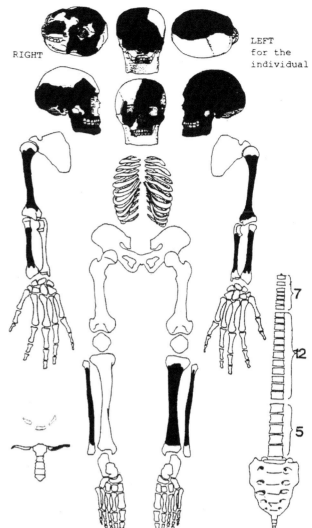

Figure 6 Individual 3 from Merv, Gyaur Kala Trench 6

a convenient place of extramural burial and open body exposure; it was used as a place of public execution between 342 and 484 AD, a martyrion is attested from the early 5th century AD and finds of magic bowls and jars containing lead scrolls are consistent with finds at other sites or places believed to have been haunted (Fiey 1967, 8–9).

The human remains found during the excavations of the fortifications at Merv are less conclusive, but clearly show that a decision was made that when the galleries of the former Parthian curtain wall were no longer fit for purpose and infilled prior to the construction of a new curtain wall, clean sand was brought in. This was probably primarily to ensure a solid secure foundation for the reconstruction of the upper defences, but the choice of sand over mudbrick or recycled refuse may have had a symbolic significance. At the same time, this spot was selected as a suitable place for the deliberate placing of bundles of disarticulated human remains belonging to several individuals of different ages and genders. This was clearly part of a decision-making process and not a random act. Nor is this consistent with a sudden response to a disaster, whether natural or military, and instead appears to reflect a view that the sandy matrix within the old walls would provide a dry environment protected from the elements and future disturbance. An identical situation was found at Shahr-i Qumis where the

excavators found the highly fragmented remains (two ribs, five vertebrae, four teeth, two small pieces of cranium and some 140 assorted bone fragments) of what appeared to be a single individual wrapped in pieces of cloth within a leather bag which was placed on a felt rug together with offerings 'including a pomegranate, almonds, feathers, plant material, a coin, a knife and horse remains' (Hansman and Stronach 1970). No evidence was found that might indicate how or where the bones came to be de-fleshed, but the fact that they were gathered up with a long bone, hoof, teeth and lower mandible of a horse and additional donkey teeth suggest that they may have been exposed in proximity to other large carcasses. Normal household refuse was thrown out in the streets, but the urban management of the equivalent of municipal tips at cities such as this is clear from repeated references in the Babylonian Talmud and is supported by other archaeological evidence (Simpson 2005).

The implication of these analyses is that it is possible to demonstrate a relationship between the archaeological context and the method of disposal. In both cases they are best explained as local responses to the need to carefully gather and inter remains which had been previously exposed and/or fragmented. The conclusion is that both data sets belonged to Zoroastrian communities and that the local definition of an *astodan* could vary from reuse of a much older building, whereby the human remains were effectively interred within a hidden vault (as at Merv and Shahr-i Qumis) to being placed in a reused pottery or purpose-made stone container which was then interred in the ground, but protected from contaminating the earth or conversely from further decay by the elements. The burial rite appears to be the same for children, men and women alike.

Notes

1   The authors are grateful to Dr R. Boucharlat and I. Smith respectively for their comments on the archaeological and taphonomic aspects of this paper. All faults and interpretations remain the responsibility of the authors.
2   In the previous literature one of the stone ossuaries was said to come from Susa but, in the absence of any others found at that site, it seems more likely that this is erroneous and that it was found at Bushehr.
3   The capacities of these were measured by means of refilling them with inert plastic packaging chips and builds on earlier use by one of the authors (Simpson) of glass micro-balloons for the accurate measurement of the capacities of pottery, metal and glass vessels.
4   I am very grateful to Dr M. Farjamirad for these insightful observations.

Bibliography

Adams, R.McC., 1965. *Land Behind Baghdad. A History of Settlement on the Diyala Plains.* Chicago.
—, 1981. *Heartland of Cities. Surveys of Ancient Settlement and Land Use on the Central Floodplain of the Euphrates.* Chicago.
Akira, H., 1981. 'Dailaman and Shahpir. Re-examination of their chronology', *Bulletin of the Ancient Orient Museum* 3, 43–61.
Alexander, J.E., 1827. *Travels from India to England: Comprehending a Visit to the Burman Empire, and a Journey through Persia, Asia Minor, European Turkey, &c. In the Years 1825–26.* London.
Andersen, S.F., 2007. *The Tylos Period Burials in Bahrain. Volume 1. The Glass and Pottery Vessels.* Manama and Moesgård.
Azarpay, G., 1981. 'Cairns, *kurums,* and *dambs.* A note on pre-Islamic surface burials in eastern Iran and central Asia', *Acta Iranica* 21 [= 2nd series VIII], 12–21, pls III–XII.
Balcer, J.M., 1978. 'Parthian and Sasanian coins and burials (1976) [at Tal-i Malyan]', *Iran* 16, 86–92, pls. 1–2.
Baqir, T., 1945. ''Iraq government excavations at 'Aqar Quf. Second interim report 1943–1944', *Iraq Supplement.*
Barasi, M.E. and Mottram, R.F., 1987. *Human Nutrition.* London (4th edn).
Barnicot, N.A., 1950. 'The local action of vitamin A on bone', *Journal of Anatomy* 84, 374–87.
Binford, L.R., 1981. *Bones, Ancient Men and Modern Myths.* New York.
Bivar, A.D.H., 1970. 'Appendix: The Sasanian coin from Qūmis', *The Journal of the Royal Asiatic Society of Great Britain and Ireland* 1970/2, 156–8.
Boucharlat, R., 1989. 'Cairns et pseudo-cairns du Fars. L'utilisation des tombes de surface au 1er millénaire de notre ère', in *Archaeologica Iranica et Orientalis. Miscellanea in honorem Louis Vanden Berghe,* ed. E. Haerinck and L. de Meyer, 675–712. Gent.
—, 1991. 'Pratiques funéraires a l'époque sasanide dans le sud de l'Iran', in *Histoire et cultes dans l'Asie centrale préislamique,* ed. P. Bernard and F. Grenet, 71–8, pls XXII–XXV. Paris.
Boyce, M., 1987. *Zoroastrians. Their Religious Beliefs and Practices.* London and New York (reprint).
Budge, E.A.W., 1920. *By Nile and Tigris. A Narrative of Journeys in Egypt and Mesopotamia on behalf of the British Museum between the years 1886 and 1913,* 2 vols. London.
Burney, C.A., 1970. 'Excavations at Haftavan Tepe 1968: first preliminary report', *Iran* 8, 157–71, pls I–VIII.
—, 1973. 'Excavations at Haftavan Tepe 1971: third preliminary report', *Iran* 11, 153–72, pls I–VIII.
CAIS Archaeological News 2007. '3rd century Sasanian woman diagnosed with syphilis', http://www.cais-soas.com/NewsUpdate.htm [accessed 15 January 2007].
— 2008. 'Discovery of a new Sasanian burial method in Pahlauj', http://www.cais-soas.com/NewsUpdate.htm [accessed 21 September 2008].
Casartelli, I.C., 1890. 'Astodans, and Avestic funeral prescriptions', *The Babylonian and Oriental Record* IV/VII (June), 145–52.
Cavallero, M., 1966. 'The excavations at Choche (presumed Ctesiphon) – Area 2', *Mesopotamia* 1, 63–81, figs 16–25, pls V–X.
Coningham, R. et al., 2006. *Anuradhapura. The British-Sri Lankan Excavations at Anuradhapura Salgaha Watta 2. Volume II: The Artefacts.* Oxford – BAR International Series 1508 = Society for South Asian Studies Monograph 4.
Cribb, J. and Herrmann, G. 2007 (eds). *After Alexander: Central Asia before Islam.* London: Proceedings of the British Academy 133.
Curtis, V.S. and Simpson, St J., 1997. 'Archaeological news from Iran', *Iran* 35, 137–44.
Curzon, G.N., 1892. *Persia and the Persian Question,* 2 vols. London.
Dickson, V., 1938. Unpublished letter dated 31 October, addressed to Sidney Smith. British Museum, Department of the Middle East (1938 Correspondence, q.v. Dickson).
Dupree, L., 1958. *Shamshir Ghar: Historic Cave Site in Kandahar Province, Afghanistan.* New York: The American Museum of Natural History, Anthropological Paper 46/2.
Ehrich, R.W., 1939. 'The later cultures at Yorgan Tepa', in *Nuzi,* ed. R.F.S. Starr et al., vol. I, appendix E: 545–69. Cambridge, MA.
Erskine, W., 1819. 'Observations on two sepulchral urns found at Bushire in Persia', *Transactions of the Literary Society of Bombay* I, 191–7.
Fiey, J.-M., 1967. 'Topography of Al-Mada'in (Seleucia–Ctesiphon area)', *Sumer* 23, 3–38.
Frye, R.N., 1970. 'Funerary inscriptions in Pahlavi from Fars', in *W.B. Henning Memorial Volume,* ed. M. Boyce and I. Gershevitch, 152–6. London.
Ghasemi, P., 2012. 'Tal-e Khandagh ("moated mounds") – military structures in ancient Fars', *Near Eastern Archaeology* 75/4, 240–51.
Gibson, McG., 1972. *The City and Area of Kish.* Coconut Grove [Miami].
— (ed.), 1981. *Uch Tepe. Tell Razuk, Tell Ahmed al-Mughir, Tell Ajamat.* Chicago.
Gignoux, P., 1975. 'Notes d'épigraphie et d'histoire sassanides', in *Mélanges linguistiques offerts à Émile Benveniste,* 213–24. Paris.
—, 2008. 'Le site de Bandiān revisité', *Studia Iranica* 37, 163–74.
Gotch, P., 1972. 'New light on rock-carved monuments at Naqsh-i Rustam and Istakhr', *Summaries of Papers to be delivered at The Sixth International Congress of Iranian Art and Archaeology, Oxford, 10th–16th September 1972* (Organizing Committee of the Sixth International Congress of Iranian Art and Archaeology, ed.), 27–8. Oxford.
Gotch, A., Simpson, St J. and Taylor, H., forthcoming. *Mapping the Marv Dasht: A Personal Account, Diary and the Archive of an Archaeological Surface Survey carried out by Paul Gotch in Southern Iran.* Oxford.
Grenet, F., 1984. *Les pratiques funéraires dans l'Asie centrale sédentaire de la conquête grecque à l'islamisation.* Paris: Publications de l'URA, Mémoire 1.
Gropp, G. and Nadjmabadi, S., 1970. 'Bericht über eine reise in west- und südiran', *Archaeologische Mitteilungen aus Iran* (N. F.) 3, 173–230, pls 78–109.
al-Haditti, A-M.M.A.R., 1995. 'Umm Keshm – summary report', *Mesopotamia* 30, 217–39.
Hansman, J. and Stronach, D., 1970. 'A Sasanian repository at Shahr-i Qumis', *Journal of the Royal Asiatic Society,* 142–55, pls I–IV.
Huff, D., 1988. 'Zum Problem zoroastrischer Grabanlagen in Fars. I. Gräber', *Archaeologische Mitteilungen aus Iran* 21, 145–76, pls 44–55.
—, 1991. 'Observations at minor monuments in the Persepolis area (summary)', *Mésopotamie et Elam. Actes de la XXXVIème Rencontre Assyriologique Internationale, Gand, 10–14 juillet 1989,* 197–200. Gent: Mesopotamian History and Environment, Occasional Publication I.
—, 1992a. 'Zum Problem zoroastrischer Grabanlagen in Fars. II. Das Saülenmonument von Pengan', *Archaeologische Mitteilungen aus Iran* 25, 207–17, pls 48–51.
—, 1992b. 'Nachtrag zur zoroastrischen Grabarchitektur in der Persis: die sogenannten Feuerlöcher', *Koldewey-Gesellschaft* 31–3. Berlin.
—, 1998. '"Fire altars" and *astodans*', in *The Art and Archaeology of Ancient Persia. New Light on the Parthian and Sasanian Empires,* ed. V. Sarkhosh Curtis, R. Hillenbrand and J.M. Rogers, 74–83, pls VIII–X. London.

—, 2004. 'Archaeological evidence of Zoroastrian funerary practices', in *Zoroastrian Rituals in Context*, ed. M. Stausberg, 593–630. Leiden.

Insoll, T., 1999. *The Archaeology of Islam*. Cambridge.

Johnson, J., 1818. *A Journey from India to England, through Persia, Georgia, Russia, Poland, and Prussia, in the year 1817*. London.

Kamada, H. and Ohtsu, T., 1988. 'Report on the excavations at Songor A – Isin-Larsa, Sasanian and Islamic graves', *Al-Rafidan* 9, 135–72, pls 39–54.

Kästner J.-M., 1987. 'Circular tomb SH 100', in *Shimal 1985/1986. Excavations of the German Archaeological Mission in Ras Al-Khaimah, U.A.E. A Preliminary Report*, ed. B. Vogt and U. Franke-Vogt, 45–8, figs 29–30. Berlin.

King, G.R., 2001. 'The coming of Islam and the Islamic period in the UAE', in *The United Arab Emirates: A New Perspective*, ed. I. Al Abed and P. Hellyer, 70–97. London.

Lamberg-Karlovsky, C.C., 1972. 'The cairn burials of south-eastern Iran', *The Memorial Volume of the Vth International Congress of Iranian Art & Archaeology, Tehran–Isfahan–Shiraz, 11th–18th April 1968*, vol. I, 102–10. Tehran.

— and Humphries, J.H., 1968. 'The cairn burials of southeastern Iran', *East and West* 18/3–4, 269–76.

Loginov, S.D. and Nikitin, A.B., 1993. 'Sasanian coins of the late 4th–7th centuries from Merv', *Mesopotamia* 28, 271–312.

McNicoll, A., 1996. 'Site H: The Achaemenid building', in *Excavations at Old Kandahar 1974 and 1975. The First Two Seasons at Shahr-i Kohna (Old Kandahar) Conducted by the British Institute of Afghan Studies*, ed. A. McNicoll and W. Ball *et al.*, 233–61. Oxford: BAR International Series 641; Society for South Asian Studies Monograph No 1.

Malcolm, Colonel Sir John, 1815. *The History of Persia from the Most Early Period to the Present Time: Containing an Account of the Religion, Government, Usages, and Character of the Inhabitants of that Kingdom*, 2 vols. London.

Meitarchiyan, M., 1990. 'The funeral rites of the Iranian Zoroastrians in the modern period', *IASCCA Information Bulletin* 17, 139–53.

Mir Fattah, Seyyed Ali Asghar, 1374/1996. 'Gurastan-i Shuqab 'arzeh dashtan dar havay-i azad va dafn beh shiveh-yi ustukhandan [The necropolis of Shuqab: practices of exposure with ossuaries]', *Athar* 25, 41–61.

Modi, J.J., 1889. *Astodan, or A Persian Coffin said to be 3,000 years old, sent to the Museum of the Anthropological Society of Bombay, by Mr. Malcolm, of Bushire*. Bombay.

Molleson, T., 2009. 'Two Sasanian ossuaries from Bushehr, Iran. Evidence for exposure of the dead', *Bioarchaeology of the Near East* 3, 1–16.

—, forthcoming. 'The human remains', in *The Fortifications and Urban Development of Gyaur-Kala (Ancient Merv)*, ed. St J. Simpson *et al.* Louvain.

Morier, J., 1818. *A Second Journey through Persia, Armenia, and Asia Minor, to Constantinople, between the years 1810 and 1816*. London.

Mouton, M., 2008. *La Péninsule d'Oman de la fin de l'Age du Fer au début de la période sassanide (250 av. – 350 ap. JC)*. Oxford: BAR International Series 1776 = Society for Arabian Studies Monograph 6.

Nasrollah Zadeh, S., 2007. *Pahlavi Inscriptions of Kazeroun* [in Persian]. Tehran.

Negro Ponzi, M.M., 1968/9. 'Sasanian glassware from Tell Mahuz (North Mesopotamia)', *Mesopotamia* 3/4, 293–384, figs 153–61, appendices A–G.

—, 2005. 'Mesopotamian glassware of the Parthian and Sasanian period: some notes', *Annales du 16e Congrès de l'Association Internationale pour l'Histoire du Verre (London 2003)*, 141–5. Nottingham.

Northedge, A., 1985. 'Planning Samarra: a report for 1983–4', *Iraq* 47, 109–28, pls XVI–XIX.

O'Shea, R., 1947. *The Sand Kings of Oman, being the experiences of an R.A.F. Officer in the Little Known Regions of Trucial Oman Arabia*. London.

Omrani Rekavandi, H., Sauer, E. and Wilkinson, T. *et al.*, 2008. 'Sasanian walls, hinterland fortresses and abandoned ancient irrigated landscapes: the 2007 season on the Great Wall of Gorgan and the Wall of Tammishe', *Iran* 46, 151–78.

Ouseley, Sir William, 1819/23. *Travels in Various Countries of the East; more particularly Persia* (3 vols, 1819: vol. I, 1821: vol. II, 1823: vol. III). London.

Peli, A. and Téreygeol, F., 2007. 'Al-Radrād (al-Jabalī): a Yemeni silver mine, first results of the French mission (2006)', *Proceedings of the Seminar for Arabian Studies* 37, 187–200.

Potts, D.T., 1997. 'Late Sasanian armament from southern Arabia', *Electrum* 1, 127–37 [reprinted as Article XVIII in D.T. Potts, *Mesopotamia, Iran and Arabia from the Seleucids to the Sasanians*, Farnham: 2010; Variorum Collected Studies Series CS962].

Rahbar, M., 2004. 'Le monument sassanide de Bandiān, Dargaz: un temple du feu d'après les dernières découvertes 1996–98', *Studia Iranica* 33/1, 7–30.

—, 2007. 'A Tower of Silence of the Sasanian period at Bandiyan: some observations about *dakhmas* in Zoroastrian religion', in Cribb and Herrmann 2007, 455–73.

—, 2008. 'A new glimpse at Zoroastrians' beliefs on burial practice based on excavations at Shaghab'. Unpublished lecture given at international workshop on 'The Persian Gulf in Prehistory and History', sponsored by the Iranian Cultural Heritage, Handicraft and Tourism Organisation, the British Institute of Persian Studies and Durham University, 1–2 July 2008.

Roaf, M., 1984. 'Excavations at Tell Mohammed 'Arab in the Eski Mosul Dam Salvage Project', *Iraq* 46, 141–56, pls X–XIII.

Salles, J.-F. and Sedov, A.V., 2010. *Qāni'. Le port antique du Hadramawt entre la Méditerranée, l'Afrique et l'Inde. Fouilles Russes 1972, 1985–89, 1991, 1993–94. Preliminary reports of the Russian Archaeological Mission to the Republic of Yemen*. Brepols.

See, A.W., Kaiser, M.E., White, J.C. and Clagett-Dame, M., 2008. 'A nutritional model of late embryonic vitamin A deficiency produces defects in organogenesis at a high penetrance and reveals new roles for the vitamin in skeletal development', *Dev Biol.*, 316(2), 171–90.

Shaffer, J.G. and Hoffman, M.A., 1976. 'Kinship and burial among Kushano-Sasanians: a preliminary assessment', *East and West* 26/1–2 (March–June), 133–52.

al-Shams, M.A., 1987/88. 'The excavations of the Hira cemetery', *Sumer* 45, 42–56 [Arabic section].

Simon, C., 1989. 'La tombe à incineration (tombe 1, locus 21)', *Northern Akkad Project Reports* 2, 54–6.

Simpson, St J., 1987. 'Umm Kheshm', *Iraq* 49, 250–1.

—, 1995. 'Death and burial in the late Islamic Near East: some insights from archaeology and ethnography', in *The Archaeology of Death in the Ancient Near East*, ed. S. Campbell and A. Green, 240–51. Oxford.

—, 1998. 'Gilt-silver and clay: a Late Sasanian skeuomorphic pitcher from Iran', in *Entlang der Seidenstrasse: Fruhmittelalterliche Kunst zwischen Persien und China in der Abegg-Stiftung*, ed. K. Otavsky, 335–42. Riggisberg.

—, 2003. 'From Mesopotamia to Merv: reconstructing patterns of consumption in Sasanian households', in *Culture through Objects: Ancient Near Eastern Studies in Honour of P.R.S. Moorey*, ed. T. Potts, M. Roaf and D. Stein, 347–75. Oxford.

—, 2005. 'Glass and small finds from Sasanian contexts at the ancient city-site of Merv: understanding patterns of circulation and retrieval of ancient material culture at a multi-period mudbrick site', in *Central Asia from the Achaemenids to the Timurids: Archaeology, History, Ethnology, Culture. Papers from an International Scientific Conference dedicated to the Centenary of Alexander Markovich Belenitsky, St. Petersburg, 2–5 November 2004*, ed. V.P. Nikonorov, 232–8. St Petersburg: Institute of the History of Material Culture of the Russian Academy of Sciences / State Hermitage / Oriental Department of the St Petersburg State University.

—, 2007a. 'Bushire and beyond: some early archaeological discoveries in Iran', in *From Persepolis to the Punjab: Exploring Ancient Iran, Afghanistan and Pakistan*, ed. E. Errington and V.S. Curtis, 153–65. London.

—, 2007b. *Excavations at Tell Abu Dhahir*. Oxford.

—, 2008. 'Suburb or slum? Excavations at Merv (Turkmenistan) and observations on stratigraphy, refuse and material culture in a Sasanian city', in *Recent Advances in Sasanian Archaeology and History*, ed. D. Kennet and P. Luft, 65–78. Oxford.

—, forthcoming. 'Sasanian funerary practices on Bushehr: a review of the archaeological evidence', *Bulletin of the Asia Institute* (N.S.).

Simpson, St J. *et al.*, forthcoming. *The Fortifications and Urban Development of Gyaur-Kala (Ancient Merv)*. Louvain.

Sono, T. and Fukai, S., 1968. *Dailaman III. Excavations at Hassani Mahale and Ghalekuti 1964*. Tokyo, The Institute of Oriental Culture, The University of Tokyo; The Tokyo University Iraq–Iran Archaeological Expedition, Report 8.

Stavisky, B.J., 1988. 'Kara-Tepe in Old Termez (Southern Uzbekistan). Summary of the work done in 1978–1982', in *Orientalia Iosephi Tucci Memoriae Dicata*, ed. G. Gnoli and L. Lanciotti, 1391–1405. Rome: Istituto Italiano per il Medio ed Estremo Oriente; Serie Orientale Roma LVI, 3.

Stein, A., 1936. 'An archaeological tour in the ancient Persis', *Iraq* 3, 111–225, pls I–XXX.

—, 1937. *Archaeological Reconnaissances in North-western India and South-eastern Iran*. London.

Steve, M.-J. et al., 2003. *L'Île de Khārg. Une page de l'histoire du Golfe Persique et du Monachisme Oriental*. Neuchâtel.

Stronach, D., 1966. 'The Kūh-i-Shahrak fire altar', *Journal of Near Eastern Studies* 25/4 (October), 217–27.

—, 1978. *Pasargadae*. Oxford.

Tafazzoli, A., 1991. 'L'inscription funéraire de Kāzerun II (Parišān)', *Studia Iranica* 20, 197–202.

— and Sheikh-al-Hokamayi, E., 1994. 'The Pahlavi funerary inscription from Mashtān (Kāzerun III)', *Archaeologische Mitteilungen aus Iran* 27, 165–7, pl. 58.1.

Tofighian, H., Nadooshan, F.K. and Mousavi, S.M., 2011. 'Sasanians in the Persian Gulf According to Archaeological Data', *e-Sasanika Archaeology* 2 [accessed October 2012].

Tomber, R., 2007. 'Rome and Mesopotamia – importers into India in the first millennium AD', *Antiquity* 81, 972–88.

Trümpelmann, L., 1984. 'Sasanian graves and burial customs', in *Arabie orientale, Mesopotamie et Iran méridionale de l'Age du fer au début de la période islamique*, ed. R. Boucharlat and J-F. Salles, 317–29. Paris.

Turgunov, B., 2006. 'The early medieval burial ground on the Dalverzin's city wall', *Bulletin of the Ancient Orient Museum* 26, 55–65.

Whitcomb, D.S., 1985. *Before the Roses and Nightingales. Excavations at Qasr-i Abu Nasr, Old Shīrāz*. New York.

—, 1987. 'Bushire and the Angali Canal', *Mesopotamia* 22, 311–36.

Whitehouse, D. and Williamson, A., 1973. 'Sasanian maritime trade', *Iran* 11, 29–49.

Yamauchi, K., 1997. 'New discoveries of Iranian archaeology (2)', *Bulletin of the Ancient Orient Museum* 18, 233–57.

Zarins J., al-Mughannam A.S. and Kamal, M., 1984. 'Excavations at Dhahran South – the tumuli field (208–92), 1403 AH/1983. A Preliminary Report', *Atlal* 8, 25–54, pls 18–59.

Zavyalov, V.A., 2007. 'The fortifications of the city of Gyaur Kala, Merv', in Cribb and Herrmann 2007, 313–29.

Chapter 8
Beneath the Surface
Imaging Techniques and the Jericho Skull

Alexandra Fletcher, Jessica Pearson, Theya Molleson, Richard Abel, Janet Ambers and Crispin Wiles

The Jericho skull in the British Museum collection (BM 127414) is one of seven Neolithic plastered human skulls found by Kathleen Kenyon at Jericho in 1953 (Kenyon 1953, 83–7, pls XXXVI–XXXVII). The site of ancient Jericho, a mound which lies about 2km to the north-west of the modern town in the State of Palestine, was excavated by Kathleen Kenyon on behalf of the British School of Archaeology in Jerusalem from 1952 to 1958. Her work at the site was pivotal to the study of the Neolithic and Bronze Age in the Middle East. The skull occupies a position of relative isolation within the Middle Eastern department at the British Museum, being much older in date than most of the collection. It has also been separated from the other skulls it was placed in the cache with, which were subsequently distributed among other institutions (see **Table 1** for the present location of the other skulls). It is nevertheless important as archaeologists have long considered 'Skull Cult' (a range of mortuary rituals involving removal, decoration and caching of skulls) to be a key component in understanding the mortuary and social practices of the Neolithic period (Kuijt 1995; Goring-Morris 2000, 124–5; Croucher 2012, 97–8). Artificial cranial modification (the permanent alteration of a skull's shape by intentionally moulding growth in early childhood) has also been linked to cultic activities. Identifying and investigating such practices through modified human remains is challenging, as often the decoration obscures areas of the skull that would otherwise be observed and the whole cannot be split into constituent parts (plaster, human remains and shell) simply to make the analytical process more convenient. Non-invasive radiographic imaging techniques are therefore vital for capturing the internal structure of rare and valuable cultural artefacts such as the Jericho Skull (Abel et al. 2011). The most relevant of these techniques are micro-CT scanners and associated software which can be used to create 3D computer models for virtual dissection of tissues and/or anatomical features (see Abel et al. 2012).

Archaeological and cultural context of the Jericho skull

The Jericho skull was deposited in a cache during the Middle Pre-pottery Neolithic B (c. 10100–9250 calibrated ^{14}C years BP) (Kenyon 1953, 84). The skulls appear to have been deposited in no particular order and this was interpreted as a careless form of disposal, as other skull caches recovered at Jericho showed deliberate arrangement in lines or circles (Kurth and Röhrer-Ertl 1981, 436; Kenyon 1956, 75, pl. XIII.). It was originally suggested that the cache represents the disposal of cultic equipment at the end of its useful life (Kenyon and Holland 1981, 77), as has been suggested for other Pre-pottery Neolithic B (PPNB) ritual objects, such as plaster statues (Garfinkel 1994; Simmons et al. 1990, 109). There is little evidence, however, that the burial of plastered skulls at Jericho was entirely associated with the disposal of waste. The skulls within the cache were in remarkably good condition and arguably, like other more structured burials, the cache formed a symbolic expression of a community's beliefs and values (Kuijt 2000b, 148).

The PPNB period saw significant changes in the lifestyles of the inhabitants of the Levant (modern Syria, Lebanon and Jordan) with a marked population increase and

Excavation number (Kenyon and Holland 1981)	Location	Accession number
D110	Jordan Archaeological Museum, Amman	J5756
D111	Ashmolean Museum, Oxford	AN1955.565
D112	Jordan Archaeological Museum, Amman	J5758
D113	British Museum, London	BM 127414
D114	Jordan Archaeological Museum, Amman	J5757
D115	Royal Ontario Museum, Toronto	1955.165.1
D116	Birmingham Museum and Art Gallery, Birmingham	1964A27
D117	University of Sydney, Sydney	57.03
D118	University of Cambridge, Museum of Archaeology and Anthropology, Cambridge	1957.159
E22	Rockefeller Museum, Jerusalem	JPE 121.32

Table 1 Locations of other plastered skulls from Jericho

movement to inhabit drier regions (Bar-Yosef and Alon 1988, 28; Bar Yosef 1986, 159–62; Rosenberg and Redding 2000, 39–40; Rollefson *et al.* 1992, 444). Ritual practices were focused on skull modification, removal and caching, alongside the creation of clay figurines, stone masks and plaster anthropomorphic statues (Bar-Yosef and Belfer-Cohen 1989, 61–8; Cauvin 2000, 75–116; Garfinkel 1994, 182; Rollefson 1990; Bar-Yosef and Belfer-Cohen 1991, 192–3; Kuijt and Goring-Morris 2002, 387–98, 399–404; Kuijt 2000b, 142; Cauvin 1972, 43–66; Verhoeven 2002, 236–47). Following skull removal, further treatments include the application of bitumen on the upper skull (Rollefson 2000, 171) and the modelling of facial features in plaster. Cranial removal was also expressed through wall paintings and the decapitation of figurines (Kuijt 2000b, 149). Recent work at Çatalhöyük and Köşk Höyük now attests that plaster remodelling of skulls was also practised in central Anatolia in later periods (9th and 8th millennia calibrated ^{14}C years BP) (Hodder 2004, 10; Lichter 2007, 250–1; Yakar 1991, 192; Silistreli 1988, 62, 65, pl. 7). In most examples, plaster covers the face, sides and base of the head, but not the cranial vault, which has led to suggestions that some skulls originally also had a wig or other form of head covering (Griffin *et al.* 1998, 66; Goring-Morris 2000, 124–5; Arensburg and Hershkovitz 1988, 53–4; Arensburg and Hershkovitz 1989, 117–23; Yakar and Hershkovitz 1988, 60–2).

Imaging techniques and museum collections

The British Museum Jericho skull (BM 127414) consists of a human cranium, with the lower jaw removed and facial features remodelled in plaster (**Pl. 1**). These modifications and additions presented several challenges for its analysis. It is axiomatic within a museum context that non-destructive and non-invasive techniques should be used to unravel the details of an artefact's construction wherever possible (see Chapter Three, this volume, for a commentary on this subject). To achieve this, it is often necessary to attempt to look beneath the surface of an artefact in a way that does not cause damage. This is particularly important for human remains that have been modified, as in the case of the plastered skull discussed here, or are held in a complex relationship with other objects and materials, such as

Egyptian mummies. In these instances, while it is important to know how those human remains have been treated and what lies beneath their outer surface, a direct internal investigation would cause irreversible alteration and might even mean their permanent disassembly. The public mummy unwrapping displays of the Victorian era (see for example Tapp 1979) have been left behind. Not only might a researcher wish to know how a modification has been made or what lies within a funerary shroud, but they may also seek more fundamental biological data such as the age, sex and state of health of an individual to help understand the social context. A number of techniques have been used to resolve these problems, but two imaging methods – conventional radiography and computerized tomography (CT) – stand out as being regularly employed within museums.

Radiography is one of the earliest and most frequently used techniques available for the internal investigation of museum collection material (Lang and Middleton 2005). It facilitates the non-invasive examination of a range of materials without physical damage. Radiographic images have been available for over 100 years (Spiegel 1995) and the technique has been used by the British Museum to research artefacts since 1949. The methods used in museums are very similar to those used in a medical context, although the quantity of radiation used is adapted to the density of the specimens and can sometimes exceed the levels which are safe for living organisms.

Radiography involves firing a stream of radiation, usually in the form of X-rays, at the subject under examination. Some of this radiation will pass through, some will be absorbed and some will be scattered. The amount which passes through depends on a number of factors, but mostly on the composition and thickness of the subject being examined. Radiographic images were traditionally captured on film or, less frequently, on fluorescent screens, but digital formats are now generally the first choice for image collection or examination (for discussions of the reasons for this, see Lang and Middleton 2005).

Despite the availability of radiographic equipment, when the skull first arrived at the Museum in 1954 no attempt was made to undertake a radiographic study. This was because plaster and bone have similar radio-opacities which makes it

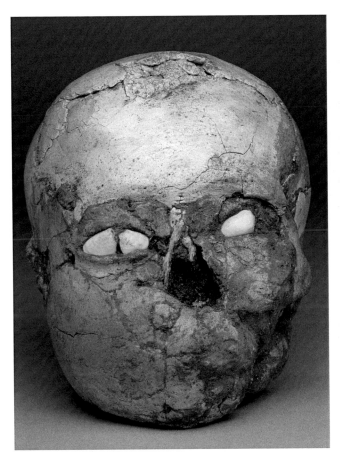

Plate 1 Front view of the Jericho skull, 10100–9250 calibrated ¹⁴C years BP. British Museum, London (BM 127414)

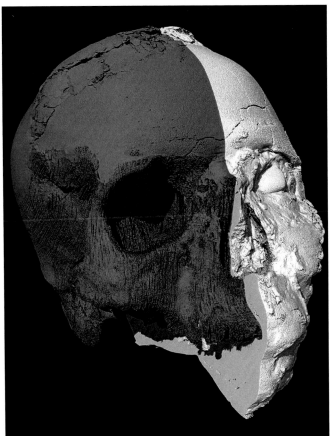

Plate 2 Computer assisted 3D reconstruction of the Jericho skull showing the structure of the cranium below the plaster face

difficult to distinguish between them by using this technique. The soil fill of the cranium posed further problems; the sheer density of this material was certain to make it difficult to penetrate the skull, while the scatter generated by the fill would be likely to fog the image and complicate its interpretation. However, success in using digitized X-radiographs to examine skeletal material from the Royal Cemetery at Ur encouraged us in 2005 to experiment by examining the British Museum Jericho skull through the use of this technique (Irving and Ambers 2002; Molleson and Hodgson 2003, 108–12). A number of radiographs of the skull were therefore produced under different voltage and exposure conditions allowing the interior to be examined at different depths and levels of contrast. These provided much information about the skull, particularly with regard to pre-mortem modification, but could not answer all questions for a number of reasons; the geometry of the skull and the equipment limited the angles at which the skull could be examined and the detail that could be achieved; the similarities in the radio-opacity of bone and plaster remained a problem despite digital adjustment of the images produced; and images of the central parts of the skull were largely obscured by the superposition of different elements and the soil packing. However, the information gained from the radiographic images allowed us to make a strong case that the skull should be the subject of a computerized tomography (CT) study.

X-ray computed tomography (CT) has been available since the 1970s and uses X-rays in conjunction with computing algorithms to create sub-surface images. Digital geometry processing is used to generate a cross-sectional image (tomogram) of the interior of an object from hundreds of two-dimensional X-ray images taken around a single axis of rotation. Computer-assisted reconstruction can also be used to generate a 3D representation of the scanned subject (**Pl. 2**).

CT scans have several advantages over traditional radiography. As it operates in the form of a series of slices, CT permits the differentiation and isolation of specific areas and substances, eliminating the problem of superposition within the subject being studied. In addition, the inherently high-contrast resolution of CT means that slight differences in the density of materials (less than 1%) can be distinguished, while the ability to reconfigure the data from a single CT scanning procedure means that images of the object can be viewed as through three different planes: axial (horizontal), coronal (vertical, front to back) or sagittal (vertical, left to right) (see **Pl. 3**). In the case of the British Museum Jericho skull, this allowed us to examine areas that could not otherwise be seen in detail such as the inner and outer surfaces of the cranial bones, the teeth, the soil packing and the plaster.

Methods

Other plastered skulls have been the subject of sub-surface investigations which have offered opportunities for comparison with the British Museum Jericho skull (Hershkovitz *et al.* 1995; Hershkovitz *et al.* 1996; Bonogofsky 2002; Goring-Morris 2000, 126; Goring-Morris *et al.* 1994–5,

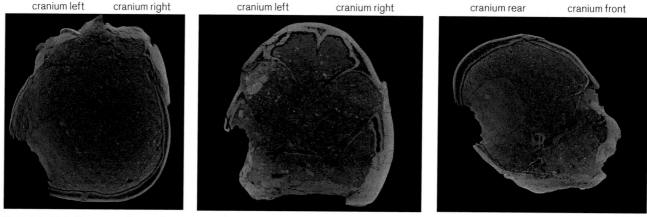

cranium left   cranium right   cranium left   cranium right   cranium rear   cranium front

Plate 3 Axial (left), coronal (middle) and sagittal (right) views of the Jericho skull created by CT scan

112). A detailed physical and anthropological study was therefore carried out (Fletcher *et. al.* 2008) using surface investigations and sub-surface examinations conducted by radiography and CT scanning. The CT scan images were assembled to show a single point in three views (axial, coronal and sagittal; **Pl. 3**). The skull was scanned sitting on its plaster base. This combined with its inherent asymmetry owing to cranial modification (see below) means that the axial, coronal and sagittal slices are not placed at right angles with the skull. This makes their interpretation more challenging and means that sometimes several images need to be compared to obtain all the information about a specific area. A list of skull treatments was compiled from published examples, with which the British Museum Jericho skull was compared and the presence or absence of specific features noted. Sex was evaluated through traditional methods; examination of the supraorbital margins, mastoid process, occipital crest, zygomatic arches and the presence of a temporal line (Workshop of European Anthropologists 1980). Age was estimated following cranial suture observation (Meindl and Lovejoy 1985). Epigenetic traits (skeletal variations between individuals thought to result from genetic inheritance or environmental factors) were also recorded (Berry and Berry 1967).

Micro-CT scanning was performed using an HMXST 225 CT system (Nikon Metrology, Tring, UK). Due to the density and size of the Jericho skull, the X-ray penetration was very low. Accordingly the X-ray energy had to be set to a high level (45,000W). X-rays were generated from a tungsten target using a voltage and current of 225kV and 200μA respectively. A total of 6,284 angular projections were collected at 0.057° intervals in a single 360° rotation. The radial projections were reconstructed into a three-dimensional matrix of 2000 × 2000 × 1000 (length × width × height) 250μm cubic voxels using the software package CT-Pro (Version 2.0, Metris X-Tek, Tring, UK). Due to the high density of the skull and plaster (>2.6 g/cm3), the reconstructed scan data contained beam hardening artefacts, evident as a ring of increased brightness (representing false density enhancement) on the margins of an object and decreased brightness at the centre, giving the shape commonly referred to as a 'cupping' artefact. Beam hardening artefacts are caused by the process of selective removal of low energy X-rays from the polychromatic X-ray beam. As X-rays pass through an object, lower energy

X-rays are removed so that the beam becomes progressively harder, or more penetrating. In order to reduce beam hardening artefacts, a copper filter was used to remove low energy X-rays, and the scan data was post-processed using CT-Pro 2.0 to remove cupping by normalizing the grey values at the edge and centre of the reconstructed scan (following Ronan *et al.* 2010; 2011).

The data was exported as a stack of TIF files for visualization and segmentation using VG Studio Max (Volume Graphics, Heidelberg, Germany). Reconstruction, thresholding, segmentation and rendering were carried out following the ten-step process recommended and described in detail by Abel *et al.* (2012)

Results: surface examination

The skull does not appear to have been significantly compressed after it was buried as all the sutures and facial features remain intact. This suggested that any modification to skull shape discovered during examination occurred in life and not due to factors such as distortion caused by the weight of soil above the burial cache. There was some damage observed above the left eye and at the top of the head (near craniometric point bregma), where impact damage was suggested by splintering of the bone with radiating fractures, indicative of the breaking of fresh bone. This may not have been related to the individual's death and could have occurred during peri-mortem (i.e. around death) treatments, handling or burial. There is a large area on the left side towards the back of the skull, which initially appeared to have been sliced off during excavation (**Pl. 4**). The evidence from the CT scans contradicted this theory (see **Pls 11, 12**), as will be discussed below, illustrating why it is advisable to apply different imaging techniques to a single specimen in order to achieve a more accurate data set.

Plaster had been applied to the area of the face finishing at the eye sockets and temples. All the edges of the plastered zone are rough and broken, indicating that when complete, it extended over a greater area than is now preserved. Although other examples from Jericho showed partial plastering with the crown of the skull left bare (Kenyon and Holland 1981, pls 51–9), the practice of full cranial plastering is attested elsewhere (Lechevallier 1978, 151, fig. 2) and therefore cannot be ruled out. The broken plastered margins surrounding the nasal cavity suggest that this example did once boast a modelled nose. The remaining ear is stylized,

Plate 4 Left lateral view of the British Museum Jericho skull showing the sub-circular opening cut into the left parietal bone

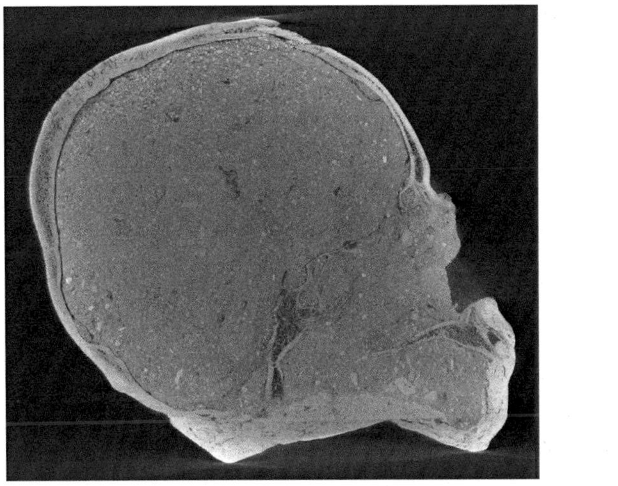

Plate 5 Sagittal CT scan on the mid-line showing that the sagittal and coronal sutures are fused which indicates a mature age adult. The image also shows the profile of the hard palate

as are the lips. The eyes are represented by shells that appear to be from a small marine bi-valve (*Donax* sp.) (Fletcher *et al.* 2008). The modelling of the eyelids covers the edges of the shells, obscuring diagnostic features and making identification of the species difficult. On the left side, one intact shell is in place while another portion is missing, suggesting another shell had originally been placed alongside it. On the right side there is a single shell that had been broken into two pieces.

Removal of the lower jaw means the face is foreshortened, a characteristic seen in other examples (Lechevallier 1978, 151, fig. 2; Goren *et al.* 2001, 674, table 1; de Contenson 1967, pl. 1 A–B). Plaster covers the full extent of the skull's base and the modelling of the plaster chin means that the skull sits upright without support as do other examples from Jericho (Strouhal 1973, 236, 238, 240). The British Museum Jericho skull shows no visible evidence for painted decoration or facial features in contrast to some other skulls (Strouhal 1973, 235–6; Goren and Segal 1995, 157–8; Goren *et al.* 2001, 673, 680; Kingery *et al.* 1988, 232; Hodder 2004, 10; Butler 1989, 143, fig. 2).

Biological characteristics and results: sub-surface examinations

Age was estimated by examining how far the cranial sutures had closed. The points where the sagittal and coronal sutures at the top (bregma) and the lambdoid and sagittal sutures at the back (lambda) of the skull meet are no longer complex and are nearing obliteration. The fused sagittal and coronal sutures can be further observed through the CT scans (**Pls 5, 15**) as can the unfused squamous suture around the top of the temporal bone (**Pl. 15**). These observations are consistent with a mature adult. The majority of plastered skulls appear to be adult, but age estimations vary (compare Strouhal 1973, 244 and Kurth and Röhrer-Ertl 1981, 437) and cranial suture ageing can only provide an approximate age at death. During the visual examination a slight linear depression was observed running approximately from ear to ear (perpendicular to the sagittal suture at the bregma). This suspected artificial cranial modification was later confirmed by radiography and CT

scan (see below). It is possible that the alteration may have contributed towards atypical suture closure and as such, the age of other individuals may have been over or underestimated; the possibility of skull modification may not have been considered where it was not immediately apparent. During previous examinations of the British Museum Jericho skull for example, it was not noted or recognized by other researchers (Kurth and Röhrer-Ertl 1981, 436–9). Extra ossicles were identified in the lambdoid suture, with cranial modification being one possible cause of the formation of accessory bones in the cranium (Hanihara and Ishida 2001). Extra ossicles were also seen in the Nahal Hemar Homo 9 specimen, but were not a feature of all skulls at this site (Arensburg and Hershkovitz 1989).

The skull was originally classed as female (Kurth and Röhrer-Ertl 1981, 437), but the sex of this individual is ambiguous with both male and female characteristics present. Indicators that the sex is possibly male are the rounded margin and shallow roof of the orbit (eye socket) (**Pl. 6**), thick orbit ridge, large mastoid (**Pl. 6**), deep palate (**Pl. 5**) and large cheek bones indicative of a robust individual. In contrast, the generally gracile form of the cranium and lack of nuchal crest or temporal line are female traits. It is possible that the skull was deliberately selected because it had no distinctively male or female attributes visible and it is perhaps significant that the plaster face has little indication of gender either. The lips are barely defined and there is no indication of features such as facial hair. The smoothing of the plaster also means the face does not reflect the age of the individual at death. Either deliberately or coincidentally, owing to the nature of the plaster that has been used, the skull has what appears to be an ungendered, young face reproduced upon it.

Sub-surface investigation allowed observation of the object's construction and further illuminated the cranial morphology. The radiographic investigation was particularly useful in looking at the linear depression thought to relate to artificial cranial modification. This had not been noted for this skull previously, although it had been identified in skulls within the same burial group (Kurth and Röhrer-Ertl 1981, 438–9). In an individual without a

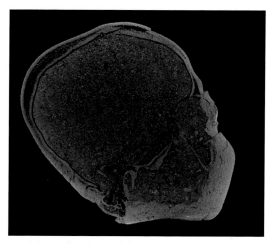

Plate 6 Sagittal CT scan off the mid-line showing variation in thickness of diploë on the vertex and frontal regions where the outer table was deflected towards the inner table. The image also shows the rounded margin and shallow roof of the orbit (eye socket) and a large well-pneumatized mastoid

modified skull, the middle layer of the cranial bone (the diploë) is a constant thickness, thinning only towards the sutures. Pressure exerted on the bone during artificial cranial modification causes deflection of the outer cranial table imposing variations in the thickness of the diploë (Merkle *et al.* 1998), which can only be observed non-destructively through radiography or CT scanning (Molleson and Campbell 1995). Both imaging techniques revealed variations in the thickness of the diploë of this individual (**Pl. 6**) in the same location as the linear depression observed by eye, confirming that this individual had experienced cranial modification. Since human skulls cannot be modified in adulthood, this must have happened at an early age. Further asymmetry in the shape of the cranium (**Pl. 15**) probably resulted from this modification.

Some clues as to the method used to artificially modify skulls at Jericho may be gained by another skull from the same cache (Strouhal 1973, 237, pl. 2). This has painted

stripes running across the parietal bones from ear to ear, which could be interpreted as a representation of how the head was bound to change the shape of the skull (compare with Özbek 1974, 473, fig. 2; Meiklejohn *et al.* 1992, fig. 2). Changes identified in other skulls from Jericho have been ascribed to post-mortem agents (Strouhal 1973, 232–4), but the variation in diploë thickness in this example is a strong indicator of pre-mortem artificial modification. Radiography of other Jericho specimens to examine diploë thickness could reveal the extent of this practice.

The radiographic investigation also revealed that there is an upper jaw and some teeth present within the soil/plaster matrix surrounding the lower portion of the face. It was not clear from the radiographs whether the teeth were in anatomical position. The CT scans, however, were able to illustrate the position and condition of the teeth in more detail. Some teeth are still in position, albeit broken and two abscesses were identified; one on the cranium's right side (first molar) and one on the left side (first premolar) (**Pls 7–8**). Dental caries (tooth decay) can be visualized in the crown of the left side first premolar. Both the first molar on the right and the left of the upper jaw were broken. The overall evidence from this example suggests that the teeth were in poor condition and that the individual had suffered from worn and damaged teeth, caries, abscesses and tooth loss during their lifetime. This fits well with the age of a mature adult. The tooth sockets for the first incisors were plugged with plaster (**Pl. 9**). The practice of destruction and remodelling of dentition has previously been noted for examples from Jericho (Strouhal 1973, 243), Beisamoun (Lechevalier 1978, 180), Kfar HaHoresh (Goren *et al.* 2001, 674), Ain Ghazal (Butler 1989, 145) and Tell Ramad (Ferembach 1969, 66–7), but their deliberate removal (avulsion) in order to mimic toothless (thereby elderly) ancestral males is doubtful (Bonogofsky 2002) and can be ruled out as an in-life practice in this case as the alveolus (tooth socket) would have healed and closed. The second and third molars were completely absent (**Pl. 10**), having never

a

b

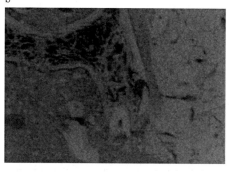

Plate 7 Axial (a) and enlarged coronal (b) CT scans showing the first molar on the right side of the cranium which is broken at the crown and has an abscess on the mesiobuccal root

a

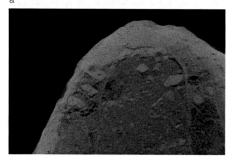

b

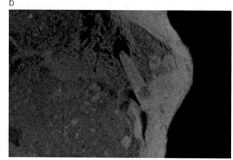

Plate 8 Axial (a) and enlarged sagittal (b) CT scans showing the first premolar on the left side of the cranium with an abscess on the palatal root and dental caries in the crown

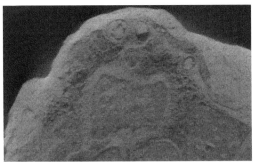

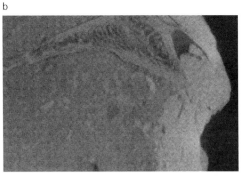

Plate 9 Axial (a) and enlarged sagittal (b) CT scans showing left incisor cavity plugged with plaster

developed. The second incisor on the right side is missing with no alveolus (tooth socket) present. The canine appears to have moved to close the gap. This additional example of a tooth failing to develop (hypodontia) supports the possibility that the missing second and third molars may be inherited (see Alt *et al.* 2013). It is difficult to assess the significance of the failure of these teeth to develop without a comparative population, although their identification in other examples could further the discussion surrounding plastered skulls, inherited social status and ancestor cult (Bonogofsky 2002; 2003, 1–2; 2004, 118; 2005, 133–4).

Damage to the plastered nose and the left parietal of the skull revealed that the cranium contains a brown soil matrix. Since all potential paths for soil to penetrate the skull had been closed over during plastering, it appears that soil was deliberately used to fill the skull, rather than accumulating as part of post-depositional processes. The radiographic images were unable to help further elucidate this, but CT scanning confirmed this theory as the images clearly showed different phases of filling for the interior (**Pl. 11**). The concentric alignment of the grit inclusions within the soil matrix suggested that the hole at the rear of the skull on the left side had been cut in antiquity and subsequently was used as the access point to fill the skull's interior. A final ball of soil of slightly finer and therefore firmer texture appears to have been used to pack down the filling as shown by the patterns of concentric cracking around it. The inclusion alignments and the patterns of cracking suggest the filling was moistened before being applied and there may have been a gap in deposition between the two phases. The first layer of filling also appears to have pulled away from the interior surface of the skull, again probably whilst drying (**Pl. 12**). The pattern of bone breakage at the edge of the access hole suggest the bone was relatively fresh when it was cut (**Pl. 12**) and it is possible that the roundel of bone was

originally replaced after the cranium had been filled. Although it was subsequently lost, its presence during the use-life of the skull may explain why the friable (easily broken up) soil filling has survived so well. The soil filling would have given support to the outer surface of the cranium as the plaster modelling was being added. Other skulls from Jericho reportedly have a plaster fill (Strouhal 1973, 232, 235, 240), suggesting there may have been variation in practices of cranial filling. As there has been no systematic study of this phenomenon across the Jericho examples, it is difficult to draw firm conclusions about the significance of these differences, if any.

Soil was also used to fill the eye sockets before the plaster used to create the face was applied (**Pl. 13**). No layering can be distinguished by eye in the plaster of the British Museum Jericho skull, in contrast to others from the same cache (Strouhal 1973, 232, 235, 240). Sub-surface studies of a plastered skull from Kfar HaHoresh, northern Israel, also showed that it was constructed in several stages with four different plaster mixtures applied to the skull (Goring-Morris 2000, 126; Goring-Morris *et al.* 1994–5, 112; Hershkovitz *et al.* 1995, 783–7). Goren *et al.* (2001, 679–85) have identified differences in the technical properties of plaster layers used on skulls from Jericho and Kfar HaHoresh. Such variation in plaster type is not discernible in the CT scans of the British Museum's Jericho skull, although the use of soil to fill the interior may reflect efforts to conserve the resources associated with obtaining or recycling materials to make plaster. The plaster for the British Museum's Jericho skull does appear to have been applied in sequence (**Pl. 14**). Cracks between plaster layers suggest that the base was plastered first, followed by the sides of the skull. An initial plug of plaster also appears to have been applied to the foramen magnum (the hole in the skull through which the spinal cord connects to the brain) (**Pl.**

Plate 10 Axial and enlarged coronal CT scans demonstrating the absence of second and third molars at the back of the right dental arcade (a–b), axial CT scan demonstrating the absence of second and third molars at the back of the left dental arcade (c)

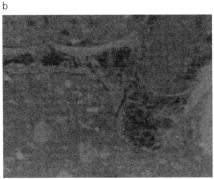

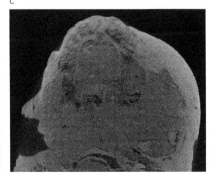

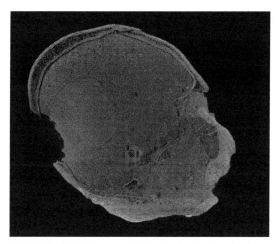

Plate 11 Sagittal CT scan of lateral left side showing layers of clay packing within the British Museum Jericho skull

15). The plaster was applied directly to the bone and the burnished finish on the surface of the face of the British Museum example was probably achieved by polishing the plaster with a smoothing tool (see Strouhal 1973, 232, 238).

The interpretation of the skull cult and social relationships in Pre-pottery Neolithic B society

The selection of skulls for plastering

There is considerable debate surrounding what factors may have influenced the choice of skulls for plastering. A number of authors have been keen to attribute this to biological sex (see Strouhal 1973; Kurth and Röhrer-Ertl 1981; Arensburg and Hershkovitz 1989), but no patterning can be seen in the current sex assignments and some are still debated (Strouhal 1973, 231–41, 244; Kurth and Röhrer-Ertl 1981, 437). Artificial cranial modification identified for some examples (Arensburg and Hershkovitz 1989, 127–8; Strouhal 1973, 241, 244; Özbek 1974) may account for difficulties encountered in determining the sex of remodelled crania. Indicators of sex and age on the skull can also be obscured by the plastering itself and post-depositional site-formation processes such as compression, which also means that sexing and population typing of such skulls should be treated with caution,

especially as the pelvis is a more accurate indicator of biological sex. This is significant because studies linking plastered skulls with an ancestor cult based on the veneration of elder males would therefore appear to be based on insubstantial evidence (see Bonogofsky 2003, 2 for examples).

Other studies have suggested that skulls were selected post-mortem for plastering according to their shape. Crania with a low wide face and broad vault, similar to the elongated shape seen in modified skulls, tended to be chosen (Garfinkel 1994, 166–70; Strouhal 1973, 243; Arensburg and Hershkovitz 1988, 55–7; Meiklejohn *et al.* 1992, 95; Arensburg and Hershkovitz 1989, 127; Verhoeven 2002, 249). The repetition of elongated head shapes on some figurines may also indicate that these were viewed as aesthetically pleasing (Meiklejohn *et al.* 1992, 95; Cauvin 2000, 147, 149, fig. 48; de Contenson 1969, 33, figs 13–14; 1971, 285; Daems and Croucher 2007, 7–13). Plaster faces were frequently modelled with little regard for the underlying bone structure and are often stylized, undermining the importance of morphological characteristics within the selection process (Garfinkel 1994, 165; Strouhal 1973, 241–4; Ferembach and Lechevallier 1973, 224–6; Lechevallier 1978, 150; Ferembach 1978, 179–80; Arensburg and Hershkovitz 1988, 55–7; Arensburg and Hershkovitz 1989, 127–9; Bienert 1991, 15, 19; Griffin *et al.* 1998, 62, 66; Goring-Morris *et al.* 1995, 47–8). As regards to the British Museum Jericho skull, it is not immediately obvious to the naked eye whether the individual underwent cranial modification or not. It is therefore unlikely that this would have been a significant factor in the selection process without prior knowledge that the individual had experienced modification through processes such as head binding in childhood. If cranial modification was an important factor in choosing skulls for plastering, the British Museum example suggests that the knowledge of an individual having undergone this process was more important than its physical result.

The occurrence of skull removal, caching and plastering within archaeological contexts is rare in relation to other burial types. This has been interpreted as indicating that

Plate 12 Axial (left), coronal (middle) and sagittal (right) CT scans. The thin dark line between the soil matrix and inner surface of the cranium shows that the clay filling contracted as it dried and pulled away from the bone. The bevelled edge of the broken bone in the coronal and sagittal views suggests the cutting/chipping of relatively fresh bone to gain access to the cranial vault rather than the accidental breakage of dry bone at a much later date

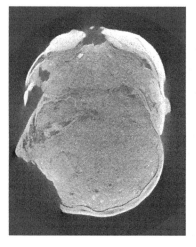
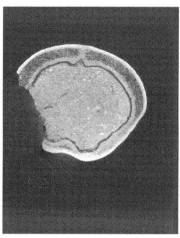
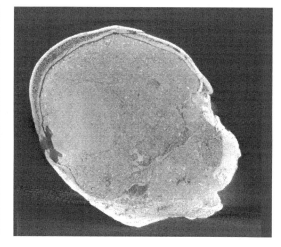

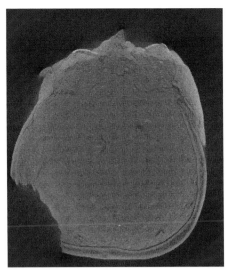

Plate 13 Axial CT scan showing soil packing within the eye sockets and overlying shell

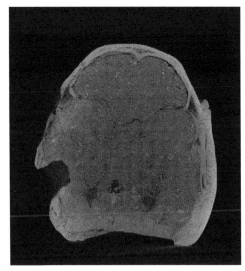

Plate 14 Coronal CT scan at the mid-point of the eye sockets (orbits) showing that a layer of plaster was applied to the base of the cranium before the sides

removal and treatment of the skull may have related to inherited or achieved status as only a small segment of the population was selected (Goring-Morris 2000, 130; Rollefson 2000, 184; Kuijt 2001, 94). The stylized rendition of facial features suggests that the skulls were not intended to look like realistic representations of the deceased (Goren *et al.* 2001, 686), which undermines arguments (Kenyon 1960, 51–4; Simmons *et al.* 1990, 109) that the skulls could be portraits of revered members of the community. It seems that the use of plastered skulls as ritual objects was more complex than simply acknowledging an individual's status (Verhoeven 2002, 251) and a general consensus of opinion has emerged that relates skull removal and associated practices to ancestor worship or ancestor cult (Cauvin 1972, 62–4; 2000, 93, 114; Bienert 1991, 20; Hershkovitz and Gopher 1990, 19–23; de Contenson 1971, 281; 1985, 22; Bar-Yosef and Alon 1988, 14, 20–8; Bar Yosef and Belfer-Cohen 1991, 193; Arensburg and Hershkovitz 1988, 55–7; Simmons *et al.* 1990, 109; Strouhal 1973, 244; Lechevallier 1978, 150; Bonogofsky 2003).

Ancestor-cult and cranial modification

Like the term 'skull cult', ancestor cult is broadly defined owing to the many different ways of practising ancestor worship identified in anthropological studies (Hardacre 1987). The representation of the dead among the living is regarded as important by archaeologists, although opinions differ regarding the exact relationship between material culture and a community's ancestral past (compare Parker-Pearson 1999, 158–61; Kuijt 2001, 82; Arensberg and Herschkovitz 1989, 129). It appears that modern scholarship has created a false impression that the plastered skulls represent venerated elderly males (Bonogofsky 2002; 2003, 1–2; 2004, 118; 2005, 133–4). Examples of post-mortem cranial removal from child skeletons in PPNA (Pre-pottery Neolithic A) and Middle PPNB contexts at Jericho (Kurth and Röhrer-Ertl 1981, 444–5, pl. VIIc; Kenyon and Holland 1981, 9, 49–50, 74, 287, 300; Kenyon 1956, 75; Cornwall 1956, 116–23, pls XX 4a–b, XXI 5b; 1981, 399–400; Naveh 2003, 86, 90) and at 'Ain Ghazal (Rollefson *et al.* 1992, 461–3;

Rollefson 2000, 169–71) point to the existence of forms of veneration that were more varied than the worship of adults alone.

Ritual activities based around skulls in the Middle PPNB encouraged the development of belief systems that cut across household and kin groups, which may reflect attempts to cope with the social and economic stresses associated with Middle PPNB population growth (Kenyon 1960, 54–6; Naveh 2003, 94). At Jericho, many of the skull caches were buried in publicly accessible locations, facilitating community participation (Kuijt 2000b, 148). Participation in such practices for the wider community would have been more easily accepted through reference to a generalized group of ancestors and standardized social rules, hence children as well as adults could have assumed a significant role in linking living communities with their past (Kuijt 1996, 315–32; Kuijt 2000b, 138–56; Kuijt 2001, 80–95; Kuijt

Plate 15 Coronal CT scan in the region of the petrous (ear) bones and foramen magnum. Layers of plaster applied to the base of the British Museum Jericho skull can be seen as can the plaster plug placed within the foramen magnum The sagittal suture is fused; the squamous suture around the temporal bone is not fused. Asymmetry caused by the modification of the cranium can also be seen

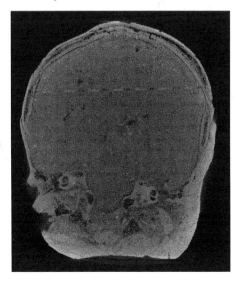

and Goring-Morris 2002, 419; Croucher 2006, 34, 36). Thus, the post-mortem treatment of skulls promoted the idea of a community's shared history and restricted the creation of inherited social status (Kuijt 2000b, 157–9; 2000c, 95–9; Byrd 1994, 656–61; Banning and Byrd 1987, 321–3; Kuijt and Goring-Morris 2002, 420–3).

The link between skull modification and status is both significant and complex (Verhoeven 2002, 249; Goring-Morris 2000, 130; Rollefson 2000, 184; Simmons et al. 1990, 109; Kenyon 1960, 51–4; Kuijt 2001, 94). The selection of modified skulls for plastering creates a link between physical alteration and social position. It is particularly important that modification must be done whilst the skull is still growing, suggesting that the affected person was probably too young to have a choice regarding whether their skull was reshaped or not (Croucher 2006, 33). The debate cannot progress because there is currently no accurate data regarding the frequency of cranial modification within Middle PPNB populations. The analysis of the Jericho skull shows that cranial modification is not always easily discernible by eye, yet attempts to quantify the proportion of modified crania present in a population have not used sub-surface examination to quantify the presence of this practice (e.g. Daems and Croucher 2007, 5–8, table 1; Croucher 2006, 32). Therefore, it is possible that deformation is present in more skulls, both plastered and not, than currently recognized, which makes a discussion of the social significance of this practice premature for the time being. In the case of the British Museum Jericho skull, the subtlety of its alteration suggests that the decision to plaster this skull was associated with a collective knowledge of the experiences an individual had undergone during their life. Future work must therefore utilize imaging techniques such as radiography and CT scanning to assess whether modified skulls are disproportionately represented in plastered skulls when compared with undecorated skulls from contemporary burials.

Conclusions

This research highlights the significance of non-destructive imaging techniques and the importance of sub-surface examination for revealing new data concerning existing collections and suggesting further avenues of research for related collections elsewhere. The work has significantly advanced our knowledge concerning how the skull was modified both during life and after death. The previously anonymous individual is now known to be a mature male who most likely suffered from poor dental health. This research has prompted a re-evaluation of the ways in which skulls were selected for plastering, with implications for the interpretation of mortuary practices within the Neolithic period of the Middle East. It is clear that the study of cranial deformation has a crucial role to play in the understanding of skull cults, ancestor worship and their role in social cohesion; perhaps plastered skulls should be viewed as primarily representing life practices, rather than death rituals. Sub-surface imaging has shown that artificial cranial modification can be identified in skulls that were not previously considered as having undergone such treatment and knowledge of this change appears to have influenced the

choice of this skull for special treatment after death. This suggests that physical and social alteration may have been linked, but conflicting social messages were also expressed by plastered skulls as they also signified aspects of community-wide ancestor worship.

Acknowledgements
The authors would like to thank the Imaging and Analysis Centre, Science Facilities, Natural History Museum, for providing the CT scan and Caroline Cartwright, British Museum, for identification of the shell species.

Bibliography
Abel, R.L., Parfitt S.A., Ashton. N.M., Lewis, S.G. and Stringer, C.B., 2011. 'Digital preservation and dissemination of ancient lithic technology with modern micro-CT', Computers and Graphics 35, 878–84.
—, Laurini, C. and Richter, M., 2012. 'A biologist's guide to "virtual" micro-CT preparation', Palaeontologia Electronica 15, 1–16.
Alt, K.W., Benz, M., Müller, W., Berner, M.E., Schultz, M., Schmidt-Schultz, T.H., Knipper, C., Gebel, H-G.K., Nissen, H.J., and Vach, W., 2013. 'Earliest evidence for social endogamy in the 9,000-year-old-population of Basta, Jordan', PLoS ONE 8(6): e65649. doi:10.1371/journal.pone.0065649 [accessed 24 September 2013].
Arensburg, B. and Hershkovitz, I., 1988. 'Nahal Hemar cave. Neolithic human remains', Atiqot 18, 50–8.
—, 1989. 'Artificial skull "treatment" in the PPNB period: Nahal Hemar', in Hershkovitz 1989, 115–31.
Banning, E. and Byrd, B., 1987. 'Houses and the changing residential unit: domestic architecture at PPNB 'Ain Ghazal, Jordan', Proceedings of the Prehistoric Society 53, 309–25.
Bar-Yosef, O., 1986. 'The walls of Jericho – an alternative interpretation', Current Anthropology 27, 157–62.
— and Alon, D., 1988. 'Nahal Hemar cave. The excavations', Atiqot 18, 3–30.
— and Belfer-Cohen, A., 1989. 'The Levantine "PPNB" interaction sphere', in Hershkovitz 1989, 59–72.
— and Belfer-Cohen, A., 1991. 'From sedentary hunter-gatherers to territorial farmers in the Levant', in Between Bands and States, ed. S.A. Gregg, 181–202. Carbondale.
Berry, A.C. and Berry, R.J., 1967. 'Epigenetic variation in the human cranium', Journal of Anatomy 101, 361–79.
Bienert, H.-D., 1991. 'Skull cult in the prehistoric Near East', Journal of Prehistoric Religion 5, 9–23.
Bonogofsky, M., 2002. 'Reassessing dental evulsion in Neolithic plastered skulls from the Levant through the use of computed tomography, direct observation, and photographs', Journal of Archaeological Science 29, 959–64.
—, 2003. 'Neolithic skulls and railroading epistemologies', Bulletin of the American Schools of Oriental Research 331(3), 1–10.
—, 2004. 'Including women and children: Neolithic modelled skulls from Jordan, Israel, Syria and Turkey', Near Eastern Archaeology 67(2), 118–19.
—, 2005. 'A bioarchaeological study of plastered skulls from Anatolia: new discoveries and interpretations', International Journal of Osteoarchaeology 15, 124–35.
Butler, C., 1989. 'The plastered skulls of 'Ain Ghazal: preliminary findings', in Hershkovitz 1989, 141–5.
Byrd, B.F., 1994. 'Public and private, domestic and corporate: the emergence of the south-west Asian village', American Antiquity 59(4), 639–66.
Cauvin, J., 1972. Religions Néolithiques de Syro-Palestine. Paris.
—, 2000. The Birth of the Gods and the Origins of Agriculture, trans. T. Watkins. Cambridge.
Cornwall, I.W., 1956. 'The Pre-Pottery burial at Jericho', Palestine Excavation Quarterly 88, 110–24.
—, 1981. 'Appendix A. The Pre-Pottery Neolithic burials', in Excavations at Jericho, vol. 3, The Architecture and Stratigraphy of the Tell, ed. K.M. Kenyon, 395–406. Oxford.

Croucher K., 2006. 'Getting ahead: exploring the meanings of skulls in the Neolithic Near East', in *Skull Collection, Modification and Decoration*, ed. M. Bonogofsky, 29–44. Oxford (British Archaeological Reports International Series 1539).

—, 2012. *Death and Dying in the Neolithic Near East*. Oxford.

Daems, A. and Croucher, K., 2007. 'Artificial cranial modification in Prehistoric Iran: evidence from crania and figurines', *Iranica Antiqua* 42, 1–21.

de Contenson, H., 1967. 'Troisième campagne de fouilles à Tell Ramad, 1966. Rapport préliminaire', *Annales Archaeologiques Arabes Syriennes* 17, 17–24.

—, 1969. 'Sixième campagne de fouilles à Tell Ramad en 1969. Rapport préliminaire', *Annales Archaeologiques Arabes Syriennes* 19, 31–5.

—, 1971. 'Tell Ramad, a village of Syria of the 7th and 6th millennia B.C.', *Archaeology* 24, 278–85.

—, 1985. 'La region de Damas au Néolithique', *Annales Archaeologiques Arabes Syriennes* 35, 9–29.

Ferembach, D., 1969. 'Étude anthropologique des ossements humains Néolithiques de Tell-Ramad (Syrie)', *Annales Archaeologiques Arabes Syriennes* 19, 49–70.

—, 1978. 'Étude anthropologique, les crânes surmodelés', in *Abu Ghosh et Beisamioun: Deux Gisements du VIIe millénaire avant l'ère Chrétiene en Israël*, ed. M. Lechevallier (Mémoires et Travaux du Centre Recherches Préhistoriques Français de Jérusalem no. 2), 179–81. Paris.

— and Lechevallier, M., 1973. 'Découverte de crânes surmodelés dans une habitation du VIIème millénaire, à Beisamoun Israël', *Paléorient* 1, 223–30.

Fletcher, A., Pearson J. and Ambers J., 2008. 'The manipulation of social and physical identity in the Neolithic. Radiographic evidence for cranial modification at Jericho and its implications for the plastering of skulls', *Cambridge Archaeological Journal* 18 (3), 309–25.

Garfinkel, Y., 1994. 'Ritual burial of cultic objects: the earliest evidence', *Cambridge Archaeological Journal* 4(2), 159–88.

Goren, Y. and Segal, I., 1995. 'On early myths and formative technologies: a study of Pre-Pottery Neolithic B Sculptures and modelled skulls from Jericho', *Israel Journal of Chemistry* 35, 155–65.

—, Goring-Morris, N. and Segal, I., 2001. 'The technology of skull modelling in the Pre-Pottery Neolithic B (P.P.N.B.): regional variability, the relation of technology and iconography and their archaeological implications', *Journal of Archaeological Science* 28, 671–90.

Goring-Morris, A.N., 2000. 'The quick and the dead. The social context of aceramic Neolithic mortuary practices as seen from Kfar HaHoresh', in Kuijt 2000a, 103–36. New York.

—, Goren, Y., Horwitz, L.K., Hershkovitz, I., Lieberman, R., Sarel, J. and Bar-Yosef, D., 1994–5. 'The 1992 season of excavations at the Pre-Pottery Neolithic B settlement of Kfar HaHoresh', *Mitekufat Haeven: Journal of the Israel Prehistoric Society* 26, 74–121.

—, Goren, Y., Horwitz, L.K., Bar-Yosef, D. and Hershkovitz, I., 1995. 'Investigations at an early Neolithic settlement in lower Galilee: results of the 1991 season at Kfar HaHoresh', *Atiqot* 27, 37–62.

Griffin, P.S., Grissom, C.A. and Rollefson, G.A., 1998. 'Three late eighth millennium plastered faces from 'Ain Ghazal, Jordan', *Paléorient* 24(1), 59–70.

Hanihara, T. and Ishida, H., 2001. 'Frequency variations of discrete cranial traits in major human populations. I. Supernumerary ossicles variations', *Journal of Anatomy* 198, 689–706.

Hardacre, H., 1987. 'Ancestor worship', in *Death, Afterlife and the Soul*, ed. L.E. Sullivan, 62–9. New York.

Hershkovitz, I. (ed.), 1989. *People and Culture in Change*. Oxford (BAR International Series 508).

— and Gopher, A., 1990. 'Paleodemography, burial customs, and food-producing economy at the beginning of the Holocene: a perspective from the southern Levant', *Mitekufat Haeven: Journal of the Israel Prehistoric Society* 23, 9–47.

—, Zohar, I., Segal, I., Spiers, M.S., Meirav, O., Sherter, U., Feldman, H. and Goring-Morris, N., 1995. 'Remedy for an 8500 year-old plastered human skull from Kfar HaHoresh, Israel', *Journal of Archaeological Science* 22, 779–88.

—, Zohar, I., Wish-Baratz, S., Goren, Y., Goring-Morris, N., Spiers, M.S., Segal, I., Meirav, O., Sherter, U. and Feldman, H., 1996.

'High resolution computerised tomography and micro-focus radiography on an eight-thousand year old plastered skull: how and why was it modelled', in *Culture et Nature Actes du Colloque International de Liège, 13–17 Decembre 1993*, ed. M. Otte (Etudes et Recherches Archéologiques de L'Université de Liège no 68.), 669–82. Liège.

Hodder, I., 2004. 'A season of great finds and new faces at Çatalhöyük', *Anatolian Archaeology* 10, 8–10.

Irving, A. and Ambers, J., 2002. 'Hidden treasure from the Royal Cemetery at Ur. Technology sheds new light on the Ancient Near East', *Near Eastern Archaeology* 65(3), 206–13.

Kenyon, K.M., 1953. 'Excavations at Jericho 1953', *Palestine Excavation Quarterly* 85, 81–96.

—, 1956. 'Excavations at Jericho 1956', *Palestine Excavation Quarterly* 88, 67–82.

—, 1960. *Archaeology in the Holy Land*. London.

— and Holland T.A. (eds), 1981. *Excavations at Jericho*, vol. 3, *The Architecture and Stratigraphy of the Tell*. Oxford.

Kingery, W.D., Vandiver, P.B. and Prickett M., 1988. 'The beginnings of pyrotechnology, part II: production and use of lime and gypsum plaster in the pre-pottery Neolithic Near East', *Journal of Field Archaeology* 15(2), 219–44.

Kuijt, I., 1995. 'New perspectives on old territories: ritual practices and the emergence of social complexity in the Levantine Neolithic', Ph.D dissertation, Harvard University. Ann Arbor, University Microfilms.

—, 1996. 'Negotiating equality through ritual: a consideration of Late Natufian and Pre-Pottery A mortuary practices', *Journal of Anthropological Archaeology* 15(4), 313–36.

— (ed.), 2000a. *Life in Neolithic Farming Communities: Social Organization, Identity and Differentiation*. New York.

—, 2000b. 'Keeping the peace. Ritual skull caching and community integration in the Levantine Neolithic', in Kuijt 2000a, 137–64.

—, 2000c. 'People and space in early agricultural villages: exploring daily lives, community size and architecture in the late Pre-Pottery Neolithic', *Journal of Anthropological Archaeology* 19, 75–102.

—, 2001. 'Place, death and the transmission of social memory in early agricultural communities of the Near Eastern Pre-Pottery Neolithic', in *Social Memory, Identity and Death: Anthropological Perspectives on Mortuary Rituals*, ed. M. Chesson, 80–99. Washington, D.C. (Archaeological Papers of the American Anthropological Association 10).

— and Goring-Morris, A.N., 2002. 'Foraging, farming and social complexity in the Pre-Pottery Neolithic of the southern Levant: a review and synthesis', *Journal of World Prehistory* 16(4), 361–440.

Kurth, G. and Röhrer-Ertl, O., 1981. 'On the anthropology of the Mesolithic to Chalcolithic human remains from the Tell es-Sultan in Jericho, Jordan', in Kenyon and Holland 1981, 407–93.

Lang, J. and Middleton, A., 2005. *Radiography of Cultural Material*. Oxford and Burlington, MA.

Lechevallier, M., 1978. 'Les sépultures', in *Abu Ghosh et Beisamioun: Deux Gisements du VIIe millénaire avant l'ère Chrétiene en Israël*, ed. M. Lechevallier (Mémoires et Travaux du Centre Recherches Préhistoriques Français de Jérusalem no. 2.), 147–51. Paris.

Lichter C., 2007. 'Geschnitten oder am stück? Totenritual und Liechenbehandlung im Jungsteinzeitlichen Anatolien', in *Die Ältesten Monumente der Menschheit*, ed. C. Lichter, 246–57. Karlsruhe.

Meiklejohn, C., Agelarakis, A., Akkermans, P.A., Smith, P.E.L. and Solecki, R., 1992. 'Artificial cranial deformation in the Proto-Neolithic and Neolithic Near East and its possible origin: evidence from four sites', *Paléorient* 18(2), 83–97.

Meindl, R.S. and Lovejoy, C.O., 1985. 'Ectocranial suture ageing scheme', *American Journal of Physical Anthropology* 68, 57–66.

Merkle, E.M., Parsche, F., Vogel, J., Brambs, H.J. and Pirsig, W., 1998. 'Computed tomographic measurements of the nasal sinuses and frontal bone in mummy-heads artificially deformed in infancy', *American Journal of Rhinology* 12(2), 99–104.

Molleson, T.I. and Campbell, S. 1995. 'Deformed skulls at Tell Arpachiyah: the social context', in *The Archaeology of Death in the Ancient Near East*, ed. S. Campbell and A. Green, 45–55. Oxford (Oxbow Monograph 51).

— and Hodgson D., 2003. 'The human remains from Woolley's exacavations at Ur', *Iraq* 45, 91–129.

Naveh, D., 2003. 'PPNA Jericho: a socio-political perspective', *Cambridge Archaeological Journal* 13(1), 83–96.

Özbek, M., 1974. 'A propos des deformations craniennes artificielles observees au Proche-Orient', *Paléorient* 2(2), 469–76.

Parker-Pearson, M., 1999. *The Archaeology of Death and Burial*. Stroud.

Ronan, R., Abel R.L., Johnson, K., Perry, C., 2010. 'Quantification of porosity in Acroporapulchra (Brook 1891) using X-ray micro-computed tomography techniques', *Journal of Experimental Marine Biology and Ecology* 396: 1–9.

—, Abel, R.L., Johnson, K. and Perry, C., 2011. 'Spatial variation in porosity and skeletal element characteristics in apical tips of the branching coral Acropora pulchra (Brook 1891)', *Coral Reefs* 30: 195–201.

Rollefson, G.O., 1990. 'The uses of plaster at Neolithic 'Ain Ghazal, Jordan', *Archaeomaterials* 4, 33–54.

—, 2000. 'Ritual and social structure at Neolithic 'Ain Ghazal', in Kuijt 2000a, 165–90.

—, Simmons, A. H. and Kafafi, Z., 1992. 'Neolithic cultures at 'Ain Ghazal, Jordan', *Journal of Field Archaeology* 19, 443–70.

Rosenberg, M. and Redding, R., 2000. 'Hallan Çemi and early village organization in eastern Anatolia', in Kuijt 2000a, 39–61.

Silistreli, U., 1988. '1987 Kösk Höyük', *Kazı Sonuçları Toplantısı* X(1), 61–6.

Simmons, A.H., Boulton, A., Roetzel Butler, C., Kafafi, Z. and Rollefson, G.O., 1990. 'A plastered human skull from Neolithic 'Ain Ghazal, Jordan', *Journal of Field Archaeology* 17, 107–10.

Spiegel, P.K., 1995. 'The first clinical X-ray made in America – 100 years', *American Journal of Roentgenology* 164, 241–3.

Strouhal, E., 1973. 'Five plastered skulls from Pre-Pottery Neolithic B Jericho. Anthropological study', *Paléorient* 2, 231–47.

Tapp, E. 1979, 'The unwrapping of a mummy', in *The Manchester Museum Mummy Project: Multidisciplinary Research on Ancient Egyptian Mummified Remains*, ed. A.R. David, 83–94. Manchester.

Verhoeven, M., 2002. 'Ritual and ideology in the Pre-Pottery Neolithic B of the Levant and southeast Anatolia', *Cambridge Archaeological Journal* 12(2), 233–58.

Workshop of European Anthropologists, 1980. 'Recommendations for age and sex diagnoses of skeletons', *Journal of Human Evolution* 9, 517–49.

Yakar, J., 1991. *Prehistoric Anatolia: The Neolithic Transformation and Early Chalcolithic Period*. Tel Aviv (Monograph Series 9 of the Institute of Archaeology).

Yakar, R. and Hershkovitz, I., 1988. 'Nahal Hemar cave. The modelled skulls', *Atiqot* 18, 59–63.

Chapter 9
The Collection of Egyptian Mummies in the British Museum
Overview and Potential for Study

John H. Taylor

Introduction

The collection of Egyptian mummies at the British Museum is one of the most comprehensive of its kind in the world and enjoys a high public profile. These embalmed bodies have long been a prominent feature of the permanent displays, with the 'mummy galleries' attracting more visitors per year than any other area of the Museum's public space. While they have had a major impact on public perceptions about ancient Egypt, the mummies as a whole have not been consistently studied. Earlier handbooks to the collection (British Museum 1924; British Museum 1938) are far from exhaustive, and even the definitive catalogue of the mummies (Dawson and Gray 1968) offers only selective coverage, omitting many incomplete bodies. A consistent research strategy for this important collection is therefore needed. This chapter aims to provide some of the groundwork, by presenting a brief profile of the collection, tracing the history of its formation and outlining previous research on the mummies. Finally, it offers observations on the potential for future research on this collection, highlighting some of the factors which may impose constraints on investigators.

Formation and growth of the collection

The development of the British Museum's collection of Egyptian mummies followed a course similar to that in other large and long-established European national museums, such as that of the Rijksmuseum van Oudheden in Leiden, reflecting the changing patterns of access to mummies and the differing priorities and interests of collectors, archaeologists and anthropologists. As the following summary will make clear, the available documentation on the recent history of the mummies is often incomplete.

1753–1820

The first mummy to enter the British Museum was part of the founding collection of Hans Sloane, acquired by the nation in 1753. It comprised a small wrapped bundle in a painted wooden coffin, and was an example of a type which has been subsequently shown to be (at least in part) a fabrication made from ibis bones and scraps of ancient mummy wrappings (Blumenbach 1794). This was followed in 1756 by two complete and authentic mummies – one the bequest of Colonel William Lethieullier (1701–56) and the other donated by his nephew Pitt Lethieullier. William Lethieullier's mummy and its coffin had been obtained in Egypt in 1721 (Bierbrier 1988, 220) and were well documented through engravings made by George Vertue in 1724 and by Alexander Gordon in 1737. The mummy EA 6694 appears to be one of those presented by the Lethieulliers; on the evidence of its outer trappings it has been identified as the 'Pitt Lethieullier mummy' (Bierbrier 1988, 223), but the body actually bears two different sets of cartonnage coverings, evidently put in place following a crude opening and investigation of the mummy (perhaps that made by Blumenbach in 1792, see below p. 108), so its identity cannot be satisfactorily proven. The second of the two Lethieullier mummies is not traceable in the collection today. In 1766 another mummy, sent from Egypt by Edward

Plate 1 Small 'pseudo-mummy' in a case made from pieces of ancient coffins – one of a number of forgeries which entered the collections of European antiquaries in the 18th century. British Museum, London (EA 6952)

Wortley Montague (1713–76), was presented to the British Museum by King George III (EA 6696). All of these mummies probably came from the Memphite necropolis, near to Cairo, the principal source of such remains in the 18th century when Upper Egypt was as yet rarely visited by Europeans. Another mummy in the collection, donated by the Earl of Bessborough (EA 6957), may have been brought from Egypt even earlier, as anecdotal evidence states that it was once in the possession of Nell Gwyn (1650–87), mistress of Charles II (British Museum 1924, 135), but this was not acquired until 1836.

Records of acquisitions of other mummies in the 18th century are lacking, but by 1792 the collection included four 'large' mummies and two additional small ones besides the Sloane specimen – these latter two (EA 6952–3) were obtained probably in 1772 from the collection of Sir William Hamilton and, like the Sloane example, were also 'pseudo-mummies' (Blumenbach 1794, 179; Quirke 1997, 254–6) (**Pl. 1**). In Montagu House, the British Museum's first home, Egyptian antiquities were displayed to visitors very much in the style of elements in a cabinet of curiosities, without context or relation to any historical framework. Prominent among these were two large and two small mummies, which attracted much attention (Moser 2006, 46–53).

1820–1840

Napoleon Bonaparte's expedition to Egypt (1798–1801) and the discovery of the Rosetta Stone opened the country's rich heritage to the wider world. The end of the Napoleonic wars coincided with a phase of increasing stability in Egypt under Mohammed Ali, and in the following decades European travellers visited the ancient sites and collected antiquities. The cemeteries of Thebes became the main focus for the acquisition of well-preserved mummies, many of which

entered the collections of prominent diplomats such as the consuls Henry Salt, Bernardino Drovetti and Giovanni Anastasi. The British Museum subsequently obtained some of these collections in whole or in part, with a view to extending the comprehensiveness (and thereby the instructional value) of its holdings, although the desire to maintain national status in a rapidly advancing field of knowledge also drove acquisition. Mummies were also obtained from other collectors and travellers, some of which were ultimately sourced from the same antiquities dealers and agents who supplied the consuls, and hence some of the mummies which passed into public collections at this time can be traced to a common find context.

Prominent among the sources of mummies which were acquired by the British Museum during this period were four substantial collections.

The first collection of the British Consul in Egypt, Henry Salt (1780–1827) (acquired piecemeal between 1816–21, purchase finalized in 1823), probably included at least six mummies, but only two (EA 6707, 6713) are clearly identifiable in contemporary documents. A list of items dispatched to England clearly identifies EA 6707, and in letters written by Salt from Alexandria dated 5 and 10 October 1821 he mentions that he was sending to England four large cases containing 'mummy cases' (British Museum, Department of Ancient Egypt and Sudan archives, AES Ar. 235). One of these shipment cases contained 'two Greek mummies', one with a portrait in tempera which is recognizable today as EA 6713. Salt adds: 'two of the other Egyptian mummies are very fine, & having been found by my Greek servant [i.e. his agent Giovanni d'Athanasi], have never been open'd'. Early museum records suggest that EA 6659, 6660, 6666 and 6723–4 were part of the first Salt collection, so these and perhaps others may have been among the mummies dispatched to England in October 1821.

The first collection of the traveller and collector Joseph Sams (1784–1860) was purchased in 1834. The *List of Additions* (1837, 427) records that this collection contained 'six human mummies, with cases' (cf. Anonymous 1833, 313). Although there are two contemporary manuscript lists of this collection, neither give full descriptions of the mummies or their coffins, with the result that only two of the mummies can be firmly identified today: EA 6662 and 6676 (recognizable by the descriptions of their coffins, and by the fact that the coffin of 6676 bears an old paper label, 'SM', used as an abbreviation for 'Sams'; the 'Salt 1835' label painted on this coffin is erroneous). There was also a seventh mummy, enclosed within a Late Period stone sarcophagus (Anonymous 1833, 312), which a manuscript list notes had been added by Sams (British Museum, Department of Ancient Egypt and Sudan archives, AES Ar. 257). This could be EA 6697, a mummy attributed to Sams but not associated with an identifiable coffin; however, it could equally well be one of the 'six human mummies, with cases'.

Six mummies were acquired from the third collection of Henry Salt, auctioned by Sotheby's in London in 1835 (his second collection having been sold to the French). Five of them are easily identifiable from the descriptions in the sale catalogue and from records which show that these particular lots were purchased by the British Museum (EA 6665, 6679, 6704, 6711, 6715 = Sotheby & Son 1835, lots 150, 852, 580, 1269, 149 respectively). The sixth mummy is EA 6680, identified as from 'Salt 1835' in Samuel Birch's manuscript catalogue of the British Museum's Egyptian antiquities. Although it has no coffin, it can be plausibly identified with the mummy described under lot 986 in the sale catalogue, which was at that time associated with the much earlier coffin of Nubkheperre Intef (EA 6652; Sotheby & Son 1835).

The second collection of the Swedish-Norwegian consul Giovanni Anastasi (1780–1860), purchased in 1839, also contained six mummies, five of which are clearly identifiable from contemporary manuscript lists: EA 6669, 6673, 6682, 6699 and 6714 (British Museum, Department of Ancient Egypt and Sudan archives, 'Acquisitions of Antiquities 1839'). The sixth mummy was contained within the cartonnage case EA 6686, but the case is now empty and the mummy is no longer identifiable; a note in the minutes of the Trustees' Standing Committee authorized the destruction of a mummy from the Anastasi collection in 1843 because it 'had been attacked and rendered worthless by insects', and this was presumably the specimen in question.

Among mummies acquired individually was that of a child, obtained from an unnamed source in 1831 (*List of Additions* 1833, 119). It is not identifiable today, although it might be equated with either EA 6709 or EA 6717, neither of which has a secure provenance. Another mummy (EA 6692) was acquired in 1835, having been purchased in Egypt from Giovanni d'Athanasi by Alexander Turnbull Christie in 1832. The Earl of Bessborough presented the mummy said to have belonged to Nell Gwyn in 1836 (EA 6957) and in 1838 Richard Howard Vyse donated a naturally preserved body, of medieval date, which he had discovered in the Third Pyramid at Giza (EA 18212).

Mummies and coffins occupied a prominent place in a new display of Egyptian antiquities which was opened at the British Museum in 1838. Here the exhibits were arranged on a taxonomic basis, and since hieroglyphs could now be translated, many of the mummies were identified by name from the inscriptions on their coffins and tentatively dated, but little attention was paid to provenance and the circumstances of their discovery. The 1840 *Synopsis of the Contents of the British Museum* lists more than 30 mummies that were displayed in the Egyptian galleries in that year (*Synopsis* 1840, 268–71, 286–96). The majority are identifiable today, but several mummies which are known to have been acquired before that date lack secure provenance, including EA 6681, 6709, 6712, 6716, 6717 and 6718. Most of these should probably be attributed to the first collections of Henry Salt and Joseph Sams, for which fully reliable lists do not exist. The mummies acquired between 1820 and 1840 reflect the principles of selection which motivated the collectors of the time, who generally sought only specimens with fine or decorated wrappings and visually attractive painted coffins. Few, if any, were collected on account of their 'archaeological' significance.

1840–1930

Between 1840 and 1880, when the Egyptian collection was under the authority of Samuel Birch, the Keeper of Oriental Antiquities, fewer mummies were acquired by the British Museum. With the advent of Auguste Mariette, the founder of Egypt's *Service des Antiquites* in the 1850s, Egyptians were encouraged to value their own pharaonic heritage, and greater restrictions were imposed on the export of antiquities. Moreover, papyri and objects of daily life were increasingly regarded as more desirable for European museums than mummies and sarcophagi. However, after the death of Mariette in 1881, excavations intensified not only at Thebes, but at Akhmim as well as at cemetery sites in the Faiyum, and relaxation of restrictions led to a larger number of antiquities again leaving Egypt. Many mummies passed on to the art market and some were disposed of officially through the 'sale room' of the Cairo Museum. E.A. Wallis Budge (Assistant Keeper and subsequently Keeper of the Department of Egyptian and Assyrian Antiquities) pursued an active policy of collecting for the British Museum, making regular visits to Egypt between 1886 and 1913, and acquired 27 mummies in line with a clear strategy: in 1898 the Trustees recorded: 'It has been Mr Budge's aim during some years to form a complete typical collection of mummies and coffins of the various periods of Egyptian history' (Minutes, Trustees' Standing Committee 12 March 1898).

Budge acquired mainly from dealers, and he viewed the mummies primarily as potential exhibits, paying little attention to provenance and archaeological context. The huge volume of material which he collected, together with his often unreliable recording, makes it difficult to trace the sources of his purchases, many of which were offered to the Museum through the shipping company of R.J. Moss of Alexandria (Bierbrier 2012, 388). They acted as Budge's agents, holding items in their warehouses until funds became available, with the consequence of masking the

Plate 2 Naturally preserved body of an adult male from Gebelein, Predynastic period, c. 3500 BC. British Museum, London (EA 32754)

identities of some of the true suppliers. Among the items which were acquired from Budge's visits to Egypt from 1886 to 1899 were two Middle Kingdom mummies bought at a village north of Asyut (EA 23425, 29574: Budge 1925, 211; Filer 1999); four Third Intermediate Period specimens (EA 20744, 29577, 29578, 30720); a large number of Late Period, Ptolemaic and Roman mummies from Akhmim (EA 20650, 20745, 29588, 29782, 29776, 29777, 29581); one probably from the Faiyum (EA 24800); and others of unknown provenance (EA 29783, 30362–4). The most striking group of mummies acquired by Budge were the six naturally preserved bodies of the late Predynastic period from Gebelein, although data on their discovery is regrettably meagre (Budge 1920, vol. II, 359–61) (**Pl. 2**). Archival sources indicate that these mummies had been acquired as early as 1898, although they

Plate 3 Mummy of Ankhef, an adult male, in original coffin inscribed with his name. From Asyut, 12th Dynasty, c. 1950 BC. This is one of the few mummies in the British Museum which has a precise archaeological context. British Museum, London (EA 46631)

were not formally accessioned until 1900. A seventh was added in 1923 (see Chapter Three, this volume).

During this period, mummies from several archaeological expeditions were presented to the British Museum. In 1888–9, four Roman period mummies came from W.M.F. Petrie's excavations at Hawara – those of the Greek youth Artemidorus (EA 21810), an unidentified youth (EA 13595) and two children (EA 21809, 22108), three of them donated by Petrie's sponsor H. Martyn Kennard and the fourth by the Reverend W. Lawson. Work conducted by the Egypt Exploration Fund at Deir el-Bahri produced two female mummies of the 11th Dynasty, which were acquired in 1904–5, one in fragments (EA 40924–7), the other, that of the lady Kemsit, now lost (EA 41853: see note to **Table 1**). In 1905, from the excavations of John Garstang at Speos Artemidos near Beni Hasan, came an unusual small cartonnage coffin containing a mummy which the excavator hesitantly identified as a monkey, but which is now recognized as a child who suffered from the rare pathological condition *osteogenesis imperfecta* (brittle bone disease) (see Chapter One, **Pl. 1**). From the 1906–7 excavations of D.G. Hogarth at Asyut, came a mummy of the 12th Dynasty (EA 46631) (**Pl. 3**), and from Petrie's 1912–13 excavations at Tarkhan, come two contracted Early Dynastic bodies, one in a reed coffin (EA 52887), the other in a wooden coffin (EA 52888), both of which have precise archaeological contexts (Petrie 1914, 6, pl. XLVII); from the same site, but without context, comes a Roman child mummy (EA 52889). Another find from Petrie's work at Sedment, acquired in 1923, was a mummified head which the excavator identified as that of Meryrehashtef, owner of an important 6th Dynasty tomb at the site (EA 55725).

The Museum also acquired mummies during these years from a variety of other sources: two were presented in 1869 by the Prince of Wales (later King Edward VII) (EA 15654, 22814) and others by the Duke of Sutherland (EA 24957), Lady Amherst (EA 48971) and Captain E.L. Gruning. Another mummy (EA 22812) was obtained from the dispersal of the India Museum in London in 1880 and two were acquired at sales – EA 22939 from the collection of the French consul Raymond Sabatier (**Pl. 4**) and EA 25258 from the dealer Claude Camille Rollin.

The majority of the mummies were exhibited in a taxonomic display which was relocated to the northern upper Egyptian galleries in the early 1880s which were renewed and expanded in 1898. After this date the display of mummies and coffins underwent relatively little change until the 1990s.

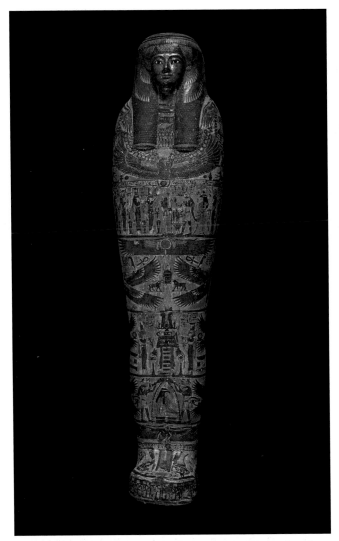

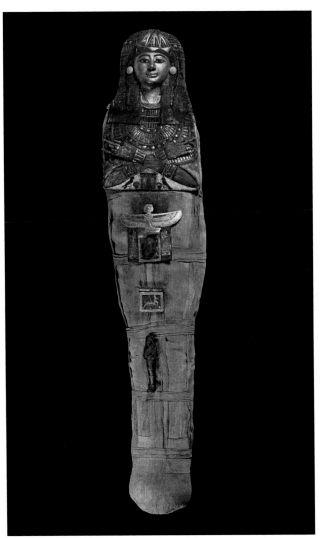

Plate 4 Mummy of a female named Tayesmutengebtiu, enclosed within original cartonnage case and securely identified by inscriptions, 22nd Dynasty, *c.* 900 BC. British Museum, London (EA 22939)

Plate 5 Mummy of an adult female named Katebet with original mask, pectoral ornaments and shabti figure, late 18th or early 19th Dynasty, *c.* 1300–1280 BC. British Museum, London (EA 6665)

Post-1930

Changing priorities in archaeological fieldwork, together with more rigorous control of the traffic in antiquities, led to a significant reduction in the numbers of mummies being brought from Egypt in this period. Only one complete Egyptian mummy has been acquired by the British Museum since 1930 – a specimen donated by St Bartholomew's Hospital, which may have been brought to England in the 19th century and which had been unwrapped at some unspecified date (EA 74303: Serpico 1998, 1044–6). A completely new permanent display of mummies, which opened in 1999, placed the remains in context with associated grave-goods and gave prominence to their significance as sources of bioanthropological information about past societies.

Overview of the collection

Table 1 is a chronological listing of 87 human bodies, comprising all the extant mummies from Egypt (both naturally and artificially preserved) which are in a complete or near-complete state. Also included are a few fragmentary bodies which have a secure provenance and date, such as the head of Meryrehashtef (EA 55725) and the remains of an 11th

Dynasty female (EA 40924–7). Although the Museum's collection also includes numerous other fragments of mummies (heads, hands and arms, feet and legs and other parts including hair samples), most of these lack reliable data as to their date, provenance and acquisition, and have therefore been omitted from the present list.

Sex and age

Sex is indicated where known, on the basis of anatomical criteria. Age is given only as A (adult) and S/A (sub-adult), since more precise estimates are subject to change.

Chronological range

With one exception (EA 18212, a medieval body from Giza), the mummies span a chronological range of nearly 4000 years (mid-4th millennium BC to early 1st millennium AD), but diachronically the evidence is unevenly spread. The seven late Predynastic bodies from Gebelein (EA 32751–6, 57353) from around *c.* 3500 BC constitute an important group from a single context. The succeeding period of 2,500 years to the end of the New Kingdom (*c.* 1070 BC) is thinly represented in the collection, consisting only of two skeletal bodies of Early Dynastic date (EA 52887–8), a single

Plate 6 Soft tissues from the mummy of a female named Irtyersenu, 26th Dynasty, *c.* 550 BC, including lungs and heart (top right) and a benign ovarian tumour (lower left), extracted and prepared by A.B. Granville in 1821. British Museum, London (EA 75991)

fragment of an identifiable mummy of the Old Kingdom (EA 55725), three complete mummies of the Middle Kingdom (EA 46631, 23425, 29574, two of them unwrapped and skeletonized), together with parts of a fourth (EA 40924–7), and one complete mummy of the New Kingdom (EA 6665) (**Pl. 5**). The majority of the collection dates between the Third Intermediate Period and the Roman era, from the 1st millennium BC to the early 2nd century AD.

The chronological profile of the British Museum collection reflects a broader picture also seen in other major museum collections, such as that of the Rijksmuseum, Leiden, all of whose 27 mummies date to the Third Intermediate to Roman periods (Raven and Taconis 2005, 53). The scarcity of well-preserved mummies from the period before the end of the New Kingdom is well attested, and several reasons for this can be postulated. Mummification by artificial processes was a mark of high status in the earlier periods and was probably available only to a relatively small proportion of the population, and the techniques used appear to have been less effective in preserving soft tissues and maintaining the physical integrity of the corpse than in later centuries. There was systematic destruction of older burials through plundering and/or reuse of tombs, while the existence of a more organized system of cemetery management during the later centuries of pharaonic culture seems to have allowed a higher proportion of later mummies to survive undisturbed to modern times.

Geographical range
Here too the picture is unbalanced, with a preponderance of mummies from Upper Egyptian sites such as Thebes and Akhmim, and very few from the historically important regions of the Delta and northern Upper Egypt. This is due to the variation in the degree of preservation of organic remains in different parts of Egypt, and to the fluctuating accessibility of burial sites between the 18th century and the present day in addition to the changing priorities of those who collected mummies.

In the Delta environmental conditions are not generally conducive to the good preservation of organic remains, and

those mummies which have been found there are usually reduced to bones. In other areas too, such as the Faiyum, groundwater destroyed many bodies. Generally, the dry conditions in cemeteries along the Nile valley in Upper Egypt promote good preservation, and it is from these areas that the majority of well-preserved mummies come.

Most of the mummies that were brought to Europe in the 16th to 18th centuries came from the Memphite necropolis, as it was relatively easy to access from Cairo and penetration further into the interior to sites such as Thebes was still considered too dangerous by most travellers. This changed in the 19th century when the whole of Egypt and northern Sudan became more accessible, and Thebes became the focus of a flourishing mummy trade. Other cemeteries along the Nile, however, remained little exploited until the late 19th and early 20th centuries. Since 1900 anthropological studies of human remains from Egypt have tended to focus on skeletal material (often in the field, rather than in the museum), with a consequent reduction in the addition of mummies to museum collections.

Previous research on the British Museum mummies
The earliest documented studies of the British Museum mummies were carried out in 1792 by the distinguished German anthropologist Johann Friedrich Blumenbach (1752–1840). His examination of small mummies in private collections had raised questions of authenticity; they did not contain, as expected, the bodies of children, but a bundle of resin-soaked wrappings and ibis bones respectively (Blumenbach 1794). To elucidate this problem Blumenbach was granted permission to open one of the three small mummies then in the British Museum (that from the Sloane collection). He found that it contained the humerus of a child and concluded that such 'mummies' (contained in coffins secured with iron nails) were 'deceptions' (Blumenbach 1794; more have been identified subsequently: Germer, Kischkewitz and Lüning 1994; Quirke 1997). Blumenbach was also allowed to examine two of the Museum's four large mummies, one of which 'had already been opened in several places'. His observations on the larger mummies relate to the state of their preservation (in both cases only the bones survived), the ethnicity of the bodies, determined from the skulls, and the absence of amulets or other objects (Blumenbach 1794).

It is not clear whether the large mummies 'opened' by Blumenbach survived this process. By 1809 only two large mummies and one 'mummy of a child' were displayed. One of the large specimens was said to be that bequeathed by William Lethieullier, but the description in the 1809 *Synopsis*, which mentions a gilded face and painted ornaments, does not match the 1724 illustration of the mummy by Vertue, suggesting that there had been some confusion of identities. The William Lethieullier mummy cannot be identified in the collection today and may have been reduced to unrecognizable fragments by Blumenbach. The 1840 *Synopsis* mentions 'Mummies, unrolled and wrapped up again; one in a very incomplete state' (1840, 268).

The period 1820–40 was characterized by many unwrappings of mummies in England. The momentum had been begun by the explorer Giovanni Belzoni (1778–1823), and the practice was taken up mainly by men of medical background, notably Thomas Joseph Pettigrew (1791–1865) (the chief exponent of mummy 'unrollings') and Augustus Bozzi Granville (1783–1872). Their investigations were directed towards increased understanding of mummification procedures, retrieving evidence for the ethnicity of the ancient Egyptians and the recovery of amulets and other objects placed within the wrappings. Although some crude scientific tests were applied, most of the mummies that were opened in this manner suffered severe and irreversible damage, and in consequence the British Museum refused Pettigrew permission 'to examine one or two of the specimens' in its collection (Pettigrew 1834, xix). A meticulously mounted and labelled set of samples from a female mummy which Granville had carefully dissected was sold to the Museum in 1853, but the authorities considered them unsuitable for display, much to Granville's displeasure (Granville 1874, vol. II, 210–11) (**Pl. 6**). Although the mummy collection was considerably expanded in the late 19th and early 20th centuries, none of the bodies were unwrapped (Budge 1920, vol. II, 395) and there is no record of any research being carried out on them until the 1960s.

An extensive radiological survey of the mummies was carried out in 1963–5 by P.H.K. Gray using portable X-ray equipment. This study of 78 mummies yielded the first significant assessments of sex, age, state of health, pathological conditions and mummification techniques, and revealed the presence of objects beneath the wrappings and within the body cavities. The results of this study were published selectively (Dawson and Gray 1968). The Trustees of the British Museum still refused for any of the mummies to be unwrapped, but permission was granted to make a small incision in mummy EA 6659 in order to extract an enigmatic object that had been revealed by X-ray; this proved to be a crude clay figurine (Dawson and Gray 1968, pls XXIc, XXXc).

Since 1991 more than 30 mummies in the collection have undergone CT scanning, carried out using a variety of scanning equipment in numerous hospitals in London, Manchester and Brisbane, while six were scanned using portable equipment when on loan to a museum in California in 2005. The studies have yielded both CT data in DICOM medical imaging format and 3D reconstructions, which have provided substantial new information about sex, age, state of health, pathology and mummification procedures, but the results have been published only selectively so far (Taylor 1994; Filer 1997; Taylor 2004). These exercises have also raised several issues concerning the long-term storage of CT data, image rights and intellectual property, which have informed subsequent discussions on the development of watertight protocols for future studies.

From the 1980s to the present day, bioanthropological and other scientific studies of Egyptian mummies have proliferated worldwide. However, comparatively little invasive study has been carried out on the British Museum mummies. The investigations which have been undertaken have been limited to the analysis of small samples from unwrapped or fragmentary bodies, chiefly in order to preserve the integrity of the wrapped mummies which constitute the major part of the collection.

Investigations have focused on three main areas: the extraction of ancient DNA, palaeopathological studies and analyses of embalming materials. In 1989 Svante Pääbo reported the successful extraction of a short sequence of mitochondrial DNA from the Predynastic natural mummy EA 32753 (Pääbo 1989), but subsequent studies on bone and ligament from mummies EA 23425, 29574, 32752, 32754, 32755, 32756, 40924–5, 57353, 52887 and 52888, carried out at the University of Munich, yielded negative results and no further investigations of this kind have been conducted on British Museum specimens.

A tissue sample from EA 32753 revealed the presence of an antigen produced by the body to combat schistosomiasis (Miller *et al.* 1993, 58–9, pl. 6). Two other natural mummies from Gebelein and the unwrapped mummies of children of the Roman period have been examined purely by visual inspection for evidence of dermatological conditions, a study which showed signs of eczema on skin and stress lines on fingernails; the same researchers identified egg cases of head louse in the hair of mummy EA 32752, in addition to reddish colouring of hair and nails which has been tentatively interpreted as 'consistent with the use of henna' (Leslie and Levell 2006). Study of soft tissues and bone from the female mummy dissected by Augustus Bozzi Granville in 1821 (EA 75991) has demonstrated that the subject suffered from tuberculosis (Donoghue *et al.* 2009); further analytical investigations on this mummy have been conducted in recent years, but as of yet are unpublished.

Several studies of the chemical composition of embalming agents from mummies have been carried out, using samples from the British Museum as the basis of Gas Chromatography/Mass Spectrometry (GC/MS) and other techniques. These studies have used small samples mainly from the exposed surfaces of incomplete bodies, from the wrappings of mummies or in some cases from the deposits exuded from mummies, retrieved from the surfaces of coffins (Serpico and White 1998; Buckley and Evershed 2001).

Future research: potential and limitations

Although the possibilities of conducting research based on tissue sampling from wrapped mummies remain limited, non-invasive imaging has and continues to furnish much new data. While these techniques greatly expand the amount of information which the British Museum mummies can yield, special care is needed in interpreting the findings. It is recognized that the value and usefulness of scientific studies depends heavily on obtaining samples from mummies which have a secure provenance and date (Buckley and Evershed 2001, 837) and, if possible, are the remains of identifiable persons. The extent and reliability of such data should be rigorously assessed as they are often less secure than they may appear to be at first sight.

Provenance

Comparatively few of the British Museum mummies have a contemporary record of their discovery or exact provenance. This is available for most of those from controlled excavations such as the bodies from Tarkhan, Asyut or Hawara, but the majority of mummies acquired before the

Table 1 Egyptian mummies in the collection of the Department of Ancient Egypt and Sudan at the British Museum, arranged in chronological sequence. 'Acquired' records the date of formal registration (which may in some cases be one or more years later than the arrival of a mummy at the Museum). 'Date' is based on recent studies of embalming techniques, coffins and associated objects, and supersedes the datings given in Dawson and Gray 1968. Under 'Wrappings etc.', 'cartonnage' denotes a complete mummy-case, from which the body has not been removed, rather than separate trappings, such as mask, collar, footcase etc. The list omits fragments of mummies without secure date and provenance (A=Adult, S/A=Sub-adult)

BM No.	Date	Provenance	Acquired	Sex	Age	Name	Description	Wrappings etc
32751	Predynastic	Gebelein	1900	M	A		Flexed	None
32752	Predynastic	Gebelein	1900	F	A		Flexed	None
32753	Predynastic	Gebelein	1900	?	A		Flexed	None
32754	Predynastic	Gebelein	1900	M	A		Flexed	Textile fragments
32755	Predynastic	Gebelein	1900	?	A		Flexed	Textile fragments
32756	Predynastic	Gebelein	1900	?	A		Flexed	Textile fragments
57353	Predynastic	Gebelein	1923	M	A		Flexed	Textile fragments
52887	1st Dyn.	Tarkhan	1913	?	A		Flexed	None
52888	1st Dyn.	Tarkhan	1913	?	A		Flexed	Textile fragments
55725	6th Dyn.	Sedment	1923	M	A	Meryrehashtef	Skull	None
40924-7	11th Dyn.	Deir el-Bahri	1904	F	A		Skull, r. arm, feet	None
46631	12th Dyn.	Asyut	1907	M	A	Ankhef	Extended	Wrapped
23425	12th Dyn.	Asyut	1895	M	A	Heny	Extended	None
29574	12th Dyn.	Asyut	1895	M	A	Khety	Extended	None
6665	19th Dyn.	Thebes	1835	F	A	Katebet	Extended	Wrapped
48971	21st Dyn.		1909	F	A		Extended	Wrapped
22939	22nd Dyn.	Thebes	1891	F	A	Tayesmutengebtiu	Extended	Wrapped, cartonnage
6659	22nd Dyn.	Thebes	1823?	M	A	Hor	Extended	Wrapped
6660	22nd Dyn.	Thebes	1823?	M	A	Denytenamun	Extended	Wrapped
6662	22nd Dyn.	Thebes	1834	M	A	Djedkhonsiufankh	Extended	Wrapped, cartonnage
30720	22nd Dyn.	Thebes	1899	M	A	Nesperennub	Extended	Wrapped, cartonnage
25258	22nd Dyn.		1894	F	A		Extended	Wrapped, cartonnage
20744	22nd Dyn.		1888	F	S/A	Tjayasetimu	Extended	Wrapped, cartonnage
6697	21st-22nd D.		1834	F	A		Extended	Wrapped
22812	21st-22nd D.		1880	M	A		Extended	Wrapped
41603	22nd Dyn.	Sp. Artemidos	1905	M?	S/A		Extended	None
29577	22nd Dyn.		1897	M	A	Djedameniufankh	Extended	Wrapped, cartonnage
74303	21st-25th D.		1990	F	A		Extended	Unwrapped
6681	25th Dyn.	Thebes	pre-1840	M	A	Peftjaukhons	Extended	Wrapped, cartonnage
6682	25th Dyn.	Thebes	1839	M	A	Padiamenet	Extended	Wrapped, cartonnage
6692	25th Dyn.	Thebes	1835	F	A	Takhebkhenem	Extended	Wrapped
6676	25th Dyn.		1834	M	A	Penamunnebnesttawy	Extended	Wrapped
15654	25th Dyn.	Thebes	1869	F	A	Bakrenes	Extended	Wrapped
32052	25th Dyn.	[Akhmim?]	1904	F	A	Tetjenef	Extended	Wrapped
6666	26th Dyn.		1823	F	A		Extended	Wrapped
24957	26th Dyn.		1893	F	A		Extended	Unwrapped
6669	26th Dyn.	Thebes	1839	M	A	Ameniryirt	Extended	Wrapped
6673	26th Dyn.		1839	F	A	Ankhesnefer	Extended	Wrapped
22814	26th Dyn.	Thebes	1869	M	A		Extended	Wrapped
75991	26th Dyn.	Thebes	1853	F	A	Irtyersenu	Fragments	Unwrapped
20745	26th Dyn.	Akhmim	1888	M	A	Irthorru	Extended	Wrapped
20650	26th Dyn.	Akhmim	1887	M	A	Djedher	Extended	Wrapped
6696	26th Dyn.		1766	M	A	Itineb	Extended	Wrapped
29578	Late Period?		1898	F?	A		Extended	Wrapped
6694	LP/Ptolemaic	Saqqara?	1756	?	A		Extended	Partially unwrapped
6716	Ptolemaic?			F	A		Extended	Wrapped
6679	Ptolemaic	Thebes	1835	M	A	Hornedjitief	Extended	Wrapped
6680	Ptolemaic		1835	M	A	Horemheb	Extended	Wrapped
6711	Ptolemaic	Thebes	1835	M	A	Ankh-hap	Extended	Wrapped
29581	Ptolemaic	Akhmim	1898	M	A	Nesmin	Extended	Wrapped
29776	Ptolemaic	Akhmim	1898	M	A	Djedher	Extended	Wrapped
29777	Ptolemaic	Akhmim	1898	M	A	Padikhonsiin	Extended	Wrapped
29778	Ptolemaic		1898	M	A		Extended	Wrapped
6957	Ptolemaic		1836	?	A		Extended	Partially unwrapped
6699	Ptolemaic		1839	?	S/A		Extended	Wrapped
6718	Ptolemaic		?	F	A		Extended	Wrapped
6704	Roman		1835	M	A		Extended	Wrapped
29782	Roman	Akhmim	1897	M	A		Extended	Wrapped

BM No.	Date	Provenance	Acquired	Sex	Age	Name	Description	Wrappings etc
6717	Roman?		?	?	S/A		Extended	Wrapped
6707	Roman	Thebes	1823	F	S/A	Cleopatra	Extended	Wrapped
13595	Roman	Hawara	1888	M	S/A		Extended	Wrapped
21810	Roman	Hawara	1888	M	A	Artemidorus	Extended	Wrapped, cartonnage
21809	Roman	Hawara	1888	?	S/A		Extended	Wrapped
22108	Roman	Hawara	1889	M	S/A		Extended	Wrapped
24800	Roman	Faiyum?	1893	M	A		Extended	Wrapped
29783 (1)	Roman		1898	M	A		Extended	Wrapped
29783 (2)	Roman		1898	?	S/A		Extended	Wrapped
29783 (3)	Roman		1898	?	S/A		Extended	Wrapped
29783 (4)	Roman		1898	?	S/A		Extended	Wrapped
6709	Roman		pre-1840	M	S/A		Extended	Wrapped
6712	Roman		pre-1840	M	A		Extended	Wrapped
6713	Roman	Thebes	1823	M	A		Extended	Wrapped
6714	Roman		1839	M	A		Extended	Wrapped
6715	Roman		1835	M	S/A		Extended	Wrapped
6723	Roman		1823	M	S/A		Extended	Wrapped
52889	Roman	Tarkhan	1913	?	S/A		Extended	Wrapped
29588	Roman	Akhmim	1897	?	S/A		Extended	Wrapped, cartonnage
54052	Roman		1915	?	S/A		Extended	Wrapped
54053	Roman		1915	M	S/A		Extended	Wrapped
30362	Roman		1898	?	S/A		Extended	Unwrapped
30363	Roman		1898	F	S/A		Extended	Unwrapped
30364	Roman		1898	M	S/A		Extended	Unwrapped
54055 (1)	Roman		1915	?	S/A		Extended	Wrapped
54055 (2)	Roman		1915	?	S/A		Extended	Wrapped
54051	Roman?		1915	?	S/A		Extended	Wrapped
6724	Roman?		1823	?	S/A?		Extended	Wrapped
18212	Medieval	Giza	1838	?	A		Extended	None

NB The mummy of Kemsit, one of the wives of Mentuhotep II, was accessioned in 1905 (as EA 41853 = 1905-10-14, 237), but it cannot now be located. The description in the original acquisition register reads: 'Upper portion (legs missing) of the mummy of a woman, with head turned over to left. Found in the tomb of the negress priestess Kemsit, and probably her body (with cloth). 2 ft 4 ins L.' A note adds that it was 'packed in wooden case & put in Carthaginian Basement, May 1 '06'. Presumably it had already disappeared by the 1960s since it was not included in Dawson and Gray's X-ray survey of the Egyptian mummy collection then.

1880s lack such information. The keeping of such records was not generally practised at that time, and thus no provenances are attached to the descriptions of the mummies in the 1840 *Synopsis*. However, by the 1890s the Museum's guidebooks give this information in most cases (as in British Museum 1898), the 'missing' data having been apparently supplied by museum staff either from paper records or on the basis of stylistic assessments. These published provenances have been repeated in later publications, but should where possible be tested by archival research since they are not always accurate. For example, mummy EA 32052 was registered in 1904 together with a group of objects from John Garstang's excavations at Beni Hasan, and it has been assumed to come from that site and published as such (Dawson and Gray 1968, 17). However, recent archival research has shown that the mummy was not originally associated with the objects from Beni Hasan, and stylistic evidence from the coffins points instead to Akhmim as a more likely provenance.

In fact many of the attributions to sites are based mainly on inscriptional evidence from the coffins in which the mummies were obtained. These often bear official titles identifying the owners as members of the priesthoods of the gods Amun at Thebes and Min at Akhmim, and in some cases genealogical information enables an individual to be linked to a documented family which is known to have resided in one of those centres.

Dating

Until recently, scientific techniques such as radiocarbon dating have not made a significant contribution to the study of Egyptian mummies, owing largely to the destructive nature of the procedure, the potential for the contamination of samples and the known practice of ancient embalmers and undertakers of reusing older organic materials for wrappings and coffins. Moreover, the margin of error inherent in radiocarbon dates has often proved unacceptably broad. The dating of the British Museum mummies is based on archaeological context, where known. If this data is unavailable (which is the case for most of the mummies), techniques of mummification and inscriptional or stylistic evidence from coffins have been used as guides, but uncertainty about the chronology of technical and stylistic trends can limit the reliability of these deductions.

Identities

Although mummies of some historical personages (particularly the New Kingdom pharaohs and their families) have survived, these are the exceptions. The majority of Egyptian mummies are either unidentified or are those of

Plate 7 Pectoral ornament from the mummy of a woman named Katebet. Although an original element of the mummy's trappings, this object was made for the burial of a man, as indicated by the costume of the two figures flanking the scarab beetle. British Museum, London (EA 6665)

persons not otherwise attested from written sources. It is rare for identification to be found on the mummy itself; the name may be inscribed on bandage epigraphs, mummy labels or on exterior trappings such as cartonnage coverings, but often these objects omit the name or are indecipherable. Such trappings can in any case be misleading; they may have been placed there by antiquities dealers or, even if original to the mummy, may bear the name or image of another person. Mummy EA 6665 has been identified as female from the mask and from X-rays of the skeleton, but a pectoral on the wrappings, which from the conspicuous fading of the colour of the surrounding textiles appears likely to be in its original context, depicts the deceased as a man (**Pl. 7**). The identification of the body as that of a woman named Katebet is based on the inscription on the lid of the associated coffin (itself a hybrid piece, having both male and female iconographic elements).

Association between mummies and coffins

It is clear from the above that accepted opinion as to the provenance, date and identity of mummies frequently relies heavily on the evidence offered by their coffins. One must therefore consider carefully the reliability of these associations. In many periods, Egyptian coffins were standardized in size, shape and proportion, not made to fit a particular individual. Mummies have often been found to be smaller than the coffins they occupy, and transposition of body and coffin therefore could, and did, occur. This happened in ancient times (through reuse and error), in the context of 18th and 19th century dealing and also, inadvertently, in museums when mummies were removed from their coffins for separate storage or display.

Transpositions may be detected if there is an obvious stylistic discrepancy between the trappings of the mummy and the coffin in which it lies, such as Ptolemaic cartonnage trappings with a coffin of a style several hundred years older,

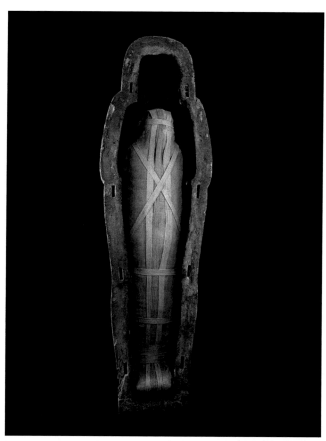

Plate 8 Unidentified wrapped female mummy, 26th Dynasty, c. 650 BC, acquired in the coffin of a male named Horaawesheb dating to the 22nd Dynasty, c. 900 BC. British Museum, London (EA 6666)

or a female mummy in a 22nd Dynasty cartonnage case, placed within a 26th Dynasty priest's coffin (Nielsen 1993). Much more difficult to detect are cases where the mummy has no exterior trappings and the arrangement of the wrappings is not distinctive. Among the collection of the British Museum, some such cases of transposition have been revealed through the determination of the sex of the mummies – both by unwrapping (female EA 24957, acquired in the coffin of man), X-ray and CT scanning (female body EA 6666 in a male coffin and male bodies EA 22812 and EA 22814 in coffins inscribed for women) (**Pl. 8**).

While these transpositions could have occurred in ancient times, it is much more likely that they reflect the deceptions which were regularly practised by antiquities dealers. Even in the early 18th century, the purveyors of 'curiosities' to European collectors broke up mummies that were found in high quality coffins so as to obtain the amulets and objects within their wrappings, substituting inferior mummies in their place (Blumenbach 1794, 133). By the early 19th century, the situation was considerably worse. Richard Robert Madden (1798–1886) recorded: 'In the sale of mummies [at Qurna], I discovered such frauds, that I have no hesitation in saying, in all the cabinets of Europe, there are not probably twenty mummies in the same coffins in which they were originally deposited.' (Madden 1829, II, 78ff). In the tomb-dwelling of one of the dealers, Madden saw 'a manufacture of mummies. Three beautiful mummy cases were laid open, an ordinary mummy was placed in the last, the original one having been previously pillaged; and, what convinced me of the fraud was several new wooden

Plate 9 Detail of the linen wrappings of the mummy of Katebet, showing remains of a reddish colouring. Descriptions of this mummy from the mid-19th century mention 'maroon' colouring on the bandages, which has now deteriorated through long-term exposure to light. British Museum, London (EA 6665)

pegs lying on the cover of the large case, undoubtedly intended as substitutes to the old ones, which had been broken in bursting open the external case.' Qurna, on the Theban west bank, was the main centre for the mummy trade in the 19th century, and a large number of the mummies now in museums came from there before the advent of scientific archaeology. Transposition was also practised by those selling their collections in Europe, thus several coffins acquired by the British Museum in the 1830s had 'intrusive' mummies inside them (above, p. 105). Indeed, absolute certainty about a mummy's identity is only possible for specimens that are still sealed within inscribed cartonnage cases which enveloped the body completely, and which could not be removed without visible damage.

Previous conservation treatments and the effects of display and storage

Scientific studies should also take into account the environments and treatments to which the mummies have been exposed since their acquisition. The majority of the British Museum mummies have been on long-term display in the public galleries (30+ in the 1840s, 42 in 1904, 24 today), exhibited in the 19th and 20th centuries in glazed cases with wood or metal frames and now currently in glass cases without microclimates or internal gases. They have been exposed to both natural and artificial light, which has caused the dyed and painted surfaces of linen wrappings to fade. The original colours are mentioned in early descriptions and may be still visible on parts of the wrappings that have not been exposed (**Pl. 9**). Fluctuating environmental conditions (temperature and humidity) have sometimes led to the growth of mould and salt efflorescence, but these instances have been successfully controlled subsequently, as has insect activity, except in the single case of a mummy which was attacked by insects and authorized for disposal in 1843 (above, p. 105). Current practice requires detailed records to be kept of all conservation treatments, but unfortunately there is little documentation on the methods which were applied to the mummies in the 19th and

early 20th centuries. Recent attempts to obtain radiocarbon dates from some of the Gebelein natural mummies have been compromised since the bodies were found to have been treated with pesticides at some unspecified date; hence the researcher must at all times be prepared to encounter difficulties arising from such undocumented treatments.

Conclusion

Experience has shown that Egyptian mummies hold the clues which may provide answers to many important questions about the life experiences and cultural practices of past societies in the Nile valley over an unparalleled time-span of more than 4,000 years. The potential which they hold as sources of scientific data is still largely untapped, but they are not an inexhaustible resource and hence any strategy for their future study must be predicated on the need to maintain their physical integrity. The trajectory of study in the short term appears likely to focus on the capture of full CT data sets of all mummies in the collection and the permanent storage of this information in readily accessible form (Taylor and Antoine 2014). Such non-invasive imaging can be expected to yield significant new data on the lifestyles of the ancient Egyptians, the incidence of disease and mummification. Much remains to be done, however, towards the study of the chemical composition of organic and inorganic substances which were used in the embalming process, and here the chief obstacle to progress at present is reluctance to subject intact mummies to destructive sampling. While research into ancient DNA from mummies continues to provoke controversy (Hawass *et al.* 2010), recent refinements in techniques for utilizing radiocarbon dating from Egyptian remains (Shortland and Bronk Ramsey 2013) may foreshadow renewed interest in the application of this methodology to the study of mummies.

Bibliography

Anonymous, 1833. 'Egyptian antiquities', *The Gentleman's Magazine*, April 1833, 312–15, pls II–III.
Bierbrier, M.L., 1988. 'The Lethieullier family and the British Museum', in *Pyramid Studies and other Essays presented to I. E. S. Edwards*, ed. J. Baines, T.G.H. James, A. Leahy and A.F. Shore, 220–8, pl. 44. London.
— (ed.), 2012. *Who was Who in Egyptology*, 4th revised edn. London.
Blumenbach, J.F., 1794. 'Observations on some Egyptian Mummies opened in London', *Philosophical Transactions of the Royal Society of London* 84, 177–95, Tab. XVI (text reprinted, *New Annual Register 1794* (London 1795), 126–35).
British Museum 1898. *A Guide to the First and Second Egyptian Rooms*. London.
— 1924. *A Guide to the First, Second and Third Egyptian Rooms*, 3rd edn. London.
— 1938. *A Handbook to the Egyptian Mummies and Coffins Exhibited in the British Museum*. London.
Buckley, S.A. and Evershed, R.P., 2001. 'Organic chemistry of embalming agents in Pharaonic and Graeco-Roman mummies', *Nature* 413, 837–41.
Budge, E.A.W., 1920. *By Nile and Tigris*, 2 vols. London.
—, 1925. *The Mummy. A Handbook of Egyptian Funerary Archaeology*, 2nd edn. Cambridge.
David, R., 2007. *The Two Brothers. Death and the Afterlife in Middle Kingdom Egypt*. Bolton.
Dawson, W.R. and Gray, P.H.K., 1968. *Catalogue of Egyptian Antiquities in the British Museum*, vol. I, *Mummies and Human Remains*. London.
Donoghue, H.D., Lee, O.Y-C, Minnikin, D.E., Besra, G.S., Taylor, J.H. and Spigelman, M., 2009. 'Tuberculosis in Dr Granville's

mummy: a molecular re-examination of the earliest known Egyptian mummy to be scientifically examined and given a medical diagnosis', *Proceedings of the Royal Society. B: Biological Sciences* 277, 51–6.

Filer, J.M., 1997. 'If the Face Fits ….A comparison of mummies and their accompanying portraits using Computerised Axial Tomography', in *Portraits and Masks: Burial Customs in Roman Egypt*, ed. M.L. Bierbrier, 121–6, pls 44–6. London.

—, 1999. 'Both mummies as *Bakshish*', in *Studies in Egyptian Antiquities: A Tribute to T.G.H James*, ed. W V Davies, 23–7, pls 3–5. London (British Museum Occasional Paper 123).

Germer, R., Kischkewitz, H. and Lüning, M., 1994. 'Pseudo-Mumien der ägyptischen Sammlung Berlin, Studien zur Altägyptischen', *Kultur* 21, 81–94, Taf. 5–9.

Granville, A.B., 1874. *Autobiography of A.B. Granville, M.D., F.R.S., – Being Eighty-eight Years of the Life of a Physician*, vols I–II. London.

Hawass, Z., Gad, Y.Z., Ismail, S., Khairat, R., Fathalla, D., Hasan, N., Ahmed, A., Elleithy, H., Ball, M., Gaballah, F., Wasef, S., Fateen, M., Amer, H., Gostner, P., Selim, A., Zink, A. and Pusch, C.M., 2010. 'Ancestry and pathology in King Tutankhamun's family', *Journal of the American Medical Association* 303, 638–47.

Leslie, K.S. and Levell, N.J., 2006. 'Cutaneous findings in mummies from the British Museum', *International Journal of Dermatology* 45, 618–21.

List of Additions made to the Collections in the British Museum in the Year MDCCCXXXI (London 1833).

List of Additions made to the Collections in the British Museum in the Year MDCCCXXXIV (London 1837).

Madden, R.R., 1829. *Travels in Turkey, Egypt, Nubia and Palestine in 1824, 1825, 1826 and 1827*, vols I–II. London.

Miller, R.L., De Jonge, N., Krijger, F.W. and Deelder, A. M., 1993. 'Predynastic schistosomiasis', in *Biological Anthropology and the Study of Ancient Egypt*, ed. W.V. Davies and R. Walker, 54–60, pl. 6. London.

Moser, S., 2006. *Wondrous Curiosities. Ancient Egypt at the British Museum.* Chicago and London.

Nielsen, E.R., 1993. 'Di-Mut-Shep-en-Ankh', *Papyrus* [Copenhagen] 13/1, 17–27.

Pääbo, S., 1989. 'Ancient DNA: extraction, characterization, molecular cloning, and enzymatic amplification', *Proceedings of the National Academy of Science, USA* 86, 1939–43.

Petrie, W.M.F., 1914. *Tarkhan*, vol. II. London.

Pettigrew, T.J., 1834. *History of Egyptian Mummies*. London.

Quirke, S., 1997. 'Modern mummies and ancient scarabs. The Egyptian collection of Sir William Hamilton', *Journal of the History of Collections* 9, 253–62.

Raven, M.J. and Taconis, W.K., 2005. *Egyptian Mummies. Radiological Atlas of the Collections in the National Museum of Antiquities at Leiden.* Turnhout.

Serpico, M. and White, R., 1998. 'Chemical analysis of coniferous resins from Ancient Egypt using Gas Chromatography/Mass Spectrometry (GC/MS)', in *Proceedings of the Seventh International Congress of Egyptologists*, ed. C.J. Eyre, *Orientalia Lovaniensia Analecta* 82 (Leuven), 1037–48.

Shortland, A.J. and Bronk Ramsey, C. (eds), 2013. *Radiocarbon and the Chronologies of Ancient Egypt*. Oxford.

Sotheby & Son, 1835. *Catalogue of the Highly Interesting and Magnificent Collection of Egyptian Antiquities, the Property of the Late Henry Salt, Esq.* London.

Synopsis 1809. *Synopsis of the Contents of the British Museum*. London.

Synopsis 1840. *Synopsis of the Contents of the British Museum*, 40th edn. London.

Taylor, J.H., 1994. 'CT scanning of a mummy', *Egyptian Archaeology* 4, 15–16.

—, 2004. *Mummy: The Inside Story*. London.

— and Antoine, D., 2014. *Ancient Lives, New Discoveries: Eight Mummies, Eight Stories*. London.

Chapter 10
The Human Remains from Tell es-Sa'idiyeh
International Custodianship, Respect and Research

Jonathan Tubb and Caroline Cartwright

Introduction

Tell es-Sa'idiyeh, identified as the biblical city of Zarethan (Josh 3:16; 1 Kings 7:45–6), lies at the heart of the central Jordan Valley, on the south side of the Wadi Kufrinjeh. The large mound occupies a key strategic position, commanding the crossroads of two major trade routes and dominating some of the richest and most fertile agricultural land east of the River Jordan.

Excavations were first conducted by James Pritchard on behalf of the University of Pennsylvania between 1964 and 1967 (Pritchard 1980; 1985), and were resumed in 1985 by a British Museum expedition directed by Jonathan Tubb (Tubb 1988; 1990; Tubb and Dorrell 1991; 1993; 1994; Tubb *et al.* 1996; 1997).

The site was initially settled in the Chalcolithic period (5th millennium BC), but the first extensive occupation phase dates to the Early Bronze Age (*c.* 3300–2150 BC). Little has been recovered of the Early Bronze I phase apart from a few traces of a well-constructed city wall, indicating that the settlement was significant and substantial, covering approximately 12 hectares. The most extensively excavated phase belongs to the Early Bronze II period. Part of a large palace complex has been uncovered, the function of which seems to have been orientated to the industrial scale production of commodities for export to Egypt. One wing of the complex (on the evidence of the bone tools) was devoted to the manufacture of fine textiles, another to the production of wine, but the most fully exposed part was found to be responsible for the extraction of olive oil. The palace was destroyed by fire around 2700 BC.

Following its destruction, and a brief, somewhat ephemeral, phase of squatter occupation in the ruins, the site appears to have been abandoned and was only reinhabited in the Late Bronze Age (1480–1150 BC). During this and subsequent periods, occupation was confined to the eastern side of the mound, giving rise to the existing topography – a high Upper Tell to the east and a lower bench-like extension to the west (**Pl. 1**).

During the 13th century BC, perhaps in the reign of Ramses II, the site was taken into Egyptian control, and at this time the Lower Tell was used as a cemetery to serve the population inhabiting the Upper Tell. This first usage of the Lower Tell as a burial place defines Phase 1 of the cemetery. Tell es-Sa'idiyeh was further developed by the pharaohs of the 20th Dynasty, and during the 12th century BC it became a major trade and taxation centre. A remarkable series of public buildings has been uncovered including a palace complex, a large residency and part of the main eastern gate – all built using Egyptian construction methods – as well as an Aegean-style external, stone-built water system. The Lower Tell continued to be used as a cemetery and a large number of graves have been excavated in Phases 2–3 of the cemetery.

Following the withdrawal of the Egyptian empire in the 12th century BC, the site reverted to local control, but the 'Egyptian phase' buildings remained in use (as did the cemetery) until some time in the 11th century BC when they were destroyed by fire. Following this destruction and a brief abandonment, occupation resumed, but on a much smaller scale. Only in the 9th century BC was the site again

Plate 1 A view of Tell es-Saʻidiyeh from the north (photo: J.N. Tubb)

extensively settled. Protected by strong fortification walls, a well-planned city was laid out on an intersecting grid of streets and alleyways, and the houses and workshops provide artefactual evidence for industrial specialization in the form of weaving and textile preparation. Towards the end of the 8th century BC, Tell es-Saʻidiyeh was again destroyed by fire, this time most probably by the Assyrians. This event effectively put an end to settlement on the site, and although a series of fortresses crowned the highest point of the Upper Tell throughout the Babylonian, Persian and Hellenistic periods, no evidence has been found for associated habitation. That there was some settlement in the vicinity, however, is indicated by the renewed use of the Lower Tell cemetery after a gap of nearly 500 years (Phase 4 of the cemetery).

During the Roman period, a solitary watchtower was built on the north-west corner of the Upper Tell. The very last traces of occupation consist of a single-roomed farmhouse on the Upper Tell and what may be a type of *khan* or caravanserai on the north side of the Lower Tell, both dating to the 7th to 8th centuries AD. It is clear from a few late period (medieval) graves (Phase 5 of the cemetery), however, that the site was visited occasionally for the purposes of burial.

The Tell es-Saʻidiyeh cemetery

As the final report volumes detailing the British Museum's excavations in the Saʻidiyeh cemetery and its human and material remains are nearing publication (Tubb *et al.* forthcoming), this paper does not seek to summarize the findings in any detail. Nevertheless, a few general remarks would seem to be appropriate.

Even before the start of the British Museum's campaign of excavations in 1985, it was known that a cemetery existed on the Lower Tell from the investigations undertaken there by James Pritchard on behalf of the University of Pennsylvania. Between 1964 and 1967, 45 graves were excavated on the north side, these having been dug into the long-abandoned remains of the Early Bronze Age city. It was partly in pursuit of investigating this underlying occupation that an excavation area was developed towards the centre of the Lower Tell in 1985. Nothing, however, prepared the British Museum expedition for the intensity and complexity of interment present in this part of the

mound, and between 1985 and 1996 some 493 graves were excavated. Although many had been grossly disturbed through the effects of intensive and repeated intercutting, it has been possible, nevertheless, to assemble a sizeable and significant corpus of burials and through detailed analysis of the internal stratigraphy to group them into 5 phases.

In Phase 1, which marks the initial use of the Lower Tell as a cemetery when the site was taken into Egyptian control, the burials consist of neatly cut pit-graves dug into the eroded remains of the Early Bronze Age occupation or the silt overlying it. The graves were laid out in rows, giving the impression of a planned graveyard. They contained individual primary inhumations, buried consistently with a west–east orientation with regards to the positioning of the head.

Phase 2, corresponding to the resumption of Egyptian control in the 12th century BC, is characterized by individual primary burials in built graves, or more properly, tombs, constructed of mud-brick and roofed over with slabs of the same material. It is this phase also that sees the introduction of double-pithos burials (two very large jars joined shoulder-to-shoulder, their necks having been removed), possibly representing the interments of a group of the Sea Peoples, who were captured and pressed into service by the Egyptians following the land battle of Ramses III in the northern Levant in the eighth year of his reign (see Tubb 2000 for a detailed discussion of this idea).

The burials of Phases 1 and 2 were found to be quite rich in grave-goods, containing fine assemblages of pottery, metal vessels and weapons, stone and ivory vessels, amulets, seals and jewellery. Many of the finds are strongly Egyptian in character, as indeed are some of the burial practices which include the 'ritual killing' of weapons, the covering of the face (or, in one case, the genitals) of the deceased with a metal bowl and the extensive use of Egyptian linen for binding, shrouds and wrapping objects.

Phase 3 represents the continued use of the cemetery following the withdrawal of the Egyptians in the mid-12th century BC and the reversion of the site to local control before its destruction by fire towards the middle of the 11th century. The burials of this phase were again made in simple sub-rectangular pits, but were much less carefully dug and were randomly disposed. Repeated use of the same burial area resulted in the considerable disruption to graves of the previous two phases and has led to the creation of a new

Specialist	Affiliation (at the time of research)	Areas of responsibility / material analysed
Janet Henderson	Institute of Archaeology, University of London*	On-site human osteoarchaeology documentation and analysis (1985 season)
Andrew Chamberlain	University of Sheffield	Supervision of human osteoarchaeology research; curation of the human skeletal remains whilst at the University of Sheffield
Charlotte Roberts	University of Bradford	Supervision of human osteoarchaeology research
Stephany Leach	University of Sheffield	On-site and post-excavation human osteoarchaeology documentation, analysis and primary publication (with E. Rega)
Elizabeth Rega	University of Sheffield	Post-excavation human osteoarchaeology analysis and primary publication (with S. Leach)
Jelena Bekvalac	University of Sheffield	On-site human osteoarchaeology documentation and analysis
Gaynor Wood	University of Sheffield	On-site human osteoarchaeology documentation and analysis
Stephen Forbes	University of Sheffield	Post-excavation human osteoarchaeology analysis and reporting
Theya Molleson	Natural History Museum, London	Post-excavation analysis of human dental remains and tooth-wear
Prisca Vareilles	University Lumière Lyon 2	Intern of T. Molleson, assisting with the post-excavation analysis of human dental remains
Caroline R. Cartwright	British Museum	Leader of environmental archaeology team and coordinator of human osteoarchaeological team; on-site and post-excavation analysis and publication of charcoal, wood, seeds, grain, mineral-preserved fibres, molluscs (with D. Reese), fish bones, ivory; also SEM examination and imaging of these materials, as well as of human tooth-wear (with T. Molleson)
David Reese	Peabody Museum of Natural History, Yale University	Identification of the marine molluscan remains (with C.R. Cartwright)
Louise Martin	University College London	On-site and post-excavation analysis of and reporting on the animal bones from non-cemetery contexts (also supervising UCL students on post-excavation analyses of animal bones)
Priscilla Lange	University of Oxford	On-site and post-excavation analysis of and reporting on the animal bones from the graves
Michela Spataro	British Museum	Analysis of and reporting on cemetery pottery
Thibaut Deviese	British Museum	Analysis of and reporting on grave pigments
Emma Passmore	British Museum	Analysis of and reporting on grave pigments
Elizabeth Crowfoot[†]	Private researcher	Early identifications of textile impressions
Michela Sandias	University of Reading	Stable isotope analysis of animal and human bones
Pascal Flohr	University of Reading	Stable isotope analysis of cereal grains
Rula Shafiq	University College London	Inter-site comparisons of the human skeletal remains e.g. those from Jericho
Joel D. Irish	University of Alaska Fairbanks	Inter-site comparisons of the human teeth with Egyptian material (dental morphometric analyses)

*In 1985, the Institute of Archaeology was part of the University of London, not part of University College London as it is now

Table 1 Internal custodianship: scientific research of the Tell es-Saʻidiyeh cemetery

burial class, 'derived secondary' which can be defined as the reburial of partial, largely disarticulated remains of pre-existing burials. In some instances bones encountered during the preparation of a new grave appear to have been dug up and simply left in disorderly piles or scatters. In other cases, however, selective bones, principally skulls and long bones, were redeposited in the newly dug grave. The grave-goods of Phase 3 are generally much poorer in quality than those of the previous two phases and show fewer Egyptian influences.

The use of the Lower Tell cemetery appears to have come to an end with the destruction of the city towards the middle of the 11th century BC, and although occupation resumed and continued throughout the Iron Age, it was not until the 6th century BC that it was used again for burials. What is remarkable about the burials of Phase 4 is their similarity to those of Phase 1, with the same strongly Egyptian influence in terms of both grave-goods and burial practices. As with Phase 1 burials, they are single, primary interments in well-fashioned sub-rectangular pits, but with one important difference. Whereas the individuals of Phases 1–3 show a consistent west–east orientation (with regards to the head), those of Phase 4 were, almost without exception, buried east–west (see Tubb 2007).

Phase 5 refers to a very few late (medieval) graves made long after the site had ceased to be a habitation centre.

Recovering the human remains from the cemetery

Having sketched the main features of the cemetery in terms of its historical context and phasing, the purpose of this chapter is to outline the collaborative processes involved in the excavation of the human remains from the graves, their international custodianship and their subsequent research. It aims to provide the 'back-story' of the collaborative decisions that have enabled the recovery of human remains from the site on behalf of the British Museum for nearly three decades.

It was clear from Pritchard's results (1980), even before the initial season of British Museum excavations in the Tell es-Saʻidiyeh cemetery in 1985, that there were several graves that were exceptionally rich in terms of their associated grave-goods (Tubb 1998). Thus, from the outset, it was envisaged that not only would there need to be specialist human osteoarchaeological input and advice (**Table 1**), but also a highly skilled team of specialist excavators working alongside experienced supervisory archaeologists, assisted by student volunteers from around the world. As each season progressed (**Table 2**) and a greater diversity of funerary

Excavation season	Tomb numbers
1985	1–40
1986	41–99 and 146–57*
1987	158–285
1989	286–384
1990	385–94
1992	395–420
1993	421–32
1995	433–80
1996	481–512

* Graves 101–45 were excavated by the University of Pennsylvania (Pritchard 1980)

Table 2 Tomb numbers excavated by the British Museum 1985–96 (Tubb *et al.* forthcoming)

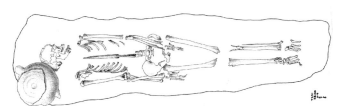

material was revealed, along with a larger quantity of human skeletal remains, procedures were constantly re-evaluated and new ones put in place.

Systems for detailed documentation, specialist photography (**Pl. 2a**) and drawing (**Pl. 2b**) were essential, as was input from the teams of conservators, environmental archaeologists and scientists on-site and at the nearby excavation headquarters at Deir 'Alla. In order to maximize the recovery of information from the human skeletal remains themselves (**Pl. 2c**), collaborations were established from 1990 onwards (**Table 1**) at the Universities of Sheffield and Bradford to provide field training and experience to students who attended courses on human osteoarchaeology. Where possible, human skeletal material was initially studied and recorded *in situ*, using purposely designed recording sheets, in order to gather as much primary information as possible. Whilst such procedures, on occasion, meant that excavation on the cemetery progressed relatively slowly, there were many beneficial outcomes which outweighed this disadvantage.

Firstly, *in situ* documentation unquestionably resulted in a very large dossier of detailed skeletal information that, even now, forms the main framework of reference for the many strands of post-excavation research and publications. Secondly, painstaking excavation protocols with regard to the Sa'idiyeh human skeletal remains, such as using a range of delicate dental tools, brushes and individual fine mesh sieves, enabled the training of a specialist team of local workmen who, season after season, were able to apply their skills in the recovery of the material (**Pl. 3a**). By being able to work alongside the human osteoarchaeologists, they were able to appreciate key skeletal changes (such as signs of palaeopathology), thus enhancing the manner in which they excavated and also their own personal understanding of the history of the people living in this area in the past – possibly their ancestors. When not engaged in excavations, most of these workmen were involved with agricultural activities such as growing onions, tomatoes or cucumbers in the fields and plastic greenhouses, which are common to that part of the Jordan Valley. As none of them owned farms and their pay for agricultural work was less than on the excavations, there was a clear financial advantage for them. The excavations benefited too, not only because many of the

Plate 2a–c: a (top) Specialist photography of the skeletal remains, 12th century BC; b (middle) Specialist drawing of Grave 251; c (bottom) Grave 364A fully excavated (photos: J.N. Tubb)

Plate 3a–b (left and right) Tell es-Sa'idiyeh cemetery during excavations (photos: J.N. Tubb)

workmen employed would return each season, but also because of their intimate understanding of and familiarity with the local soils as a result of their everyday agricultural tasks. This made them ideally placed to recognize during the excavation small changes in soil texture, colour and density that might be of archaeological significance. Their present-day knowledge of the delicate relationship between crops, stock animals, soil fertility and water availability proved invaluable to the archaeobotanists and archaeozoologists on the team. Through contacts with some of their extended families, much useful information was collated regarding local village olive oil cooperatives, inter-cropping practices of grapevines, olive and fig trees, selection of particular types of soils for cash-crops including pomegranates and sumach, and the importance of wild fruits such as *Ziziphus spina-christi* (Christ's thorn) as stock supplements to sheep and goats.

Furthermore, by having the active on-site input of archaeobotanists and archaeozoologists, the emergent skilled team of local workmen (**Pl. 3b**) was able to learn about the different recovery methods and recording techniques needed for the retrieval of categories of material other than human remains, such as tiny and fragile fish bones or organic traces in pots. Thirdly, the slow and careful pace of uncovering the human skeletal remains greatly minimized the adverse effect of rapid exposure to sunlight and temperature on the bones themselves and allowed conservation intervention when required. Although excavation commenced each day at the site very early in the morning, both human and animal bones showed a tendency to dry out and deteriorate very rapidly with increasing exposure to light and heat, particularly if the changes were sudden. If unchecked, this would exacerbate the development of salt and gypsum crystal growth just below the surface of the bone, often in spongy tissue, which could lead to splitting or cracking. Measures needed to be adopted immediately to minimize such effects. Mindful of a potentially wide range of future analytical research on the material, only minimal conservation consolidants were applied to bones or teeth. This, too, was not without its problems; applications of a thin solution of Paraloid B-72 (a proprietary brand of thermoplastic resin soluble in acetone, ethanol, toluene and xylene) resulted in a too rapid

evaporation of the consolidant and an extremely thin and ineffectual coating of the outer surface, leaving the under-surface areas vulnerable to crumbling and disintegration. Thicker solutions of Paraloid B-72 were also not effective on site as they could not penetrate the bone in order to consolidate it. The compromise for both human and animal bones was to transport key elements (such as those displaying pathological change) in their burial soils back to the excavation headquarters (some 20 minutes by road at Deir 'Alla) where consolidation could proceed under temperature controls in the environmental laboratory. In the instance of neo-natal or infant burials located in ceramic vessels, it was deemed preferable to block-lift these and to transport them to the conservation laboratory in the excavation headquarters at Deir 'Alla where each could be micro-excavated under controlled laboratory conditions there by the human osteoarchaeologist and the conservator (**Pl. 4**).

Throughout each excavation season, many soil, sediment, organic and residue samples were also taken from the graves/tombs for post-excavation analysis in the British Museum's scientific research laboratory. Depending on the conditions of preservation, it is interesting to note that even samples that were taken in the 1980s are proving viable for analysis at the present time. For example, some of the graves, notably Grave 46, revealed traces of yellow, red and purplish-red pigments surrounding the skeleton and within the confines of the internal grave-lining. Samples, taken at the time of excavation, have recently been analysed (Deviese and Passmore 2012) and the results revealed that no shellfish purple was present, but all were ochre-based pigments. Samples were taken from the graves for future phytolith (plant silica) analysis to investigate ash deposits that might represent the results of ritual fires, and possibly also matting that might have been used in the burials. Wet and dry sieving/screening and flotation of grave/tomb infills were carried out on site and in the environmental archaeology laboratory at the excavation headquarters at Deir 'Alla; such processes enabled the retrieval of biological remains, beads and other categories of small-scale material. Full descriptions of the nature and presence or absence of mudbrick and/or stone forming part of the construction of the tomb/grave, its kerb or lining were recorded and catalogued each season. These complemented the

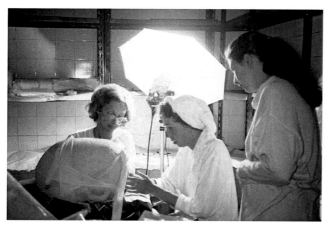

Plate 4 Micro-excavation of block-lifted and wrapped ceramic vessel containing neo-natal human skeletal remains. Left to right: conservator Jan Quinlan, human osteoarchaeologist Stephany Leach and student volunteer Jo Carter (photo: C.R. Cartwright)

photographic and illustrative archive. Such documentation, the continuity of recording and, indeed, excavating from one season to the next, was frequently complicated by the fact that the graves intercut the underlying Early Bronze Age occupation. Close attention to detail was required to avoid misattribution of material, including charcoal and other archaeobotanical remains, which had proved so diagnostic for reconstruction of the Early Bronze Age agricultural aspects of Tell es-Sa'idiyeh (see, for example, Cartwright 2002), but were scanty in the securely associated grave fills.

Compared to practices used elsewhere, several aspects of the methods adopted at Tell es-Sa'idiyeh can be highlighted. Perhaps the most important were the continually evolving aspects of theory being put into practice, season to season. This enabled the refinement of techniques used to excavate the human remains themselves as well as their grave-goods and the burial loci. The carefully selected excavation team comprising a director, an associate director, archaeologists, conservators, scientists, human osteoarchaeologists, archaeobotanists, archaeozoologists, surveyors, photographers, illustrators, students and local workmen displayed an enormous array of complementary knowledge and skills, not routinely available on every excavation. The purpose-built excavation headquarters, also rarely available on other projects, afforded facilities and equipment that enabled sustained processing, conservation, photography, illustration and more than just baseline research. The extraordinary range of specialist expertise available for consultation on and off-site (**Table 1**) offered every opportunity to apply new scientific techniques of retrieval and sampling, with the dual objectives of analyses at the present time as well as archiving samples for new, groundbreaking analyses in the future. It must be stressed that none of this would have been possible without the generous co-operation of the Department of Antiquities of Jordan and the Jordanian people.

International custodianship, post-excavation research and respect

The multi-disciplinary approach to both excavation and recording continued into the post-excavation research,

giving a greatly enriched data set and, in consequence, fuller results. The concept of 'respect' encompasses all aspects of this multi-layered and multi-faceted research. Exploring every avenue of potential research during each season and at the current time, and archiving samples for the future, ensures as far as possible that maximum respect is given to the people of Tell es-Sa'idiyeh and their possessions, now brought to light (in every sense of the words).

The agreement between the Department of Antiquities of Jordan and the expedition allowed for a division of the artefacts recovered from the cemetery (as from all other contexts excavated at the site), and this has provided the opportunity to display in the permanent galleries many of the more significant objects (**Pl. 5a–b**) and make them available to the British Museum's international audience. Furthermore, it generously permitted, for research purposes, the transfer to the United Kingdom of all the human skeletal remains excavated by the British Museum at Tell es-Sa'idiyeh since 1985, as each season's graves had been catalogued in the published interim reports (Tubb 1988; 1990; Tubb and Dorrell 1991; 1993; 1994; Tubb et al. 1996; 1997). On completion of the research, the human remains will be returned to Jordan for reburial. The agreement also allowed the transfer of all associated animal bones, archaeobotanical and molluscan material from the cemetery for identification and research, as well as the above-mentioned soil, sediment, organic and residue samples. This represents a rare and valuable opportunity for integrated, multi-disciplinary scientific research to be carried out by expert specialists under controlled laboratory conditions with the latest equipment and analytical techniques.

The specialist training of the local workforce (**Pl. 3a–b**) had already initiated the process of demonstrating respect to the people uncovered in the Sa'idiyeh cemetery, not only through the complex and careful techniques of recovery, but also by the sustained interaction with and feedback of the expertise and knowledge from all present on the excavation. This information exchange increased interest on the part of the local community that provided the workmen and also the extended community that took care of the British Museum team at the excavation headquarters at Deir 'Alla. The Department of Antiquities' inspectors, present throughout each excavation season, were well placed to facilitate a wider dispersion of knowledge to the community through daily communication, and also to visitors from further afield in Jordan and abroad, such as at archaeological conferences held in Irbid or Amman.

Once back at the British Museum, collaborative research concerning the human remains continued for the final monograph that will contain detailed analyses and interpretation of diverse materials and topics. An interim report on the human skeletal remains from the 1995 season (Leach and Rega 1996) generated useful feedback that assisted with the cemetery synthesis. A detailed catalogue and report of many of the human skeletons (Forbes 1997) provided important data for the final reports (Tubb et al. forthcoming), as did the substantial corpus of the University of Sheffield recording sheets completed on site (now archived at the British Museum). Human skeletal remains from Tell es-Sa'idiyeh remained on extended loan as a teaching

Plate 5a–b: a (left) Ivory cosmetic container in the form of a fish from Tomb 232, 1250–1150 BC. British Museum, London (1987.0727.138); b (right) wine set from Tomb 32, 1250–1150 BC. British Museum, London (1985,0714.53; 1985,0714.54; 1985,0714.55)

collection and for further student research in the Department of Archaeology, University of Sheffield. Also included in the forthcoming British Museum final report volumes are detailed analyses and interpretation of the human teeth, including variable pressure scanning electron microscope study of tooth wear on selected specimens from Tell es-Sa'idiyeh.

Other categories of funerary material have already been alluded to above and it is important to emphasize the broad diversity of research that has emerged, which has contributed to a more complete understanding of the people represented in the Sa'idiyeh cemetery and their lifeways. For example, on-site and post-excavation archaeozoological analysis has culminated in a report on the animal bone funerary offerings recovered from the British Museum's cemetery excavations. There are tantalizing references to similar material recovered from Pritchard's excavations in the 1960s, but unfortunately no detailed data or identifications (P. Lange, pers. comm. June 2010). Details of the analysis of the fish remains found in the funerary offerings of Grave 232, as well as the bone artefacts have also been presented for publication (Tubb *et al.* forthcoming). The archaeozoological results from the cemetery are already providing interesting comparisons with those from other time periods at Tell es-Sa'idiyeh.

Several considerations of the cultural significance, repertoire and chronology of the associated artefacts from the Tell es-Sa'idiyeh cemetery have been published (e.g. Green 2006, 2010; 2012), stimulating discussion into the significance of the site in a wider context of Middle Eastern and Mediterranean studies. Allied to this study is the petrographic examination (currently being prepared at the British Museum for publication) of local and imported pottery from the cemetery. Imported material in the form of wood from cedar of Lebanon trees and ivory for fine objects, including the remarkable cosmetic container in the form of a fish (**Pl. 5a**) from Grave 232 (ME 1987.7-27,138), are also currently being submitted for publication (Tubb *et al.*, forthcoming).

The forthcoming final report volumes (Tubb *et al.*, forthcoming) will naturally include detailed specialist

studies on all aspects of the cemetery finds: pottery, metalwork, seals and scarabs, ivory objects and so forth, many of them complemented by the results of scientific analyses. With regard to the metalwork, it is worth pointing out that many pieces, such as copper alloy bracelets/anklets, bowls (for example, in **Pl. 5a**) and weapons were associated with mineral-preserved textile fragments, supplying good evidence of the original shroud wrapping the body, its weave and its fibre identifications. From these we can deduce that the textile closely resembles Egyptian linen shrouds. Remains of string found in some of the beads, for example from Grave 242, have also been identified as flax.

Marine shells and shell beads (often from imported Mediterranean and/or Red Sea sources) from the Sa'idiyeh graves have been extensively studied (Tubb *et al.* forthcoming); the species represented and the use to which they were put provide interesting comparisons and contrasts to the shell use of Early Bronze Age peoples at the site (Cartwright 2003).

Given that we are asserting that the concepts of 'respect' and 'international custodianship' embrace the implementation of research as fully as possible by key specialists, we also suggest that it is important to consider novel approaches as well as tried-and-tested ones. It is not always feasible on excavation projects to refocus analyses within broader frameworks of research, but at Tell es-Sa'idiyeh, the rich and diverse evidence coupled with an extended timeframe for study has paid handsome dividends in that regard. For example, the stable isotope analyses (carbon, nitrogen and oxygen) that are being carried out on samples of human (and animal) bones from Tell es-Sa'idiyeh as part of broader research programmes will chart changes in diet and water use in Jordan from the Neolithic to the Byzantine periods, and the results are eagerly awaited. They will complement the extremely interesting results recently received (P. Flohr, pers. comm. October 2012) on the subject of reconstructing past water availability using plant carbon and nitrogen stable isotope ratios on archaeological cereal grains from Sa'idiyeh and other sites in Jordan. Inter-site comparisons between the Sa'idiyeh human skeletal remains and those from other sites, such as Jericho, have investigated the effects of rural and urban living on diet and health. Comparisons with human teeth from Egypt have recently been undertaken and several requests for DNA analyses have been considered.

Finally, we are conscious of the assertion by Leach and Rega (1996: 134) that states: 'Due to long-term site occupation, limits of the excavated area and the obvious cultural factors affecting the complete populational representation in the Tell es-Sa'idiyeh cemetery, such as segregated child and adult burial areas, traditional demographic methods of estimating life expectancy and average age at death in this cemetery are not only inappropriate but uninformative.' Whilst this observation may have been entirely valid at the time (1996), further seasons ensued with more excavation of human skeletal remains. As a result, Green (2006; 2010; 2012) sees in the evidence from the cemetery an opportunity to examine changes in status, culture and gender in the Late Bronze Age–Early Iron Age transition during a time at which the people at Tell es-Sa'idiyeh were closely integrated with the Egyptian sphere of influence. However, certain key points remain valid: interpretation of the Sa'idiyeh human remains is neither simple nor straightforward, and it is hoped that the multi-disciplinary, international scholarship reflected in the British Museum final reports (Tubb *et al.* forthcoming) will not only reflect this complexity, but also the importance of Tell es-Sa'idiyeh, its peoples and its cultural and economic influence over time.

Acknowledgements

We gratefully acknowledge the hard work of everyone involved in the British Museum's Tell es-Sa'idiyeh project during all the excavation seasons and in the subsequent post-excavation phases. Although far too numerous to be named individually here, we thank them sincerely for their valuable contributions.

Bibliography

Cartwright, C.R., 2002. 'Grape and grain: dietary evidence from an Early Bronze Age store at Tell es-Sa'idiyeh, Jordan', *Palestine Exploration Quarterly* 134, 98–117.

—, 2003. 'Unusual use of freshwater mussel (*Unio* sp.) shells during the Early Bronze Age at Tell es-Sa'idiyeh, Jordan', *Environmental Archaeology* 8, 85–9.

Deviese, T. and Passmore, E., 2012. 'Analysis of four pigment and sediment samples from Tell es-Sa'idiyeh by HPLC and Raman Spectroscopy for colorant identification', British Museum Department of Conservation and Scientific Research Analytical Request AR2012/06 (unpublished).

Forbes, S., 1997. 'Catalogue and report: human skeletons from the Tell es-Sa'idiyeh cemetery', University of Sheffield (unpublished).

Green, J.D.M., 2006. 'Ritual and social structure in the Late Bronze and Early Iron Age Southern Levant: the cemetery at Tell es-Sa'idiyeh, Jordan', Ph.D thesis, University College London.

—, 2010. 'Creating prestige in the Jordan Valley: a reconstruction of ritual and social dynamics from the Late Bronze–Early Iron Age cemetery at Tell es-Sa'idiyeh', in *Proceedings of the 6th International Congress of the Archaeology of the Ancient Near East 5 May–10 May 2009*, ed. P. Matthiae, F. Pinnock, L. Nigro and N. Marchetti, 765–79, 'Sapienza', Università di Roma vol. 1. Wiesbaden.

—, 2012. 'Forces of transformation in death: the cemetery at Tell es-Sa'idiyeh, Jordan', in *Forces of Transformation. The End of the Bronze Age in the Mediterranean*, ed. C. Bachhuber and R.G. Roberts, 78–89. Oxford (Themes from the Ancient Near East BANEA Publication Series, vol. 1).

Leach, S. and Rega, E., 1996. 'Interim report on the human skeletal material recovered from the 1995 Tell es-Sa'idiyeh excavations, areas BB and DD', *Palestine Exploration Quarterly* 128, 131–8.

Pritchard, J.B., 1980. *The Cemetery at Tell es-Sa'idiyeh, Jordan*. Pennsylvania (University Museum Monograph 41).

—, 1985. *Tell es-Sa'idiyeh: Excavations on the Tell 1964–1966*. Pennsylvania (University Museum Monograph 60).

Tubb, J.N., 1988. 'Tell es-Sa'idiyeh: preliminary report on the first three seasons of renewed excavations', *Levant* XX, 23–88.

—, 1990. 'Preliminary report on the fourth season of excavations at Tell es-Sa'idiyeh in the Jordan Valley', *Levant* XXII, 21–42.

—, 1998. *Canaanites*. London.

—, 2000. 'Sea Peoples in the Jordan Valley', in *The Sea Peoples and their World: A Reassessment*, ed. Eliezer D. Oren, 183–96. Philadelphia (University Museum Monograph 108, University Museum Symposium Series 11).

—, '2007. The sixth century BC horizon at Tell es-Sa'idiyeh', in *Up to the Gates of Ekron: Essays on the Archaeology and History of the Eastern Mediterranean in Honor of Seymour Gitin*, ed. S.W. Crawford *et al.*, 280–95. Jerusalem.

— and Dorrell, P.G., 1991. 'Tell es-Sa'idiyeh: interim report on the fifth (1990) season of excavations', *Levant* XXIII, 67–86.

— and Dorrell, P.G., 1993. 'Tell es-Sa'idiyeh 1992: interim report on the sixth season of excavations', *Palestine Exploration Quarterly* 125, 50–74.

— and Dorrell, P.G., 1994. 'Tell es-Sa'idiyeh 1993: interim report on the seventh season of excavations', *Palestine Exploration Quarterly* 126, 52–67.

—, Dorrell, P.G. and Cobbing, F.J., 1996. 'Interim report on the eighth (1995) season of excavations at Tell es-Sa'idiyeh', *Palestine Exploration Quarterly* 128, 16–40.

—, Dorrell, P.G. and Cobbing, F.J., 1997. 'Interim report on the ninth season of excavations at Tell es Sa'idiyeh, Jordan', *Palestine Exploration Quarterly* 129, 54–77.

—, Green, J., Cartwright, C.R. and Chapman, R.L., forthcoming. *Tell es-Sa'idiyeh: Excavations in the Lower Tell Cemetery*. London.

Chapter 11
The Bioarchaeology of Amara West in Nubia
Investigating the Impacts of Political, Cultural and Environmental Change on Health and Diet

Michaela Binder and Neal Spencer

Egypt and Kush

The pharaonic state defined itself as the 'Two Lands', the union of the Nile valley between modern Cairo and Aswan (Upper Egypt) with the fertile Nile Delta (Lower Egypt). Beyond lay chaotic, dangerous lands to the west (Libya) and north-east (a succession of city states and greater powers in Syro-Palestine and beyond) and to the south, Nubia. Throughout much of the 3rd and 2nd millennia BC, Egypt occupied parts of Nubia (Smith 2003; Edwards 2004) where areas of broad, fertile floodplain are interspersed with Nile cataract regions framed by outcrops of granite where the bedrock is visible on the surface or in the river, making river navigation and large-scale agriculture rather difficult. These periods of pharaonic control are attested through the inscriptions, monuments, chapels and tombs left by individuals in the area between Aswan and Kurgus at the Fifth Nile Cataract, but also through a network of towns, fortifications and cult temples.

The New Kingdom (*c.* 1550–1070 BC) control of Nubia was characterized by the construction of Egyptian towns with temples and cemeteries, such as those at Sai, Kerma (Dokki Gel), Soleb, Sesebi and Tombos. These towns housed Egyptian administrators, priests and military men (**Pl. 1**). Amara West is one of these Egyptian towns, founded in the early 13th century BC, and partly excavated by the Egypt Exploration Society in the 1930s and 1940s (Spencer 1997; 2002). Further upstream, Gebel Barkal and Kurgus feature Egyptian inscriptions and monuments, but it is unclear whether a considerable Egyptian population was ever present.

The archaeology of Nubia was long subservient to the discipline of Egyptology. The modern perspective of the conquest, settlement history and culture of the region was effectively viewed through the prism of pharaonic ideology: depicting Kush as 'wretched', an outpost of the pharaonic state with local populations 'Egyptianized' (particularly local elites; Säve-Söderbergh 1991), while the riches of the desert gold mines were exploited and exotic goods traded from further south. Fieldwork in the last four decades has prompted a considerable reassessment, with the realization that Egyptian cultural impact outside certain key centres may have been minimal. Within the pharaonic settlements, a model of cultural entanglement (Smith 2003), rather than domination, is increasingly accepted. Furthermore, it is now evident that the loss of Egyptian control of the area in the 11th century BC did not lead to the abandonment of these settlements. Indeed, a number of cemeteries house burials spanning the era between Egyptian occupation and the rise of the next great Nubian polity (the 25th dynasty that would conquer and control all of Egypt) reflecting the persistence of indigenous funerary cultures.

The British Museum instigated a research project at Amara West in 2008, in both the town and its cemeteries. Fieldwork provides the opportunity to place the collection within the context of the latest archaeological research; all artefacts remain within Sudan, with a selection entering the collection of the Sudan National Museum. The human and animal remains, in addition to selected samples of organic and inorganic materials, are exported to the British Museum for further scientific analysis. Arguably the best

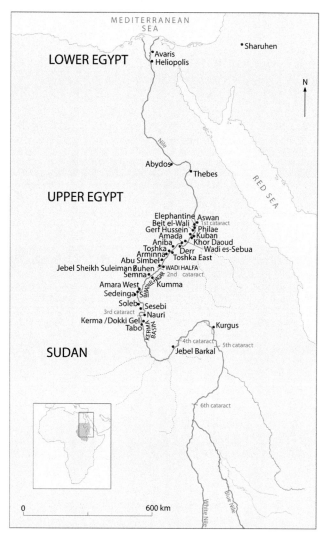

Plate 1 Map of Egypt and Nubia, showing the location of Amara West (drawing by Claire Thorne)

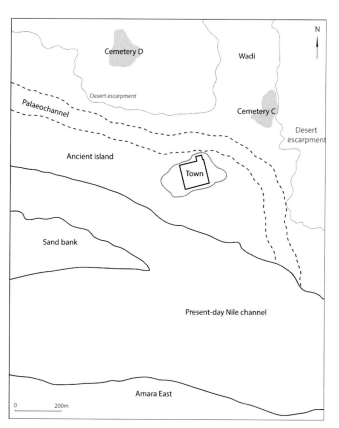

Plate 2 Key map of Amara West, with location of town and cemeteries

preserved settlement of the 13th–11th century BC anywhere in the Nile valley, Amara West allows a detailed, high resolution and interdisciplinary investigation of the nature of cultural entanglement between Egypt and Nubia in the late 2nd millennium BC, through excavation of the town and its cemeteries within a framework of bioarchaeological and environmental analyses. The findings of such research naturally resonate with colonial contexts in other regions and periods.

Town and cemetery: complementary data sets on life and death

The town was founded in the reign of Seti I (*c.* 1306–1290 BC), upon an island in the Nile (**Pls 2, 6**), initially within a walled area of 108 x 108m (**Pl. 3**). Alongside a sandstone cult temple, the town was laid out with streets that mirrored the orientation of the town wall, comprising storage magazines and the residence of the 'deputy of Kush', the senior Egyptian administrator of the region. Over the ensuing five or six generations, the town developed into a more densely occupied, less formally arranged, settlement, with a much higher proportion of the walled area given over to housing (Spencer 2014). Nile valley settlement archaeology has focused on the royal foundations associated with important temples, funerary complexes, 'workmen's villages', or the

royal residence city of Tell el-Amarna (Kemp *et al.* 2012). The rather static, normalized view of houses suggested by much research on these sites (see Tietze 1985; Kotsilda 2007), is probably misleading. Amara West offers an opportunity to consider house(hold)s as dynamic entities, particularly the role of individual and household agency in shaping the lived environment, with adjustments to house layouts and interiors, often set within a palimpsest of earlier architecture (Spencer 2014). Around a century after the town of Amara West was founded, an extramural area of housing developed beyond the west wall, notable for the presence of several large villas, approaching 500m² in area (**Pl. 5**; Spencer 2009, 50–7).

Most houses cover a ground floor area of only 25–70m² (**Pl. 4**); light filtered through roofs of matting, wooden beams and clay, as well as through stairwells and doorways: no evidence for windows has been identified. Such an arrangement was ideal for retaining heat in the cold desert nights and ensuring it stayed cool during hot summer days. The inhabitants also lived in a dense environment filled with smoke from cooking and hearths, as well as human and animal waste and occupation debris that gradually engulfed the house entrances. The 'low horizon of activity' posited for modest houses at Tell el-Amarna, given the low benches and squat furniture (Kemp and Stevens 2010, 507), is probably an apt description of aspects of the lived experience at Amara West. The artefact assemblages are largely consistent with those found in contemporary Egypt: stone tools, fishing equipment, items of adornment in faience, carnelian, steatite and copper alloy, in addition to a small number of imported Canaanite and Mycenaean pottery containers. Some houses were provided with cult

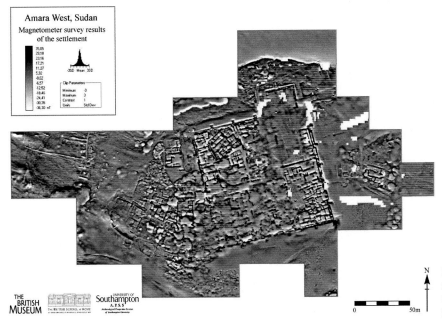

Plate 3 Magnetometry survey of the town.
Survey by Sophie Hay and Leonie Pett
(University of Southampton/British School
in Rome)

niches, statues or small stelae with depictions of deities, reflecting the spiritual concerns of the inhabitants.

The evidence for foodways in the town and cemeteries is a particular focus of research. Most houses were provided with grinding emplacements, presumably used primarily for processing cereal, alongside cylindrical ceramic ovens and circular hearths. These hearths, which were used as sources of warmth as well as for cooking, are often set in front of the low bench (*mastaba*) in the smaller houses. In one case, two houses shared a space with grinding emplacements and ovens; the town is notable for the lack of communal spaces, at least any defined by architecture. Botanical remains – including seeds but also soluble silica taken up by plants (phytoliths) – are indicative of differential food provision within the town. A pilot study of archaeobotanical samples from an extramural villa and two small houses within the walled town (Ryan *et al.* 2012), data sets of contemporary date, revealed that emmer wheat comprised the source of nearly 90% of cereal chaff in the villa, compared to 55% in the smaller houses where barley fulfilled a more important part of the diet. Clover (for fodder?), flax, lentils, figs, colocynth and watermelon were also identified in the botanical record, with both dung and charcoal being used as fuel in the ovens and hearths. Faunal and fish remains have yet to be studied in detail, but appear to be consistent with the assemblages found in Egypt: cattle, caprines and pig dominate, with a very small amount of wild species.

But was this town in Nubia entirely Egyptian? One example of Nubian architecture has been identified in the town (Spencer 2010), which indicates that individuals or groups could deploy a local indigenous architectural style. It is the presence, however, of handmade basket-impressed Nubian cooking pots that is most significant. Initially forming only around 1% of the assemblages, in the later occupation phases (12th–11th centuries BC) this rises to around 10%; the increase in number of non-textual markers, such as incised images of animals, upon storage vessels seems concurrent. Does this reflect the presence of Nubian inhabitants, perhaps partly through intermarriage? Or is it

simply reflecting a preference for, or the convenience of acquiring, local cookwares? Petrographic and chemical analyses reveal the same clay mix was being used for Nubian and Egyptian-style vessels (Spataro *et al.* forthcoming).

The cemetery provides clearer evidence for cultural entanglement and hybridity, but also for post-colonial occupation into the 9th or 8th centuries BC. Other than sherd scatters with material of 10th–8th century BC date, evidence from the town is restricted to the period of pharaonic control; surface deflation and a preference for

Plate 4 House E13.3-S at Amara West

Plate 5 Extramural villa E12.10 at Amara West

Plate 6 Looking west over Amara West town (foreground). Ernetta island, near horizon, shows the agricultural potential of islands protected from wind and sand ingression (photo: Susie Green)

continuing to occupy and modify existing buildings need to be taken into account. While the environmental setting, upon a fertile island, may have been a critical factor in leading to the foundation of Amara West, it is also likely to have been a major reason for the abandonment of the town. Investigations of the northern Nile channel, now dry, has revealed that this was no longer perennial by the late 2nd millennium BC, as indicated by Optically Stimulated Luminescence (OSL) dates (Spencer *et al.* 2012). Without water in this channel, all three barriers to considerable sand ingression would be removed (tamarisk trees, associated sand dunes and the water channel itself), resulting in the fertile island being transformed into the arid environment we see today. Alongside reflections of cultural affiliation, the excavation of the cemeteries at Amara West allows questions to be posed as regards to the effects of environmental stress on the town's population.

The cemeteries of Amara West

The cemeteries of Amara West extend to the north-east and north-west of the settlement on the opposite side of the Nile channel (**Pl. 2**). Cemetery D is set on the low desert ridge,

whereas Cemetery C is located on an alluvial terrace above a *wadi* north-east of the town. Burial grounds associated with the settlement were first identified by the Egypt Exploration Society (EES) during their field work campaign in 1938–9 (Spencer 2002). In addition to large-scale excavations in the town, they also explored a small number of graves in the area of Cemetery D and elsewhere during the 1938–9 season. The discovery of three large chamber tombs used for the interment of several individuals which feature mudbrick pyramid superstructures – similar to tombs at other New Kingdom sites in Nubia and Egypt – led H.W. Fairman to identify the cemetery as the burial ground of the elite during the Egyptian occupation of Amara West (Spencer 2002, 3). Later material was interpreted as evidence for the reuse of the burials during the Napatan period (8th–6th centuries BC; Spencer 2002, 3). The survey and excavation work in Cemetery C was carried out during a survey of the Dal Cataract area by the Centre National du Rechérche Scientifique (France) under A. Vila (1977) who assigned the excavated graves both to the New Kingdom and X-group (4th–5th centuries AD), a dating that now has to be revised.

Plate 7 Mudbrick superstructure of G309 at Amara West (view south, with base of pyramid at right)

Plate 8 Commingled human remains in the western burial chamber of G234 in Cemetery C at Amara West

In Cemetery D, two new pyramid tombs (G301, G309, **Pl. 7**) dating to the New Kingdom period were uncovered, confirming Fairman's initial dating (Binder *et al.* 2011). Radiocarbon dates obtained from bone bioapatite (mineral component of bone) of the two individuals buried in the western chamber of G301[1] (Meadows *et al.* 2012) are consistent with the dating suggested by the artefacts. The post-colonial burials comprise both the reuse of the New Kingdom tombs and the construction of new tombs; pottery suggests the cemetery was in use as late as the early 8th century BC. In 2012, fieldwork revealed evidence that the cemetery area was already used for burial much earlier during the *Kerma ancien* (2500–2050 BC) or *Kerma moyen* (2050–1750 BC) periods. Contemporary settlement evidence of these periods is so far only known from sites further north of the site (Vila 1977), while there is no indication of earlier settlement in the town of Amara West.

In Cemetery C, the earliest graves discovered date to the late New Kingdom (Binder 2011). These conform to the same chamber tomb type with underground burial chambers used for multiple burials (**Pl. 8**). Grave 244 features as many as five chambers and is the largest tomb discovered at Amara West so far. With the exception of this grave, which features a Nubian-style mound (tumulus) (**Pl. 9**), no

superstructures are preserved above the chamber tombs of Cemetery C; it is possible that any such superstructures may have been lost through surface deflation. While the chamber tombs in Cemetery C are similar in size (diameters of 2.4–3.0m across, height 0.7–0.9m), the number of interments found buried within the chambers is considerably higher than in cemetery D: 49 heavily disturbed and commingled individuals were recovered from grave G201.

While the chamber tombs continued to be constructed during the 10th and 9th centuries BC, a shift in funerary culture is discernible with some burials now placed in lateral side niches off a rectangular, east–west aligned shaft, usually ranging between 0.4–0.85m in depth. In contrast to the New Kingdom chamber tombs, these graves principally accommodated single or double burials, of both adults and children; only three examples held more than two individuals. During the New Kingdom these niche graves first appear in Lower Nubia (e.g. Qustul (Williams 1990), Wadi es-Sebua (Emery and Kirwan 1935)), then gradually spread further south, becoming common in Upper Nubian cemeteries during the 10th to 8th centuries, such as in Missiminia (Vila 1980) and Sanam (Griffith 1923; Lohwasser 2010). The niche grave remained in use throughout Nubia until the Post-Meroitic period (350–550 AD). The pottery

Plate 9 Tumulus of New Kingdom chamber tomb G244 in Cemetery C (view south) at Amara West

Plate 10 Selected Egyptian-style grave-goods (clockwise from top left: F8023, F9291, F9466, F9467, F9312 [front and back])

suggests a dating of the Amara West niche graves to the 10th to 9th centuries BC, supported by a radiocarbon date of 1030–890 calibrated BC[2] from bone bioapatite from one burial (Meadows *et al.* 2012). While evidence of superstructures is rarely found above these niche burials, several graves in the eastern central part of the cemetery feature low tumuli of alluvial silt, defined by loosely arranged schist stones. They further differ from the remainder of the niche burials in their significantly larger size, and location on a slightly elevated area overlooking the main burial ground; both aspects might reflect status differences.

As with the settlement, funerary customs in both cemeteries attest to the strong influence of Egyptian culture, both during the New Kingdom and its aftermath (Binder 2014). The tombs dating to the New Kingdom are almost exclusively of Egyptian style, both in terms of architecture and treatment of the deceased: burial in an extended body position, the use of wooden coffins and the array of artefacts placed in these tombs (**Pl. 10**). This trend continues well into the post-New Kingdom period with pharaonic funerary customs remaining prevalent, but there are indications for a revival of indigenous Nubian burial customs. This cultural mixture is particularly well exemplified by the construction of tumulus superstructures, one of the hallmark features of

Nubian burial customs, above Egyptian-style chamber tombs (e.g. G244 in Cemetery C, **Pl. 9**; G305, G314, both in Cemetery D). The use of funerary beds, and the placement of bodies in a flexed body position, further reflect the combination of Nubian and Egyptian funerary customs within the same grave.

Studying health and diet on ancient human remains

Studying health and living conditions of past human populations can be based on the occurrence of pathological changes in human remains. However, due to the unspecific nature of skeletal response to most disease processes, bioarchaeological research in this field has, in recent years, moved away from the diagnosis of specific pathological conditions to an analysis of more unspecific indicators of 'physiological stress' (e.g. Larsen 1997; Goodman and Martin 2002). This approach is based on the concept of the 'systemic stress perspective' (Goodman *et al.* 1984), a model in which health is perceived as the success or failure of populations to adapt to their biological and cultural environment. Skeletal changes resulting from failure do not necessarily correspond to a specific disease, but rather represent generalized responses to negative influences on the physiological system (see below).

However, the study of health and disease in the past through human remains demands consideration of methodological and theoretical issues, which can limit any possible conclusions. One major problem is linked to the nature of skeletal samples: these only represent a sample of the entire population, limited by a number of intrinsic (e.g. mobility, mortality rates) and extrinsic (e.g. preservation, excavation strategies) factors which are impossible to control. Therefore, frequency results gained from cemetery studies are not necessarily representative of the entire population (Waldron 2007, 27ff). Other problems are related to the limited potential of bone to respond to pathological stimulus or insult: usually, only chronic diseases affect the skeleton. Consequently, those individuals that do show skeletal signs of disease are the ones that survived long enough to develop bone responses, which presupposes a reasonably good immune system; those with a weak immune system may have died straightaway (Wood *et al.* 1992). Other underlying factors, such as individual susceptibility to disease, will always remain unknown (Wood *et al.* 1992; Wright and Yoder 2003).

With regards to 'stress markers', the systemic stress perspective has been the subject of criticism for only focusing on the biological side, while failing to acknowledge the influence of psychological factors on health and wellbeing (Bush 1991). Nevertheless, by analysing human remains within their archaeological, environmental, cultural and socio-economic context, it is possible to make inferences about health and living conditions of past human populations (Roberts and Cox 2003).

Reconstructing health and living conditions at Amara West

The time period between 1300 and 800 BC is marked by major political and environmental change: the loss of Egyptian colonial control over Nubia in the 11th century BC and a significant climatic deterioration affecting the Middle Nile valley in the later 2nd and early 1st millennium BC (Macklin and Woodward 2001). The end of Egyptian colonial rule may have had a significant impact on the socio-economic infrastructure of the colonial settlements in Nubia due to a disruption of imports. In addition, recent palaeoenvironmental research is revealing evidence for deteriorating environmental conditions that affected the entire middle Nile valley region, including the drying up of the northern channel at Amara West (Spencer *et al.* 2012). This would have limited the amount of land suitable for agriculture and been a major factor in the abandonment of the town. The health status of the people living at Amara West is being used to address questions about general living conditions and to test whether these individuals were subject to significant changes brought about by the political, cultural and environmental transformations that affected Upper Nubia around 1000 BC.

To date, 246 individuals have been excavated from the Amara West cemeteries (**Table 1**), comprising both complete individuals as well as a large number of individuals recovered from commingled contexts. Commingled human remains are problematic as disarticulated and mixed bones are difficult, often impossible, to reassociate as individual

	Complete individuals		Commingled individuals	
	adult	sub-adult	adult	sub-adult
New Kingdom	22	11	4	0
Post-New Kingdom	60	55	81	13
Total	**82**	**66**	**85**	**13**

Table 1 Assemblage of human remains excavated between 2009 and 2013 at Amara West

skeletons. Matching of elements can be based on morphological and metric criteria as well as DNA studies, and the success rate usually depends upon bone preservation, the number of commingled individuals and presence of differentiating features (Ubelaker 2008). At Amara West, most of the commingled contexts are small enough to allow for the relatively secure establishment of a minimum number of individuals and partial reconstruction of individuals. However, smaller skeletal elements such as hands, feet, ribs or vertebrae are often difficult to assign to an individual, limiting some of the palaeopathological interpretations. Therefore, only 152 individual skeletons (25 New Kingdom, 127 post-New Kingdom) have so far been included in the detailed bioarchaeological analysis. The assemblage of human remains also comprises a small number of soft tissue fragments including brain, muscle and skin, in addition to a few samples of hair.

Age and sex were established based on protocols outlined by Buikstra and Ubelaker (1994) and the recommendations of the British Association for Biological Anthropology and Bioarchaeology (BABAO; Brickley and McKinley 2004). Sex determination was carried out through visual inspection of morphological features on the skull and pelvis. Estimation of age-at-death of adult individuals was based on final epiphyseal fusion, degenerative changes on the auricular surface and pubic symphysis. The selection of 'stress indicators' included in this study is based on suggestions outlined by Goodman and Martin (2002), which are now commonly employed in bioarchaeological studies that seek to address questions of health in past human populations (e.g. Steckel and Rose 2002; Buzon 2006). Stature, though determined genetically, is also considered to be a valuable indicator of living conditions during childhood as the amount as to which one's genetic potential can be fulfilled is largely dependent on nutritional and health status during childhood (Goodman and Martin 2002). Due to problems with available stature estimation methods, mean adult femur lengths were used as a proxy (Brothwell and Zakrzewski 2004).

Inferring the presence and frequency of infectious diseases in past human populations on the basis of human remains is compromised by the slow and unspecific nature of skeletal response (Ortner 2011); the deposition of newly formed bone on the long bones is often used as a proxy (Larsen 1997, 82ff; Goodman and Martin 2002). These changes can be caused by a wide range of infections (both direct and in association with a specific systemic disease), but also by trauma, circulatory disorders and muscle activity (Larsen 1997, 82ff) which has led to some criticism over the past years (Weston 2008). New bone formation in the maxillary sinuses and on the visceral surface of the ribs is

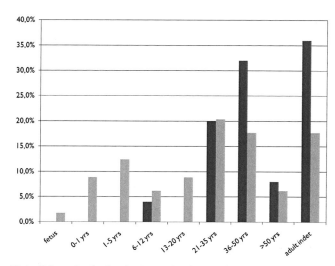

Plate 11 Age–death distribution in the New Kingdom and post-New Kingdom samples at Amara West (blue=New Kingdom, grey=post-New Kingdom)

indicative of non-specific infections of the upper and lower respiratory tract (Roberts *et al.* 1994; Roberts 2007) and was also included in this study. While infection of the maxillary sinuses is mainly caused by two different factors: poor air quality (both indoors and outdoors) which leads to an irritation and subsequent inflammation of the upper respiratory tract (Roberts 2007) or dental disease, chronic infections in the lungs are usually linked to diseases such as pneumonia, tuberculosis, brucellosis or fungal diseases. Pathological changes in the orbital roof (*cribra orbitalia*), were also assessed. Furthermore, the study included a systematic analysis of skeletal trauma, osteoarthritis as well as dental pathologies (caries, ante-mortem tooth loss (AMTL), dental calculus, periapical lesions and dental wear).

Within the framework of this study, further insights into dietary habits and possible diachronic changes occurring therein were sought through a biomolecular study of stable carbon and nitrogen isotopes. However, repeated attempts to extract collagen from samples of bones and teeth at Amara West have failed to provide suitable amounts of collagen. The poor survival rates of bone collagen in arid regions is a well-recognized problem (Grupe 1995) which, in combination with the high amount of natural salt in the burial environment, may have prompted collagen deterioration at Amara West.

Preliminary results and discussion

Demographic parameters

Comparing the age-at-death distribution of the adult individuals between the New Kingdom and the post-New Kingdom samples (**Pl. 11**), the proportion of older adults is significantly larger in the earlier sample. While in theory this could indicate better living conditions and therefore a higher life expectancy during the early phase of occupation of Amara West, the size of the New Kingdom sample is currently too small to allow such conclusions. In the larger post-New Kingdom sample, 46.0% of the adult deaths occurred in the young adult range (21–35 years), potentially suggesting a high degree of environmental pressure during the later phases of occupation, a notion that is further

supported by other markers of stress analysed in this assemblage (see below).

Childhood health

Another striking difference regarding patterns of mortality between the two groups is the apparent absence of infants from the New Kingdom sample. Infant mortality is generally considered a strong indicator of living conditions as neonates and infants are particularly susceptible to infectious diseases such as pneumonia, diarrhoea, malaria and malnutrition (WHO 2012). However, Egyptian and Nubian archaeological skeletal assemblages are known to be problematic in this regard as infants were also buried within the settlements (Zillhardt 2009) or in separate areas of the cemeteries (Brunton and Engelbach 1927; Murail *et al.* 2004). Consequently, the relatively low infant mortality rate during the New Kingdom period at Amara West is not likely to be a representative indicator of the living conditions. Above the age of five years, the risk of dying from diseases usually decreases considerably (Margerison and Knüsel 2002). The considerable number of older infants and juveniles during the post-New Kingdom period therefore suggests considerable environmental pressure, probably due to infectious diseases, affecting the population living at Amara West.

Further clues towards detecting potential causes of childhood mortality at Amara West were observed in some child remains in the post-New Kingdom sample. Of the individuals below 5 years, 92% display porosities in the orbital roof which are possibly indicative of dietary deficiencies such as anaemic conditions due to malaria, chronic diseases, dietary deficiencies (Walker *et al.* 2009) or scurvy (Ortner and Ericksen 1997). New bone formation on the endocranial side of the skull, generally caused by an inflammatory reaction of the meningeal vessels due to an infection or scurvy (Lewis 2004), was also observed in six (50%) of the infants with a preserved skull. All of those affected by endocranial changes also displayed signs of *cribra orbitalia*.

The possibility of scurvy deserves further comment as a chronic lack of vitamin C results in the weakening of the connective tissue in the walls of blood vessels, leaving them prone to rupture and consequent haemorrhaging (Ortner 2003: 383). Skeletal responses occur if haemorrhages inflame, further stimulating new bone growth and porosities. Indeed, porosity and abnormal bone formation in different locations on the skull – such as the inner and outer table of the skull vault, the orbits, sphenoids and maxilla – are generally accepted as markers for scurvy in children (Ortner and Ericksen 1997). Six of the post-New Kingdom sub-adult individuals display new bone formation in the orbits, on the maxilla and on the exterior and interior surface of the skull vault which, particularly if occurring in combination, may indicate scurvy. While it is tempting to associate these findings with deteriorating agricultural potential due to increasingly arid conditions, this remains difficult to determine in the absence of intact settlement layers and associated palaeoenvironmental data of the post-New Kingdom.

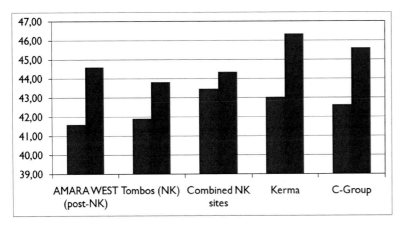

Plate 12 Mean adult femur lengths from Amara West in comparison with other Nubian sites (comparative data taken from Buzon 2006) (blue = male; red = female)

Mean femur lengths

Further indications for significant environmental stress affecting infants and children at Amara West are provided by mean adult femur lengths (male: 44.6cm, female: 41.6cm), although these were only available for the post-New Kingdom sample. In comparison to other Nubian sites (**Pl. 12**), the Amara West individuals rank at the very low end of the scale, particularly the female individuals. These findings provide additional evidence for the presence of environmental challenges, such as infectious diseases, or high levels of nutritional deficiencies affecting children during the period of growth and development.

Infectious diseases

Periosteal new bone formation (NBF) was detected in six New Kingdom and 23 post-New Kingdom individuals. Further differential diagnostic features associating the changes with a specific disease were entirely absent in the sample, thus we can only note the unspecific signs of negative environmental influences.

Pathological changes in both the ribs and maxillary sinuses regions (**Pl. 13**) are also very common findings both in the New Kingdom and in the post-New Kingdom samples (**Table 2**).

Taking the archaeological and environmental data into account, poor air quality and the presence of infectious diseases seem to be reasonable assumptions. Ovens and hearths within small roofed spaces, combined with considerable amounts of dust, dirt and windblown sand brought through doorways, stairwells and windows by strong northerly winds, increasing in later occupation phases due to climatic deterioration, would have created a living environment conducive to contracting respiratory diseases.

In addition, infections such as tuberculosis, brucellosis or fungal infections have to be considered (Roberts *et al.* 1994);

these have been tentatively identified in the palaeopathological record of the Nile valley (Ortner 2003, 254). Given the close proximity of humans and livestock, and their likely presence within the settlement itself, it seems plausible to assume that these diseases affected people living at Amara West as well. Both infectious diseases are known to cause unambiguous skeletal changes in some cases (Ortner 2003). Detection of pathogen DNA in the skeletal material could help identify the possible source of such infections, but it is doubtful whether DNA is preserved in the Amara West material given the poor bone preservation, the environmental conditions and unlikely survival of collagen.

Cribra orbitalia

Changes in the orbital cavity were observed in many adult individuals, although they seem to have been more prevalent during the New Kingdom (**Table 2**). Previously assumed to result from anaemic conditions caused by dietary deficiencies or chronic infections (Stuart-Macadam 1992), recent research indicates that lesions of similar appearance can be caused by chronic eye infections, infections of the

Plate 13 New bone formation (arrows) at the inner side of the ribs of Sk301-4 (New Kingdom)

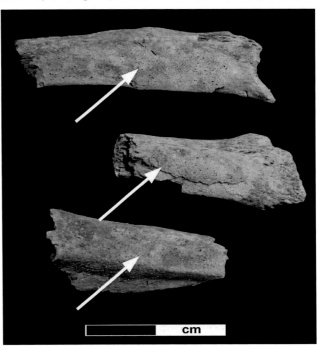

Table 2 Frequencies of major disease categories observed (n = affected, N = total number of individuals with skeletal element preserved, NBF = new bone formation)

	New Kingdom		post-New Kingdom	
	n/N	%	n/N	%
NBF Tibia	6/13	42.9%	23/61	37.7%
NBF Ribs	11/18	61.1%	29/59	42.0%
Sinusitis	10/13	76.9%	23/35	65.7%
Orbital lesions	10/14	71.4%	29/50	58.0%

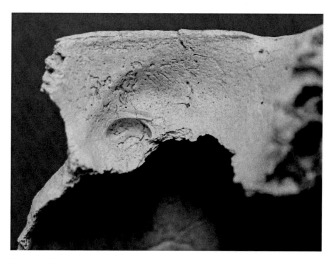

Plate 14 Circular depression in the roof of the right eye socket (Sk314-12, post-New Kingdom)

frontal sinuses or scurvy (Wapler *et al.* 2004). Differentiation between such causes would require further, invasive, histological analyses. Two more distinctive cases of orbital infection were detected in the post-New Kingdom data set, which featured circular depressions in the roof of the eye cavity, surrounded by healed new bone formation (**Pl. 14**). Such lesions are consistent with a diagnosis of trachoma (Webb 1990), a bacterial eye infection which principally affects children, though symptoms can persist into adulthood resulting in blindness. Its presence also provides clues towards hygiene within the settlement, as the transmission of trachoma is linked to factors such as poor

sanitation, inadequate access to water and closeness to animals (Wright *et al.* 2008).

Trauma

One of the most notable findings in the Amara West population so far is the high frequency of fractures (**Pl. 15**). While 37.9% (11/29) of the New Kingdom individuals had suffered at least one healed fracture, 39.8% (43/108) of the post-New Kingdom individuals were affected. High trauma frequencies have commonly been reported in Nubian samples (Kilgore *et al.* 1997; Judd 2004), but the distribution of traumatic lesions in the Amara West sample is notable for the high levels of trauma in the axial skeleton. Both groups show a particularly high frequency of trauma to the spine, comprising both of oblique fractures of the transverse and spinous processes (structures of the posterior part of a vertebra), as well as compression fractures of the vertebral bodies (**Pl. 16**). If they are not related to other underlying pathologies such as osteoporosis or cancer (neither was apparent in the individuals with fractures of the spine), fractures to the spine usually result from high-energy trauma caused by falls, crashes or direct blows to the spine (Resnick 2002). Similar mechanisms are also the cause of other rather uncommon types of complex fracture observed in the Amara West samples, such as multiple fractures to the pelvis and the scapula. Since there is no explicit evidence that inhabitants were involved in high levels of interpersonal violence, attributing the observed lesions to accidental injuries seems reasonable. The trauma profile appears to be consistent with patterns observed in farming communities, where the main

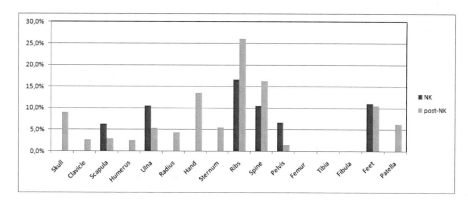

Plate 15 Frequencies of fractures in the New Kingdom and post-New Kingdom samples from Amara West

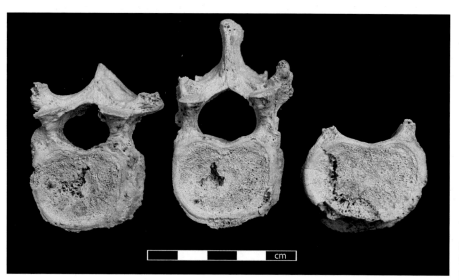

Plate 16 Compression fractures of the three lower thoracic vertebrae (Sk216-1, post-New Kingdom)

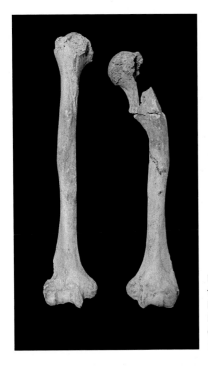

Plate 17 Poorly aligned fracture of the left humerus, with the right humerus for comparison (Sk211-7, post-New Kingdom)

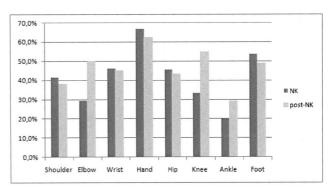

Plate 18 Frequencies of osteoarthritis in major post-cranial joints

causes of injuries are falls and blunt trauma related to the handling of large animals (Gerberich *et al.* 2001). While the topography at Amara itself does not represent an overly risky environment, additional hazards accounting for the high frequency of accidental injuries may be sought in the multi-storeyed houses where some activities would have been located on roofs made of wooden beams, plant material and mudbrick which may have occasionally collapsed. Other possibilities include activities related to agricultural activities such as palm harvesting or the handling of large animals. Comparably high values of axial skeleton trauma were also observed in the New Kingdom workmen's cemetery at Amarna, Egypt (Kemp *et al.* 2012) where they were interpreted as a testimony to the populations' involvement in the construction of Akhenaten's new city. Fractures to the long bones (**Pl. 17**) are generally less common, with no fractures to the long bones of the lower extremity yet identified, in contrast to other Nubian samples (Kilgore *et al.* 1997; Judd 2004; Buzon and Richman 2007). Fractures of the upper limb are again usually associated with falls.

Despite the severity of some observed fractures, many are well healed. Nonetheless, several of the spinal fractures are rather severe in nature and it is very likely that such injuries would have been accompanied by further complications and health impairment, due to soft tissue trauma. Thus, the high degree of healed fractures may indicate some form of medical treatment or care being provided within the community.

Osteoarthritis

Osteoarthritis, a disease of the synovial joints, was also assessed. Primary osteoarthritis is one of the most common diseases reported in human remains (Waldron 2009, 26ff). It results from general degeneration of the joints over a lifetime and can be enhanced by factors such as excessive movement. As such, the frequency of osteoarthritis can provide indications of general workload levels in a population. The condition is manifested through osteophyte formation on the joint margins, in combination with pitting and eburnation on the joint surfaces, with either of the latter having to be present (Rogers and Waldron 1995).

At Amara West, osteoarthritis of the spine and extra-spinal joints was encountered in many adults during both time periods (**Pl. 18**). The high frequencies during the post-New Kingdom period are particularly notable, given the generally much younger age-at-death at this time. Osteoarthritis in the spine was equally common with 94.4% of the New Kingdom and 82.8% of the post-New Kingdom sample displaying signs of joint disease in the intervertebral joint, alongside intervertebral disc disease resulting from degeneration of the spinal discs. These results suggest that people living at Amara West were involved in physically strenuous activities in day-to-day life, as might be expected in a largely agricultural society. Drawing reliable conclusions about any diachronic trends requires a larger New Kingdom assemblage.

Dental pathologies

The assessment of dental pathologies (**Table 3**) reveals poor levels of dental health throughout the period of occupation. The higher values in the New Kingdom sample is likely to be the result of higher ages-at-death in this group (see above). The most striking characteristic of dental health in both samples is the exceedingly high amount of ante-mortem tooth loss (AMTL) (**Pl. 19**), a phenomenon common at other sites in Nubia (Buzon and Bombak 2010). It is most likely related to a diet high in abrasive materials such as grit or sand, which is also reflected in the high degree of dental wear observed at Amara West. These findings also have to be taken into account when interpreting the occurrence of other pathologies such as caries or abscess formation, as their development and frequency is often facilitated or removed by dental abrasion

Table 3 Dental pathologies in samples from Amara West (NK = New Kingdom; AMTL = ante-mortem tooth loss)

	NK	post-NK	NK	post-NK
	teeth affected		individuals affected	
Caries	2.8%	9.7%	60.0%	42.9%
AMTL	31.7%	31.3%	78.9%	67.2%
Abscess			57.9%	46.9%

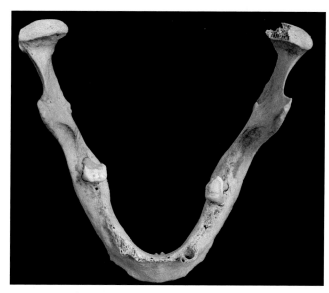

Plate 19 Severe ante-mortem tooth loss and dental wear in the lower jaw (G201, post-New Kingdom)

and consecutive ante-mortem tooth loss (AMTL; Hillson 2008). Thus, the relatively low amount of carious teeth, especially in the New Kingdom sample, is not necessarily representative. The presence of caries does attest to the availability of foods high in fermentable carbohydrates, including fruits such as dates or figs, identified in the palaeobotanical material (Ryan *et al.* 2012).

The frequent occurrence of abscesses, some of them rather severe, is also related to the high degree of dental abrasion and AMTL at Amara West. If teeth are cracked or the pulp cavity becomes exposed through micro trauma or excessive dental wear, the entry of bacteria is facilitated, usually leading to the formation of a dental abscess.

Preliminary conclusions

Due to the small size of the New Kingdom sample, it is not yet feasible to undertake a diachronic study to ascertain if, and to what degree, the proposed cultural, political and perhaps most importantly environmental changes would have affected the health and living conditions of people living at Amara West. Some tendencies can be noted in the assemblages analysed to date. The frequencies of all markers used here are generally very high in both phases, with stress markers more common in the earlier samples, with the exception of mean age-at-death. This is higher in the earlier sample and might argue for deteriorating living conditions during the post-New Kingdom period. The detailed assessment of selected pathological changes does indicate a fairly high degree of environmental pressures affecting the inhabitants of Amara West throughout the entire time period of use of the site. In addition to more unspecific stress markers, the pathological spectrum also comprises diseases such as cancer (Binder *et al.* 2014) and atherosclerosis (Binder and Roberts 2014). However, confirming any diachronic trends will require further investigation and a larger sample size.

Mobility

Further research carried out on human remains from Amara West addresses the question of human migration related to the Egyptianization of Nubia from a biomolecular perspective. Up until recently, it has been assumed that the Egyptian colonization of Nubia was brought about by large-scale migration of Egyptians resulting in a widespread Egyptianization visible in the material culture. However, this approach has become increasingly challenged in recent years (Edwards 2004, 107). Bioarchaeological data informing these research questions can be gained through stable strontium and oxygen isotope values from bone and teeth, which provide a lasting record of a person's geographic origin. Analysis of these biomolecules from archaeological remains has successfully been applied to track human migrations in the past. With regards to the Egyptianization of Nubia, analysis of individuals from the New Kingdom cemetery at Tombos tentatively identified a small number of Egyptian immigrants alongside a predominantly indigenous Nubian population (Buzon *et al.* 2007). Similar analyses have been carried out on tooth samples from Amara West by M. Buzon at Purdue University (Buzon and Simonetti 2013). However, the individuals from Amara West included in the study are largely of post-New Kingdom date, therefore further analyses are needed. Again, a larger New Kingdom data set would be essential to explore such research questions. Furthermore, Amara West may have been inhabited by individuals relocated from other Egyptian sites in Nubia and people indigenous to the region, which would not result in a distinctive strontium isotope signature.

Conclusion: life and death in colonial Kush

The detailed assessment of the ancient lived experience of Amara West through the skeletal remains of its inhabitants, as well as the traces they left behind in life and for burial (from architectural through artefactual and geochemical residues) is still at a preliminary stage. However, the site is already providing a detailed impression of how individual/ household agency was the primary factor in dictating the form of the domestic physical environment. The built environment further represents one of the major factors governing the spectrum of diseases affecting people living therein. The bioarchaeological research in the cemeteries further expands our understanding of the urban sphere, from the high number of individuals with healed fractures, suggesting care within the houses, to potentially high levels of indoor pollution causing chronic respiratory diseases, but also an increasing number of Nubian cultural markers from *c.* 1200 BC onwards. The individuals who chose tumuli, funerary beds or flexed burials – how they were to be represented in eternal life – do not seem to have lived in houses (or used objects) much different from those in contemporary Egypt.

Without the integration of town and cemetery data, the degree of cultural entanglement would be more difficult to gauge. In the near complete absence of texts relating to individuals who lived at Amara West, the study of the human remains and the bioarchaeological data enables the proposal of a more nuanced, heterogenous vision of life in a colonial town, one in which 'Egyptianization' may represent one extreme of a nuanced spectrum, which also included a degree of 'Nubianization' within a previously pharaonic town and its cemeteries. This research project therefore provides a case study of how the combined study of architectural, artefactual, environmental and bioarchaeological data from new fieldwork at archaeological sites can vastly improve our knowledge about life in the past gained.

Acknowledgements

Fieldwork at Amara West would not be possible without the permission and support of the National Corporation of Antiquities and Museums, with particular thanks to Hassan Hussein Idris, Salah Mohamed Ahmed, Abdel Rahman Ali Mohamed and our inspector, Shadia Abdu Rabo. A large team of excavators and specialists are responsible for the work described here under the direction of Neal Spencer; Michaela Binder leads the cemetery excavations and the associated bioarchaeological research. Particular thanks are due to Marie Millet, Marie Vandenbeusch, Mohamed Saad, René Kertesz, Nicole Lorenz, Dyan Semple, Åshild Vagene, Milena Grzybowska, Laurel Engbring and Carina Summerfield. Further thanks are due to Michela Spataro (ceramic fabric analyses), Philip Kevin and Rachel Swift (conservation), Caroline Cartwright and Philippa Ryan (botany) and Marei Hacke (textiles) of the British Museum, Charlotte Roberts at Durham University and to John Meadows of the University of Kiel (^{14}C dates). This research would not have been possible without generous funding from the Leverhulme Trust, for the project *Health and Diet in Occupied Nubia through Political and Climate Change*, with further support from the British Academy and the Michela Schiff-Giorgini Foundation, as well as the Institute for Bioarchaeology and Thames Valley Ancient Egypt Society. For further information on the project, visit www.britishmuseum.org/AmaraWest.

Notes

1 KIA-46312 301-3 bioapatite 2944±26 1260–1050 cal BC, p=95; KIA-46313 301-4 bioapatite 2908±24 1210–1015 cal BC, p=95.
2 KIA-46314 237 bioapatite 2807±26 1030–890 cal BC.

Bibliography

Binder, M., 2011. 'The 10th–9th century BC – new evidence from Cemetery C of Amara West, *Sudan & Nubia* 15, 39–53.

— 2014. 'Cultural traditions and transitions during the New Kingdom colonial period and its aftermath – Recent discoveries from the cemeteries of Amara West', in *Proceedings of the 12th International Conference for Nubian Studies*, ed. D. Welsby and J.R. Anderson. Leuven.

—, Spencer, N. and Millet, M., 2011. 'Cemetery D at Amara West: the Ramesside Period and its aftermath', *British Museum Studies in Ancient Egypt and Sudan* [Online], 16 (available: http://www.britishmuseum.org/research/online_journals/bmsaes/issue_16.aspx).

and Roberts, C., 2014. 'Calcified structures associated with human skeletal remains: possible atherosclerosis affecting the population buried at Amara West, Sudan (1300–800 BC)', *International Journal of Paleopathology*.

—, Roberts, C., Spencer, N., Antoine, D. and Cartwright, C., 2014. 'On the antiquity of cancer: evidence for metastatic carcinoma in a young man from Ancient Nubia (c. 1200 BC)', *PLOS One*.

Brickley, M. and McKinley, J.I. (eds), 2004. *Guidelines to the Standards for Recording Human Remains*. Reading (Institute of Field Archaeologists Paper Number 7).

Brothwell, D.R. and Zakrzewski, S., 2004. 'Metric and non-metric studies of archaeological human bone', in Brickley and McKinley 2004, 27–33.

Brunton, G. and Engelbach, R., 1927. *Gurob*. London (British School of Archaeology in Egypt 41).

Buikstra, J.E. and Ubelaker, D.H., 1994. *Standards for Data Collection from Human Remains*. Arkansas (Arkansas Archaeological Survey Research Series).

Bush, H., 1991. 'Concepts of health and stress', in *Health in Past Societies*, ed. H. Bush and M. Zvelebil, 11–21. Oxford (BAR International Series 567).

Buzon, M.R., 2006. 'Health of the non-elites at Tombos: nutritional and disease stress in New Kingdom Nubia, *American Journal of Physical Anthropology* 130, 26–37.

— and Bombak, A., 2010. 'Dental disease in the Nile valley during the New Kingdom', *International Journal of Osteoarchaeology* 20, 371–87.

— and Richman, R., 2007. 'Traumatic injuries and imperialism: the effects of Egyptian colonial strategies at Tombos', *American Journal of Physical Anthropology* 133, 783–91.

—, Simonetti, A. and Creaser, R.A., 2007. 'Migration in the Nile valley during the New Kingdom period: a preliminary strontium isotope study', *Journal of Archaeological Science* 34, 1391–1401.

— and Simonetti, A., 2013. 'Strontium isotope (87Sr/86Sr) variability in the Nile valley: identifying residential mobility during ancient Egyptian and Nubian sociopolitical changes in the New Kingdom and Napatan periods', *American Journal of Physical Anthropology* 151, 1–9.

Edwards, D.N., 2004. *The Nubian Past – An Archaeology of the Sudan*. London and New York.

Emery, W.B. and Kirwan, L., 1935. *The Excavations and Survey between Wadi es-Sebua and Adindan*. Cairo.

Gerberich, S.G., Myers, J. and Hard, D.L., 2001. *Traumatic Injuries in Agriculture. National AG Safety Database* [Online] [Accessed 8 July 2012].

Goodman, A. and Martin, D.L., 2002. 'Reconstructing health profiles from human remains', in Steckel and Rose 2002, 11–60.

Goodman, A.H., Martin, D.L., Armelagos, G.J. and Clark, G., 1984. 'Indicators of stress from bone and teeth', in *Paleopathology at the Origins of Agriculture*, ed. M.N. Cohen And G.J. Armelagos, 13–50. Orlando.

Griffith, F.L. 1923. 'Oxford excavations in Nubia. XVIII–XXV, the cemetery of Sanam', *Liverpool Annals of Archaeology and Anthropology* 10, 73–171.

Grupe, G., 1995. 'Preservation of collagen in bone from dry, sandy soil', *Journal of Archaeological Science* 22, 193–9.

Hillson, S., 2008. 'Dental pathology', in *Biological Anthropology of the Human Skeleton*, ed. M.A. Katzenberg and S.R. Saunders, 117–48. New York.

Judd, M.A., 2004. 'Trauma in the city of Kerma: ancient versus modern injury patterns', *International Journal of Osteoarchaeology* 14, 34–51.

Kemp, B. and Stevens, A., 2010. *Busy Lives at Amarna: Excavations in the Main City (Grid 12 and the house of Ranefer, N49.18), I: The Excavations, Architecture and Environmental Remains*. London (Excavation Memoir 90).

Kemp, B.J., Stevens, A., Dabbs, G.R., Zabecki, M. and Rose, J.C., 2012. 'Life, death and beyond in Akhenaten's Egypt: excavating the South Tombs Cemetery at Amarna', *Antiquity* 87, 64–78.

Kilgore, L., Jurmain, R. and Van Gerven, D.P., 1997. 'Paleoepidemiological patterns of trauma in a medieval Nubian skeletal population', *International Journal of Osteoarchaeology* 7, 103–14.

Koltsida, A., 2007. *Social Aspects of Ancient Egyptian Domestic Architecture*. Oxford (BAR Int. Ser. 1608).

Larsen, C.S., 1997. *Bioarchaeology: Interpreting Behaviour from the Human Skeleton*. Cambridge (Cambridge Studies in Biological and Evolutionary Anthropology).

Lewis, M.E., 2004. 'Endocranial lesions in non-adult skeletons: understanding their aetiology', *International Journal of Osteoarchaeology* 14, 82–97.

Lohwasser, A., 2010. *The Kushite Cemetery of Sanam – A Non-Royal Burial Ground of the Nubia Capital, c.800–600 BC*. London.

Macklin, M.G. and Woodward, J.C., 2001. 'Holocene alluvial history and the palaeochannels of the River Nile in the Northern Dongola Reach', in *Life on the Desert Edge – Seven Thousand Years of Settlement in the Northern Dongola Reach, Sudan*, ed. D. Welsby, 7–13. London (Sudan Archaeological Research Society).

Margerison, B.J. and Knüsel, C. J., 2002. 'Paleodemographic comparison of a catastrophic and an attritional death assemblage', *American Journal of Physical Anthropology* 119, 134–43.

Meadows, J., Binder, M., Millard, A. and Spencer, N., 2012. 'How accurate are radiocarbon dates from bioapatite? Dating New Kingdom and Nubian burials at Amara West, Sudan', paper presented at the 12th International Radiocarbon Conference, Paris, France.

Murail, P., Maureille, B., Peresinotto, D. and Geus, F., 2004. 'An infant cemetery of the Classic Kerma period (1750–1500 BC, Island of Sai, Sudan)', *Antiquity* 78, 267–77.

Ortner, D.J., 2003. *Identification of Pathological Conditions in Human Skeletal Remains*. London.

—, 2011. 'Human skeletal paleopathology', *International Journal of Paleopathology* 1, 4–11.

— and Ericksen, M.F., 1997. 'Bone changes in the human skull probably resulting from scurvy in infancy and childhood, *International Journal of Osteoarchaeology* 7, 212–20.

Resnick, D. 2002. *Diagnosis of Bone and Joint Disorders*. Philadelphia.

Roberts, C. and Cox, M., 2003. *Health and Disease in Britain: From Prehistory to the Present Day*. Stroud.

Roberts, C.A., 2007. 'A bioarcheological study of maxillary sinusitis', *American Journal of Physical Anthropology* 133, 792–807.

—, Lucy, D. and Manchester, K., 1994. 'Inflammatory lesions of ribs: an analysis of the Terry Collection', *American Journal of Physical Anthropology* 95, 169–82.

Rogers, J. and Waldron, T., 1995. *A Field Guide to Joint Disease in Archaeology*. Chichester.

Ryan, P., Cartwright, C. and Spencer, N., 2012. 'Archaeobotanical research in a pharaonic town in ancient Nubia', *The British Museum Technical Research Bulletin* 6, 97–107.

Säve-Söderbergh, T., 1991. 'Khet: the cultural and sociopolitical structure of a Nubian princedom in Tuthmoside times', in W.V. Davies, *Egypt and Africa*, 186–91. London.

Smith, S.T., 2003. *Wretched Kush*. London and New York.

Spataro, M., Millet, M. and Spencer, N., forthcoming. 'The New Kingdom settlement of Amara West (Nubia, Sudan): mineralogical and chemical investigation of the ceramics'.

Spencer, N., 2009. 'Cemeteries and a late Ramesside suburb at Amara West', *Sudan & Nubia* 13, 47–61.

—, 2010. 'Nubian architecture in an Egyptian town? Building E12.11 at Amara West', *Sudan & Nubia* 14: 15–24.

—, 2014. 'Amara West: considerations on urban life in occupied Kush', in J.R. Anderson and D.A. Welsby (eds), *Proceedings of the 12th International Conference for Nubian Studies. 1–6 August 2012, London*. Leuven.

—, Macklin, M.G. and Woodward, J.C., 2012. 'Reassessing the abandonment of Amara West: the impact of a changing Nile?', *Sudan and Nubia* 16, 37–43.

Spencer, P. 1997. *Amara West I: The Architectural Report*. London (Excavation Memoir 63).

—, 2002. *Amara West II. The Cemetery and the Pottery Corpus*. London.

Steckel, R.H. and Rose, J.C. (eds), 2002. *The Backbone of History: Health and Nutrition in the Western Hemisphere*. Cambridge.

Stuart-Macadam, P.L., 1992. 'Anemia in past human populations', in *Diet, Demography and Disease*, ed. P.L. Stuart-Macadam and S. Kent, 151–73. New York.

Tietze, C., 1985. 'Amarna: Analyse der Wohnhauser und soziale Struktur der Stadtbewohner', *ZÄS* 112, 48–84.

Ubelaker, D., 2008. 'Methodology in commingling analysis: an historical overview', in *Recovery, Analysis, and Identification of Commingled Human Remains*, ed. B.J. Adams and J.E. Byrd, 1–6. New York.

Vila, A., 1977. *La prospection archéologique de la vallée du Nil, au sud de la cataracte de Dal (Nubia Soudanaise), Fasc. 7 : Le district d'Amara Ouest*. Paris.

—, 1980. *La prospection archéologique de la vallée du Nil, au sud de la cataracte de Dal (Nubia Soudanaise), Fasc. 12 : La nécropole de Missiminia, I. Les sépultures napatéenes*. Paris.

Waldron, T., 2007. *Palaeoepidemiology – The Measure of Disease in the Human Past*. Walnut Creek, CA.

—, 2009. *Palaeopathology*. Cambridge.

Walker, P.L., Bathurst, R.R., Richman, R., Gjerdrum, T. and Andrushko, V.A., 2009. 'The causes of porotic hyperostosis and cribra orbitalia: a reappraisal of the iron-deficiency-anemia hypothesis', *American Journal of Physical Anthropology* 139, 109–25.

Wapler, U., Crubézy, E. and Schultz, M., 2004. 'Is cribra orbitalia synonymous with anemia? Analysis and interpretation of cranial pathology in Sudan', *American Journal of Physical Anthropology* 123, 333–9.

Webb, S.G., 1990. 'Prehistoric eye disease (trachoma?) in Australian Aborigines', *American Journal of Physical Anthropology* 81, 91–100.

Weston, D.A., 2008. 'Investigating the specificity of periosteal reactions in pathology museum specimens', *American Journal of Physical Anthropology* 137, 48–59.

WHO 2012. *Children: Reducing Mortality – Fact Sheet N° 178* [Online]. Available: http://www.who.int/mediacentre/factsheets/fs178/en/index.html [Accessed 8 July 2012].

Williams, B.B., 1990. *Twenty-Fifth Dynasty and Napatan Remains at Qustul: Cemeteries W and V*, The University of Chicago Oriental Institute Nubian Expedition Vol. VII. Chicago.

Wood, J.W., Milner, G.R., Harpending, H.C. and Weiss, K.M., 1992. 'The osteological paradox – problems of inferring prehistoric health from skeletal samples', *Current Anthropology* 33, 343–70.

Wright, H.R., Turner, A. and Taylor, H.R., 2008. 'Trachoma', *The Lancet* 371, 1945–54.

Wright, L.E. and Yoder, C.J., 2003. 'Recent progress in bioarchaeology: approaches to the osteological paradox', *Journal of Archaeological Research* 11, 43–70.

Zillhardt, R., 2009. *Kinderbestattungen und die soziale Stellung des Kindes im Alten Ägypten – Unter besonderer Berücksichtigung des Ostfriedhofes von Deir el-Medine*. Göttinger Miszellen Beihefte.

Contributors

Richard Abel is a Lecturer in Musculoskeletal Sciences, Imperial College London and Scientific Associate, Imaging and Analysis Centre, at the Natural History Museum, London.

Janet Ambers is a Scientist in the Department of Conservation and Scientific Research at the British Museum.

Daniel Antoine is the Curator of Physical Anthropology and Assistant Keeper of the Department of Ancient Egypt and Sudan at the British Museum. He is also responsible for the Museum's human remains collection.

Michaela Binder is a member of the Department of Archaeology at the University of Durham.

Caroline Cartwright is a Scientist in the Department of Conservation and Scientific Research at the British Museum.

Alexandra Fletcher is the Raymond and Beverly Sackler Curator of the Ancient Near East within the Department of the Middle East at the British Museum.

JD Hill is Research Manager at the British Museum and oversees the strategic direction, management and funding of research activities across the British Museum.

Jody Joy is Curator of the British and European Iron Age Collections at the British Museum.

Capucine Korenberg is a Conservation Scientist in the Department of Conservation and Scientific Research at the British Museum.

Clark Spencer Larsen is the Distinguished Professor of Social and Behavioral Sciences and Chair in the Department of Anthropology at the Ohio State University.

Simon Mays is the Human Skeletal Biologist for English Heritage.

Natasha McKinney is a Curator of the Oceania Collection in the Department of Africa, Oceania and the Americas at the British Museum.

Theya Molleson is a Physical Anthropologist and Scientific Associate at the Department of Earth Sciences, Natural History Museum, London.

Jessica Pearson is a Senior Lecturer in Bioarchaeology at the Department of Archaeology, Classics and Egyptology, University of Liverpool.

Julianne Phippard is a Preventive Conservator in the Department of Conservation and Scientific Research at the British Museum.

Vanessa Sáiz Gómez is a conservator who formerly worked in the Department of Conservation and Scientific Research at the British Museum.

Gaye Sculthorpe is a Curator and Section Head for Oceania in the Department of Africa, Oceania and the Americas at the British Museum.

St John Simpson is Curator of the collections from Ancient Iran and Arabia in the Department of the Middle East at the British Museum.

Neal Spencer is Keeper of the Department of Ancient Egypt and Sudan at the British Museum.

Emily Taylor is a Museum Assistant in the Department of Ancient Egypt and Sudan at the British Museum.

John H. Taylor is a Curator in the Department of Ancient Egypt and Sudan at the British Museum.

Jonathan Tubb is Keeper of the Department of the Middle East at the British Museum.

Clare Ward is a Conservator of Organic Artefacts in the Department of Conservation and Scientific Research at the British Museum.

Crispin Wiles is a Teaching Fellow for Innovation at the Department of Surgery and Cancer, Imperial College London.

Barbara Wills is a Conservator of Organic Artefacts in the Department of Conservation and Scientific Research at the British Museum.

Index